KONSPIRA

WFU
STUDIUM
PRO HUMANITATE

This volume
has benefited from
the collegial support of
The Wake Forest University Studium

MACIEJ ŁOPIŃSKI   MARCIN MOSKIT

TRANSLATED BY JANE CAVE

AFTERWORD BY LAWRENCE WESCHLER

MARIUSZ WILK

KONSPIRA

SOLIDARITY UNDERGROUND

UNIVERSITY OF CALIFORNIA PRESS   BERKELEY LOS ANGELES OXFORD

University of California Press
Berkeley and Los Angeles, California
University of California Press, Ltd.
Oxford, England
© 1990 by
The Regents of the University of California
Printed in the United States of America
1 2 3 4 5 6 7 8 9

Library of Congress Cataloging-in-Publication Data

Łopiński, Maciej.
  [Konspira. English]
  Konspira : Solidarity underground / Maciej Łopiński, Marcin Moskit,
Mariusz Wilk ; translated by Jane Cave.
    p.   cm.
  Translation of: Konspira.
  ISBN 0-520-06131-4 (alk. paper)
    1. Poland—Politics and government—1980–   2. NSZZ "Solidarność"
(Labor organization).   3. Conspiracies—Poland.   4. Dissenters—
Poland.   I. Moskit, Marcin.   II. Wilk, Mariusz.   III. Title.
DK4442.L6613   1990
322'.2'09438—dc20   89-20213

CONTENTS

ABOUT THE AUTHORS

MACIEJ ŁOPIŃSKI, born in 1947, is a journalist and has written for Gdańsk newspapers and periodicals. From 1971 to 1981 he was a member of the Polish Communist party. Following the imposition of martial law, he was banned from journalism and began working with the independent press. In December 1982 he was arrested, together with Mariusz Wilk, on suspicion of "activity in a secret structure of the Solidarity trade union." After several months, he was released on health grounds. He is now a member of the Regional Solidarity Board in Gdańsk and editor-in-chief of Solidarity's *Gdańsk Weekly*.

MARCIN MOSKIT was a pseudonym of Zbigniew Gach. Born in 1952, Gach is a journalist who worked for Gdańsk newspapers and periodicals. He is now a reporter for the new *Gdańsk Weekly*, a publication linked to the Gdańsk Solidarity organization. Maciej Łopiński is the editor-in-chief.

MARIUSZ WILK, born in 1955, is a journalist active in the democratic opposition. He is the cofounder of several independent publications in the Wrocław area. He took part in the strike in the Gdańsk Shipyard in 1980, editing the *Biuletyn Informacyjny "Solidarność,"* which he headed until December 13, 1981. He was also press spokesman for the Gdańsk Solidarity Regional Board. From the imposition of martial law, he was sought by the Security Service. He remained in hiding until his arrest on December 11, 1982. He was released just before the amnesty of July 1983. Later, he became involved in the Movement of New Entrepreneurship in Gdańsk.

NOTE

The following interviews with Solidarity activists were conducted at different times, and some activists were interviewed more than once. The dates of the interviews are as follows:

Bogdan Borusewicz	I	October 1982
	II	November 1982
	III	March 1984
Zbigniew Bujak	I	October 1982
	II	February 1984
Władysław Frasyniuk	I	June 1982
Aleksander Hall	I	February 1984
Tadeusz Jedynak	I	April 1984
Bogdan Lis	I	January 1984
	II	February 1984
Eugeniusz Szumiejko	I	February 1984

PREFACE

Konspira demands a few introductory explanations. Bearing in mind the antipathy with which the reader generally views all introductions, we shall limit ourselves to those remarks that we regard as absolutely necessary.

1. This book about underground Solidarity is drawn from interviews with the following people: Bogdan Borusewicz, Zbigniew Bujak, Władysław Frasyniuk, Aleksander Hall, Tadeusz Jedynak, Bogdan Lis, and Eugeniusz Szumiejko. Our conversations with them were structured in such a way as to cover both the course of events and a number of specific issues.

We had intended to give all participants the opportunity to go over the text before publication; this proved impossible in the case of Bogdan Lis, who was arrested in June 1984.

2. The overrepresentation of discussants from Gdańsk is due to the fact that the underground activists who accompanied Bujak and Frasyniuk during our long recording sessions with them asked to remain anonymous. For this reason, we were unable to include their opinions directly, although they undoubtedly had an impact on the book as a whole.

3. Initially we intended to write a kind of monograph on the underground that would have examined the four regions whose representatives made up the Interim Coordinating Commission at the beginning of its activity. Unfortunately, we did not manage to talk with Władysław Hardek before he left the underground. The arrest of Władysław Frasyniuk meant that we were obliged to rely on only one

interview with him, although the interview was an extensive one. For similar reasons, *Konspira* does not contain any interview with Janusz Pałubicki of Poznań, or with Frasyniuk's two successors, Piotr Bednarz and Józef Pinior. Since two of us were arrested, we were obliged to stop work on the book for some time.

4. When we sat down to edit the final version, we had the following materials: fifty-seven recorded tapes (about fifteen hundred pages of text), five hundred pages of our own notes, and a substantial collection of underground publications. In making our selection, we tried to reflect faithfully both the facts and the intentions of those who talked with us. We avoided presenting our own opinions and we deleted the questions we had asked. Of course, we alone bear responsibility for the book as a whole.

5. For some people *Konspira* offers a fragment of Poland's recent history, for others, a fragment of their own biography, and for still others, a striking journalistic topic. *Konspira* is also a metaphor made up of two interrelated parts. To appreciate this, it is enough to realize what was involved in the collection of our material: losing people who were tailing us, making use of couriers and mail drops, hiding the tape recordings. These are all elements of underground reality and simultaneously components of the creative process. In other words, in writing we engaged in conspiracy, and conspiring with each other, we wrote.

The following question then arises: Where is the boundary between the world presented in this book and the world in which its authors live?

Our thanks to all those who helped us bring our work to a happy conclusion.

Maciej Łopiński
Marcin Moskit
Mariusz Wilk

August 1984

CHRONOLOGY

1945 Yalta agreement. Formation of the Polish People's Republic.

1956 *February:* Khrushchev's "Secret Speech" to the Twentieth Congress of the Soviet Communist party signals the beginning of destalinization.
June: Striking workers in Poznań massacred.
October: Władysław Gomułka installed as new reformist Communist party head in Warsaw, launching the short-lived "Spring in October," but within a year he too begins to turn more repressive.

1968 *March:* Student protests in Poland decisively squashed.
August: "Prague Spring" comes to a bloody end with Warsaw Pact invasion of Czechoslovakia.

1970 *December:* Workers' protests along Polish Baltic coast violently suppressed. Gomułka replaced by Edward Gierek, who launches another short-lived season of reform.

1976 *June:* Workers' protests in Radom and Ursus violently suppressed. In response to the subsequent wave of repression, a group of Polish intellectuals launches KOR—the Workers Defense Committee—thus instigating an eventual alliance between Polish workers and intelligentsia.

1977 *December:* President Jimmy Carter visits Poland.

1978 *October:* Karol Wojtyła, archbishop of Krakow, becomes Pope John Paul II.

1979 *June:* Pope John Paul II makes triumphant visit to Poland.

1980 *June-August:* Labor disturbances throughout Poland culminate in the seventeen-day occupation strike of the Lenin Shipyard in Gdańsk, the emergence of Lech Wałęsa as a national leader and, on August 31, the signing of the Gdańsk agreements, which set the stage for the legalization of Solidarity, the Eastern bloc's first independent trade union. Gierek is replaced by Stanisław Kania who will himself soon be replaced by the defense minister, General Wojciech Jaruzelski.
October: Czesław Miłosz is awarded the Nobel Prize for Literature.
December: Dedication, in Gdańsk, of a monument honoring the workers massacred there a decade earlier.

1981 *March:* A police riot in Bydgoszcz leads to growing crisis, against the backdrop of the serious threat of a Soviet invasion, which is only resolved through a controversial last-minute compromise.
September: Solidarity's First National Congress, consisting of delegates representing 10 million members, convenes in Gdańsk, stipulates a program, and elects a National Commission.
December 11-12: Solidarity's National Commission meets in Gdańsk amid growing crisis.
December 13: General Jaruzelski imposes a "State of War," interning thousands of activists, including Lech Wałęsa and almost all those who attended the National Commission meeting. Among those who evade arrest are Bogdan Lis, Władysław Frasyniuk, Zbigniew Bujak, Bogdan Borusewicz and the other protagonists of this book, several of whom, during the months ahead, will form the TKK, the underground's Temporary Coordinating Commission.

1982 *May 1 and August 31:* Major demonstrations.

October 5: Frasyniuk arrested in Wrocław.

October 8: Parliament delegalizes Solidarity. TKK calls for a four-hour protest strike on November 10.

November 10: Protest strike fizzles. Leonid Brezhnev dies.

November 11: Wałęsa released.

December 31: "Suspension" of the State of War.

1983 *April 9-11:* Wałęsa holds secret meetings with the TKK.

May 1 and 3: Major demonstrations.

June: Pope's second visit to Poland.

July: "Termination" of State of War; partial amnesty, though show trial of major figures is still pending.

October 5: Lech Wałęsa is awarded Nobel Peace Prize.

1984 *June 9:* Lis arrested.

July: Limited amnesty includes Frasyniuk, Michnik, and several other key figures, but not Lis, who is facing a charge of high treason (and a possible death penalty).

August 31: Demonstrations.

October: Kidnap and murder of Father Jerzy Popiełuszko.

December: Konspira published simultaneously by an underground outfit (Spotkania) in Poland and an émigré press (Prezedwit) in Paris. Lis released.

1985 *February 13:* Frasyniuk, Lis, and Michnik rearrested while meeting with Wałęsa, face serious new charges.

March: Mikhail Gorbachev becomes new Soviet First Secretary.

May 1 and 3: Demonstrations.

June 17: Jedynak arrested.

May-June: Trial and new convictions for Frasyniuk, Lis, and Michnik.

1986 *January:* Borusewicz arrested.

May 1: Demonstrations.

May 31: Bujak arrested.

July 17: New amnesty for political prisoners announced—virtually all will be released by September.

September: Wałęsa establishes a Temporary Solidarity Council, including Borusewicz, Bujak, Frasyniuk, Jedynak, Lis, Pałubicki, and Pinior.

1987 *May 1 and 3:* Solemn masses in all cities.
June: Pope John Paul II's third pilgrimage to Poland.
August 31: Demonstrations.
October: Solidarity's National Executive Committee is formed, comprising, among others, Wałęsa, Bujak, Lis, and Frasyniuk.

1988 *March 8:* Student demonstrations commemorating twentieth anniversary of 1968 protests attacked by police in Krakow, Warsaw, and Lublin.
April: A new wave of strikes begins, this time in Bydgoszcz, though quickly spreading to Nowa Huta and the Lenin Shipyards in Gdańsk, and featuring a new generation of very young workers who nevertheless make the relegalization of Solidarity their principal demand. Major demonstrations throughout the country on May Day. Thereafter, the authorities defang the strikes one at a time, eventually leaving Gdańsk isolated. The shipworkers agree to suspend the strike without having reached any agreement, but vow they will be back.
August: Another wave of strikes, this time starting in Silesia and again spreading to Gdańsk. General Kiszczak, Jaruzelski's top aide, meets with Wałęsa and agrees to a series of negotiations on a wide range of issues, including the status of the union. With difficulty, Wałęsa convinces the young workers to suspend their strike.

1989 *February-April:* Following numerous delays, the "Round Table" negotiations between the authorities and the opposition finally get under way, with Frasyniuk, Bujak, Lis, and Hall all playing significant roles. In exchange for the relegalization of the union (which takes place April 17), Solidarity agrees to participate in a snap election, under carefully circumscribed conditions (65 percent of the seats in the key lower house of parliament will be reserved for the Communist party and its allies). Lis agrees to run for Senate, but Bujak and Frasyniuk join Wałęsa in declining to run for any parliamentary position, preferring to focus their energies on the union side of the movement.

June 4: Despite tremendous odds, Solidarity virtually sweeps the election, winning almost all the seats for which it is eligible. On the same day, in Beijing, the Chinese authorities massacre their opponents in Tiananmen Square.

July-August: The Communist parliamentary coalition unravels; Jaruzelski narrowly wins the presidency but the party proves incapable of electing its own prime minister, and presently Lech Wałęsa engineers his "Little Coalition," uniting Solidarity's delegates with those of the party's onetime allied puppet parties. Wałęsa's candidate, Tadeusz Mazowiecki, is installed as prime minister.

September-December: The Mazowiecki government, with minority Communist participation, moves rapidly toward a "shock" transition into a free market as Solidarity braces for the consequences. Meanwhile, Communist regimes start falling, one after the next, in Hungary, East Germany, Bulgaria, Czechoslovakia, and Romania.

1

The last session of the National Commission.' Things are heating up. Attack by night. "Lech is also surrounded." Apparent strength and real weakness. Why Solidarity allowed itself to be taken by surprise.

ZBIGNIEW BUJAK I.1

At about 6 P.M. on December 12, 1981, the second day of the National Commission's meeting, someone proposed a rather peculiar motion: that anyone who wanted to leave early had to get official permission from the National Commission and that the entire meeting should vote on each such request. The motion was passed by a decisive majority. This might have indicated that people subconsciously felt the seriousness of the situation (it was vital that they remain there and discuss the issues because something important was going on), but it might also have indicated something else.[2]

The bastard who proposed that motion . . . I'd like to. . . . I don't remember who it was, but in retrospect, I think the Security Service must have been watching directly what was going on in the shipyard, because what happened there was crucial for their entire strategy during the early phase of martial law.

Many observers of the last session of the National Commission noticed that at the end of the second day's discussion, Lech Wałęsa suddenly

1

stopped saying anything, that he sat there as though resigned, seemingly far away.

Lech was ready to make enormous compromises in order to preserve or save Solidarity. For this reason, every time the discussion became more radical, he looked at everyone with disapproval, even pity. He simply knew, or sensed, more than the others. In any case, it has to be admitted that outside observers, mostly those with experience in the Polish Peasant Party or Home Army,[3] had warned us long before: you have to get yourselves prepared because they're going to attack you. As early as the end of 1980 we'd had wives of Security officers coming to regional headquarters and crying on my shoulder, saying, "They're preparing camps for forty or fifty thousand people, the authorities are prepared to shoot, you have to do something." But even after the Bydgoszcz provocation I was still convinced that somehow the dynamics of the situation would enable us to keep ahead of each stage of their preparations.[4] I thought that if they really wanted to clamp down, they'd be unable to go further than charging us with overstepping the bounds of our statute.

That they could impose martial law never even occurred to me, particularly as none of our advisers had been able to say firmly whether or not this was possible. The only person I know who foresaw a military dictatorship was Wiktor Kulerski. But he kept fairly quiet about it because he didn't want—as he put it—to go around sowing defeatism. Nevertheless, as early as December 1980, he was stating firmly, "There's no question of any accord with the authorities." He was the only one who got it right. He was probably helped by his family background; his grandfather did time in a tsarist prison, his father in a Stalinist one. As an art historian, Wiktor himself had a broader historical view of many issues. He used to say that ever since he began to work in Solidarity he felt like a Jew who'd got on the wrong train—as was obvious from every station he went through—but despite that couldn't decide to get off because, after all, he was finally going.

At ten o'clock in the evening, Wiktor called me at the meeting to say that things seemed to be heating up—the telex lines had been cut and he'd heard strange things about troop movements. Then he passed the phone to the guy who was responsible in our region for collecting and analyzing all information concerning suspicious troop movements. And this guy . . . with whom I was afterward hopping mad . . . assured me, "Everything's OK, they're just normal fall maneuvers, there's nothing to worry about, you can carry on as usual." And this was just a few hours before . . .

The atmosphere of the Commission meeting was, in my opinion, a bit strange from the start; it was oppressive. The arguments in the corridors were different too. Usually we argued about every sentence, about every resolution, but this time the discussion focused on fundamental issues. On the one hand, there was Jacek Kuroń's radical proposal for an interim government;[5] on the other—the enormous caution of attorney Jan Olszewski. On the one hand, the blustering statements made by many people, and on the other—Lech looking pityingly at the whole situation.

The meeting finished at midnight, and ten minutes later there wasn't a soul left in the cloakroom. This probably came as a surprise to the other side. They must have been sure the meeting would continue the next day and that they'd therefore be able to round up everyone at their hotels. If they'd known right away that the meeting had ended, they would certainly have rounded us up in the shipyard as we were leaving. But they got the information too late.

As far as my plans went, I was going back to the hotel. But I was with Zbigniew Janas, who insisted on going home. Our wives were in close touch, so I told him, "Listen, if my Wacia finds out that you've gone home and I've stayed here, there'll be the most almighty row." But he wouldn't budge.[6]

ALEKSANDER HALL I.1

Most people decided to go back to their hotel and didn't pay much attention to the signals trickling in or to the warnings of Hall, who was wandering around the shipyard like Cassandra. Late that night he discovered that the police had been to his apartment and his remaining doubts evaporated. Something serious was underway, although how big and exactly what he couldn't yet predict. There was a lot of information floating around, but, at the time, how much of it was understood as far as those at the meeting were concerned? Today Hall can still see the scene in the conference room. Only two people understood what was going on: Jan Olszewski, who almost went pale with shock, and Antoni Macierewicz. And yet Hall talked to Wałęsa, Taylor, Wądołowski, Kuroń . . . Kuroń said something like, "So they're after Young Po-

3

land?"[7] Afterward, Hall accompanied Karol Modzelewski to the gate and told him, "The police have been to my place, to Darek Kobzdej's too, but I don't think they're just looking for us, because why should they?" Modzelewski answered, "The most stupid thing now would be to allow ourselves to be locked up." Nevertheless, he got on their chartered bus and went back to the hotel.

Wądołowski, with whom Hall was friendly because of their work together on the Committee in Defense of Prisoners of Conscience, simply suggested that they go to his room at the Monopol Hotel, where Hall would be safe. Hall insisted that it would be better if Wądołowski went with him, but at this moment they somehow parted company . . . and drove off in the last two cars to leave the shipyard that night.

BOGDAN LIS I.1

Some people seemed to sense that something was up and tried to take precautions. Lis left the shipyard with Andrzej Gwiazda, suggesting that they spend the night in a "safe" apartment. Gwiazda considered the proposal but finally decided against it, saying, "I think I'll go to the station; I'm a bit tired." In the end, Lis abandoned the idea; he too was tired.

We said goodbye. I went along Jan z Kolna Street, then Robotnicza, and suddenly I was overtaken by two trucks full of ZOMO [motorized police]. Under my arm I was carrying a file with "Solidarity National Commission" written on it, and they turned and stopped about a hundred meters in front of me. I didn't know whether to make a run for it or not, but in the end I just kept going and nobody stopped me. I got home and went to bed more or less straightaway. A half hour later a couple of friends came round (I won't mention their names here), saying that I had to get out of the apartment because something was going on—the hotels were surrounded, Solidarity's regional headquarters too. I said, "Leave me in peace!" They left, but after a couple of minutes they came back, and in the end I decided to go with them.

BUJAK I.2

By this time Bujak and Janas had bought train tickets and gone to the station bar for a coffee. Just after 2 A.M., when they were standing on the

platform, they noticed that the ZOMO were stationed all around the
Monopol. Surprised and curious they left the station to have a look; their
first thought was that the ZOMO were rounding up black-marketeers.
Suddenly Macierewicz appeared, and right away he suggested that
they were probably after Solidarity. Bujak replied, "That's impossible.
It's probably some kind of training exercise." Macierewicz nevertheless
went off in a taxi to check whether the Grand Hotel in Sopot, where the
other half of the National Commission was staying, had also been sur-
rounded. Bujak and Janas didn't see him after that, but at the taxi
stand they spotted another cab that had come from the direction of
Sopot. The driver confirmed Macierewicz's suspicion, telling them that
the Hevelius Hotel was also surrounded.

Then we thought to ourselves, hell, this might really be an attack
on the union. But I was still hesitating. At about three o'clock, the
ZOMO suddenly packed up and left. Then I said to Janas, "Let's go
and see what they've been up to." The door to the hotel was locked,
but we spotted Janusz Onyszkiewicz's assistant, who waved at us to go
away fast. I told her, "Don't get excited; find someone who'll open the
door, because we want to talk to you." We're going up the stairs, and
she says, "They've taken Janusz." To which I reply, "Have they gone
mad? Janusz Onyszkiewicz? But he's very well known. The whole region will go on strike immediately." We keep going, and she says that
she saw them leading Wądołowski out of his room, in handcuffs. Well,
when I hear that they've taken the first vice-chairman of Solidarity, I
go a bit weak at the knees. I ask who else they've taken, and she starts
crying and says they've arrested the entire presidium. She thinks only
Szumiejko and Konarski got away. My God! We ask if there's anyone
left in the hotel, and she says yes, the Security Service is checking all
the rooms. After that we don't talk any longer but rush down the stairs
to the door. It's locked again, and the concierge, who was there a
minute ago, has disappeared. I started figuring out which pane of
glass to break, but luckily it wasn't necessary.

We leaped outside. A car from the Gdańsk Regional Board approached us out of the shadows, and one of the Gdańsk employees
(whom I knew by sight) asked me what was going on. I told her,
"They've arrested the whole presidium, but what's happening in Gdańsk
apart from this?" She said, "They've surrounded and occupied the
Regional Board office, they're arresting people at the Solidarity press
agency, Lech [Wałęsa] too is surrounded and there's no way of contacting him." To which I replied, "Hell, it's finally a showdown with

the union." Janas and I gave her our briefcases, so they wouldn't get in the way, and decided each of us would try to hide out on our own and then get to Warsaw. But before that, we decided to meet once more in Gdańsk—by the altar in the Maria Basilica at two o'clock. Up till then we had absolutely no information about the situation in other parts of the country.

EUGENIUSZ SZUMIEJKO I.1

Friday and Saturday (December 11–12) Szumiejko was on the road virtually the whole time. On Friday he flew to Warsaw and attended the Congress of Polish Culture. On Saturday he returned to Gdańsk, intending to go back to Warsaw on Sunday—with Lech Wałęsa and Jan Waszkiewicz.

After the meeting of the National Commission had finished, around 12:30 at night, I went with Waszkiewicz to the Monopol Hotel to get a bit of sleep. Lech had already given up the idea of traveling to Warsaw. We woke up at 4:30. Downstairs in the lobby everything was deathly quiet; people looked at us a bit strangely. Waszkiewicz and I got in the car and set off for Warsaw. On the way we had to get some gas, so we stopped at a gas station, but the attendants there said they were closing up and, anyway, where did we think we were going now that they'd locked up Wałęsa? I made a comment to Waszkiewicz to the effect that people were so keen for something to happen finally that . . . they made up stories about how "they've locked up Lech." Without gas we couldn't get to Warsaw, so we made it as far as Tczew so we could catch a train. The train had already left, though, so Waszkiewicz said, "Well, let's get a little sleep at last; so little sleep for weeks on end is madness." We had a radio in the car. The clock struck six, and suddenly there was Jaruzelski speaking, with the national anthem playing.[8] We made a quick decision: let's go back and see if anyone's left at the hotel and then—to the shipyard!

BOGDAN BORUSEWICZ I.1

On the evening of December 12, while the National Commission was in session, there was a meeting of a faction that had earlier decided to meet every so often in order to discuss and assess the situation, to see what might still be done for the union. The meeting took place outside the shipyard, in a private apartment, and none of the members of the faction—friends and acquaintances of Bogdan Borusewicz—was any longer in the Gdańsk Solidarity leadership, with the exception of Lech Kaczyński. They had all resigned about a month before the imposition of martial law. Bogdan himself simply couldn't carry on any longer . . .

I don't have an unambiguous attitude toward Solidarity. On the one hand, I realize that this was a movement of supreme importance for Poland (and not only for Poland), something that our fathers and elder brothers had been waiting for since the war. On the other hand, it was a period of unbelievably hard work for me, several months without any private life whatsoever. Although I'd been active in the opposition previously, I'd always had enough time to do this and that, to go to the movies, to chat with friends.

It's hard even to imagine what went on in the Gdańsk Inter-Factory Strike Committee, at least at the beginning. I'd get home at night, eat something, fall into bed, and the next morning it was back to the grindstone. But this wasn't the main reason—this wasn't why I came to the conclusion that there was no point in battling on any longer. I simply began to see how people were changing, how ambition and position were going to the heads of people who used to be good friends, how colleagues who used to be unpretentious and co-operative with each other were turning into bosses who destroyed their opponents. Suddenly I realized that success by no means necessarily changes people for the better, that the social and national success of this movement was no longer my success. I felt worse and worse, but perhaps I was just being oversensitive.

Unfortunately, there was something more. The movement began to acquire all the negative characteristics of the system: intolerance toward people with different opinions, the stifling of criticism, primitive chauvinism. I can't imagine a situation in which a guy could have stood up during elections to the Solidarity leadership and said, "I'm a nonbeliever." The candidates included various people, Catholics and atheists, but every one of them raised high the cross. There wasn't one who would have said, "I won't swear by God because I'm a nonbeliever. Elect me if you want to. If not, don't."

The cult of leadership flourished. First of all, the supreme leader—Wałęsa, whom one couldn't criticize; then the leaders in every region and virtually every factory. And what was worse—just as Fromm described in *Escape from Freedom*—people wanted to rid themselves of

7

their freedom, to hand it over to these puffed-up leaders. How else can you describe the attitude when someone gets up at a regional meeting and says that his constituents have bound him to vote for everything that Wałęsa says and against everything that Andrzej Gwiazda says? More than once I felt as though I was taking part in a farce. Even at the Party congress you can't get away with something like that.

Intolerance went together with chauvinism. There emerged within Solidarity a wing that can only be compared with "Grunwald" or *Rzeczywistość*.⁹ I could see only one difference—their attitude toward communism. The "real Poles" from Solidarity represented a totalitarian ideology, but of a color other than red. Even stranger was the fact that this wing acquired considerable influence among workers. On the other hand, the so-called liberal circles, whose core was made up of the old opposition, got squeezed out—by Party propaganda, by the "real Poles," and by the Church, which was much closer in ideological terms to the totalitarian group in Solidarity.

I struggled on for a long time, until I finally realized that if society wanted to go in a completely different direction from the one I thought it ought to follow, then let it. The movement acquired its own dynamic, becoming—despite all logic—ever more radical (but only verbally). There came a point when democratically elected activists lost all contact with reality. And reality was more than Solidarity, more than radical leaflets, and Radio Free Europe; it was the USSR, the army, and the Security Service, which we knew already in the autumn of 1980 had drawn up a list of people to be interned. To my amazement, Kuroń—whom I had known as a pragmatist with his feet firmly on the ground—also lost all sense of reality, as did Modzelewski. Madness ensued. People stopped thinking in political terms and began thinking in mystical categories—that as soon as the word was spoken, it would become flesh. In other words, we only had to say "hand over power," and power would be transferred to our hands. Of course, the leaders were under enormous social pressure, but that doesn't excuse them; leaders are supposed to be leaders precisely because they can think, foresee developments, and, if necessary, swim against the tide. Either they should have spoken out while simultaneously getting ready for a confrontation or they shouldn't have run on at the mouth.

The only problem was: who was to take charge of the preparations? The people from the old opposition who knew and trusted each other could, of course, have worked out a system of interregional com-

8

munication independent of telexes and telephones, they could have got some printing equipment together. But they didn't particularly want to. For some people, I and my colleagues had become a symbol of evil, of cunning and political maneuvering. We didn't want to become symbols of theft as well. After all, if I'd wanted to hide an offset machine or a radio transmitter, I would have had to do so secretly. And I had no guarantee that in the event it were seized in a police raid, someone wouldn't say that I'd stolen it and made use of it for some kind of political game. I remember how Wałęsa once visited a common acquaintance and saw a duplicator at her place. Aha, he thought to himself, a duplicator; she must have stolen it. . . . And he gave this woman's address to Andrzej Słowik, who came from Łódź to get the duplicator, telling him, "Take it out of there, it's ours." When I heard about this I was absolutely furious with Wałęsa. I told him he should have asked first if the duplicator really belonged to the union. His reply to this was simply, "Get another one, a new one." I thought to myself, "That's a great idea; I take one, then they catch me. All duplicators have a serial number that customs make a note of, and then we'll have a real mess."

All this tells you what kind of possibilities there were—and what the atmosphere was. The atmosphere made it impossible to engage in any activity that demanded a high level of secrecy. A lot of secrecy demands a lot of trust. There wasn't any trust, so there weren't any preparations.

In addition to this, we had what was, in my opinion, a disastrous policy in the selection of the national and regional leadership. And I mean selection rather than election, because in each case people were chosen by one person only, something that was democratically accepted by the majority. And chosen according to the following principle: they weren't going to get out of line. As a rule, people who never get out of line are people who don't have their own opinion or enough civic courage to voice it. This principle came back to haunt the union with a vengeance in the most extreme fashion—on December 13, 1981.

BUJAK I.3

When union organizers in the Mazowsze region began considering how to get ready for the confrontation that the authorities were preparing, they were hindered by the basic issue of openness in the union. This openness was so far-reaching that it went beyond the bounds of security or even logic. On the one hand, it was worth it, because if they had plotted in secrecy, the accusations that official propaganda hurled at Solidarity after December 13 might have found some support; on the other hand, however, it made it impossible for Solidarity to prepare for something like martial law.

What do we mean by preparing for something like martial law? Simply that we had to hide some money, some printing equipment, paper, hundreds of things that cost money. If we were really going to keep this a secret, only I and the treasurer should have known about it. But the union engaged in normal, or even abnormal, financial management. There were constant rows over finances, accusations of misappropriation and wastefulness, demands that people account for every penny. Given this level of supervision to ensure that every penny was spent properly, how was I to conceal anything without having the presidium or the entire Regional Board vote on it? It would have been incredibly difficult. I'm not saying it would have been impossible, because some regions did manage it, although on a fairly small scale. In Mazowsze, where quarrels over money were virtually a daily occurrence, there was no way we could have hidden a large sum. We planned to hide fifty million but we only managed ten. We wanted to hide some printing equipment and hard currency, but—in light of continuing suspicions—the dollars that had long been stored under mattresses were paid into an account in a state bank, and the machines (whose location had been assiduously traced) were allocated around the region. Here, though, I had some security elsewhere: I felt that as long as the NOWa independent publishing house existed and had its equipment safe and secure, we would have access to printing equipment.

WŁADYSŁAW FRASYNIUK I.1

Because of the legendary story of the eighty million złoties withdrawn from the bank, for a long time Wrocław enjoyed the reputation of being the region best prepared for any eventuality.[10] Nevertheless, Frasyniuk considers that this wasn't entirely the case.

We weren't at all prepared for conspiratorial activity. Neither the

National Commission nor its presidium had done anything, the regions had done very little and—and this was the basic mistake—the factory commissions had done even less. In our region we issued, two or three times, special instructions detailing what to do in the event of a state of emergency. In November 1981 we sent the final version out to all union bodies, suggesting they establish alternative, clandestine commissions and work out a system of interfactory communication in case telexes and telephones were cut off, that they hide their equipment, documents, and so on. The reception these guidelines met in the enterprises was fairly typical. They didn't have much practical effect (for example, only about twenty to thirty percent of factories established alternative commissions), but they had a great psychological impact. People read them, passed them from hand to hand, pinned them on their bulletin boards, and said to one another, "There you are, we've had instructions, let the authorities know we're ready." The instructions themselves gave people a sense of security. On December 13 nearly everyone at the bus depot on Grabiszyńska Street was clutching a copy and saying, "We've done that, now we need to do this. We've dealt with point *a*, what about point *b*?"

In short, I wouldn't exaggerate the impact of this whole campaign. We Poles often say that the law exists to be broken or circumvented, and nobody ever follows the regulations, which, in any case, are usually pulled out of thin air. This is why our instructions weren't the decisive factor in this case either; more important was people's consciousness (or lack of it) of the goal of our struggle. In places where the factory commissions and regional boards functioned badly, where people were overcome by passivity, where there was no flow of information, there was no consciousness. On the other hand, if people knew what they were fighting for, everyone joined in the protest—not just workers in the large factories, not just young workers and students, but also their mothers, fathers, and grandparents, in a word, everyone who realized what it was that we were about to lose.

Technical preparations weren't the problem. More important was the fact that people weren't mentally prepared. Nobody imagined that this seemingly weak government would prove strong enough to turn the police (who had set up their own independent trade union) or the army (our workmates and neighbors) on us. We were more afraid of intervention from outside; I know that some people had even printed leaflets in Russian for Soviet soldiers. So I wouldn't exaggerate our

11

level of technical preparedness, although we did, of course, remember that once the authorities do make a move, they try to get their hands on the money before anything else. From the very beginning we concealed some funds (even some of the money collected during the August 1980 strikes) just in case. In September 1980, we had 800,000 złoties hidden, and by March 1981—10 million. Nevertheless, by the autumn, given that the situation was deteriorating, we'd come to the conclusion that this wasn't nearly enough for such a big region. It was just three of us who decided to conceal a larger sum, and this was done by Józef Pinior at the beginning of December. I advised everyone I could to do the same, but I don't know how many did. The heads of the individual sections in our region received instructions to this effect, and the guys in Legnica, for example, hid 2 million.

As far as printing equipment was concerned, we simply didn't have anything to conceal. We were barely getting by. Our guys had taken bits and pieces from ancient machines to make new ones so that we'd have something to print with. Just before martial law, we finally got some fantastic equipment from the Swedish unions, so we organized a decent place for it, and the Swedes trained our printers. We simply couldn't risk damaging these good machines that we'd been dreaming about for so long by hiding them somewhere. As for our old duplicators—we'd been planning to give them to Wałbrzych and Legnica, but in the end we (a small group of us) gave them to the non-Solidarity press. We simply felt that it was vital to have publications that were independent of both the union and the government. The only thing was, we couldn't say so openly or the union members would have torn us to pieces. As luck would have it, it was precisely these duplicators that were saved.

On the other hand, we lost all our documents, although we had prepared a special place for them. It was Zbigniew Mikoś who organized this on his own initiative. He was a veteran of the wartime underground and had never trusted the Reds. His hiding place contained radio telephones, a couple of ancient cars, and even cans of paralyzing gas and rubber truncheons made to order—all of it waiting for the right moment. He also found some people who knew how to alter official documents. Mikoś was prepared for anything, but dreadfully secretive. We always treated him with a pinch of salt because of his ideas and exaggerated caution. Nobody knew where he kept the stuff; when he died suddenly a month before martial law, he took his secret to the grave.

LIS I.2

The Gdańsk Regional Board also sensed that things were heading for a violent showdown. It was late, very late in the day, however, when they started to make the first preparations. Five days before martial law the board established a special group, whose members included Bogdan Lis.

This group, which, in addition to me, included Kłys and Samsonowicz, was supposed to make sure we had some printing equipment concealed, decide on a means of communication between factories, and withdraw as much money as possible from the bank. This last operation was particularly complicated in Gdańsk because at one time the regional conference had passed a resolution that a given percentage of union dues should go to the regional authorities. Then the resolution was rescinded, and the percentage reduced. That's why we now had to persuade the factories to transfer some of their funds into a special strike account. We even designated people who were to withdraw and hide this money, but we began everything too late. December 13 simply took us by surprise. We had assumed that any changes would be introduced through the Sejm [parliament], which would have given us another few weeks to organize countermeasures.

In my opinion, many activists believed it possible to reach some kind of agreement with the authorities. It was widely felt that the Communists weren't so bad, that conflicts were based on misunderstandings, and that it would never come to the use of force. There was also a widespread sense of our strength and people in addition wanted some psychological security, they wanted to believe that we weren't in danger. Solidarity's chief weakness, particularly toward the end of 1981, lay in the bragging of its activists, including many at the factory level. This was probably not true of the majority, but the tone was set by those who shouted loudest and pounded the table at the right moment. We lacked experience (not just the activists but the entire population), experience that would have allowed us to wield power in a democratic fashion. In Gdańsk two factions—actually, two programs [Wałęsa's and Gwiazda's]—were competing with each other. There were mistakes on both sides, but the second program, the one that lost out in the end, was probably more correct, because it envisaged democratic controls over those in power, including those who held power in the union; it envisaged the kind of activity we'd talked about in August and even earlier. The mistakes contained in these programs derived from the fact that they'd emerged at a time of sharp

13

struggle, which cast a shadow over the constructive proposals put forward by both Wałęsa and Gwiazda.

I hope that people now see clearly the behavior of many of those tub-thumpers who have either emigrated or signed declarations of loyalty or have simply pulled in their tails and fallen silent. In future we finally have to learn how to listen to people's arguments rather than just to the amount of noise they make.

Another weakness of the union was the enormous growth in the number of its paid staff, which was particularly acute in the Gdańsk region. Eighty percent of those employed in the Regional Board (and most of them also worked for the National Commission) were appointed according to the wrong criteria. At the beginning, there was some justification to employing people only on the basis of trust, but later we should have established a clear personnel policy. Because the majority of the staff lacked the appropriate qualifications and were poorly organized, they were overwhelmed, and the presidium clearly had no desire to deal with the issue consistently. In addition, the Regional Board had its own workplace Solidarity organization, and a very aggressive one at that!

Many of the region's employees had helped create Solidarity, had taken part in the August strikes; some of them had previously been involved in the opposition, in the Free Trade Unions. How could you throw them out or be hard on them? This problem was based precisely on the lack of understanding about the nature of democracy. After all, these people had been struggling for democracy and not for their right to be a decision-making cog in a democratic structure.

At the same time, activists were shouting and swaggering, the whole union was talking about a confrontation—having in mind a completely different kind of confrontation from the one the authorities were contemplating. Solidarity was shooting off at the mouth while the authorities were getting ready to shoot for real.

BORUSEWICZ I.2

In contrast to leading Solidarity activists, Borusewicz neither swaggered nor felt himself duty bound to think for others. At the meeting with his "factional" friends he made a speech about the fact that, despite everything, the authorities were relaxing the pressure: on television they had stopped transmitting recordings of the Radom meeting

*of regional chairmen (which they had obtained by bugging the con-
ference room);[11] the atmosphere had improved, the regime probably
wouldn't attack. And that was really Borusewicz's belief too—until he
heard that the sale of gasoline had been banned, that strange police
maneuvers were in progress, and that it was impossible to get through
on the phone anywhere. He left the meeting a little earlier than the
others because he wanted to ride with Krzysztof Dowgiałło in the direction of Sopot, but when he saw a police van in front of his apartment
building, all the pieces of the puzzle began to fall alarmingly into place.*

Had I felt responsible for others, I would have reacted somehow,
I'd have raised the alarm. But no, I didn't tell anyone about what I'd
seen or what I thought it meant. As much out of my usual caution as
anything else, since I didn't want to look like an idiot again, like
someone who raises a panic every so often. A couple of times before,
I'd warned that we needed to get ready because there was an attack on
the way. When I heard in November that the Politburo was going to
discuss imposing a state of emergency, I rushed to a meeting of the
presidium that was then taking place. Of course, they were a bit
alarmed, but they didn't really react. And when nothing happened
during the next few days, I looked like an idiot. Now that I was . . .
how shall I put it . . . an out-patient, at least I had the luxury of not
having to think for everyone else.

NOTES

1. On December 11, 1981, Solidarity's National Commission met in the Gdańsk
Shipyard to decide how the union should respond to the government's apparent determination to provoke an all-out confrontation. After months of increasing tension, the
Central Committee of the Polish United Workers' party had, on November 28, passed
a resolution proclaiming the need to equip the government with emergency powers to
counteract the threat to "the socialist state and public order and security." The Solidarity leadership assumed—mistakenly, as it turned out—that the necessary legislation would be debated at a meeting of the Sejm (parliament) scheduled for December
15. On December 3, the presidium of the National Commission, meeting in Radom,
issued a statement calling for a 24-hour warning strike should the Sejm accord the
government emergency powers and an all-out general strike should the government
actually implement such measures. This statement was to be discussed and voted on
by the full Solidarity leadership at the Gdańsk meeting of the National Commission.
The Polish leadership, however, decided to circumvent debate in the Sejm, and the
decision to impose martial law was ratified by the Council of State, a body empowered
to issue decrees between sessions of the Sejm. Solidarity thus had no time to prepare
for a strike, and its leadership was taken by surprise.

2. Here and throughout the book, the text in italics is the authors' summary of statements made either by the person being interviewed or by other Solidarity activists who were present during the interview.

3. Polish Peasant party—a prewar political party; the Home Army—the non-Communist war-time resistance.

4. In March 1981, a Solidarity meeting in Bydgoszcz was attacked by police, and several union members were injured. The ensuing conflict was the most serious confrontation between the government and Solidarity, solved with a compromise leading to the official recognition of Rural Solidarity.

5. In the fall of 1981 Jacek Kuroń proposed the formation of what he then called a Committee of National Salvation, in which representatives of the Party, the Church, and Solidarity would share power. This idea was subsequently endorsed by those within the Solidarity leadership who hoped for a compromise with the authorities.

6. Thus Bujak decided to go home, and escaped arrest at the hotel.

7. A reference to the Young Poland Movement, an independent group based in Gdańsk and led by Alexander Hall. Kuroń was obviously trying to minimize the importance of the fact that the Security Service was looking for Hall.

8. In his radio address, General Jaruzelski declared that Poland found itself "on the edge of an abyss," fast approaching a "national catastrophe." To save the country from this "catastrophe," the Council of State had passed a decree imposing martial law (referred to in Polish as a "state of war") from midnight, December 12. Jaruzelski informed his listeners that a Military Council of National Salvation had been formed to function as an emergency government, military commissars had been appointed at all levels of the state administration and in some factories, restrictions on civil liberties had been introduced, and a number of people "representing a threat to the security of the state" had been interned. The "restrictions" on civil liberties referred to by Jaruzelski were spelled out in the decree passed by the Council of State. They included the "suspension" of Solidarity and many other organizations; a ban on all publications not approved by the state authorities; a ban on strikes and public meetings (including theater and cinema performances) held without permission of the state authorities; and provisions for the internment of anyone over the age of seventeen about whom there were "justified suspicions" that they represented a threat to state security. In addition, "the appropriate state authorities" were empowered to impose a curfew, ban travel to and from the region under their jurisdiction, limit or stop all postal and telecommunication services, and censor the mail and telephone conversations. Prison sentences of up to ten years' imprisonment would be imposed on anyone found guilty of infringing martial law regulations.

9. Grunwald—a hard-line, nationalist Party faction with strong anti-Semitic elements. *Rzeczywistość*—an official weekly with a similar ideology.

10. The eighty million złoties referred to here were withdrawn from the Lower Silesia Solidarity bank account by Józef Pinior, the regional treasurer, on December 3, 1981, ten days before the imposition of martial law. When martial law was imposed, Pinior went into hiding, and the money was used to finance underground activity. Despite the fact that there was nothing illegal about the withdrawal, the Polish authorities alleged that Pinior had embezzled the money. Pinior was finally arrested

16

on April 24, 1983, and subsequently sentenced to four years' imprisonment on charges of being a member of the ICC.

11. Unbeknownst to Solidarity, the Polish authorities had recorded the National Commission presidium meeting in Radom on December 3. Three days later, Warsaw radio began broadcasting edited extracts purporting to show that Solidarity was planning to use force to overthrow the government.

2

Fighting in the factories. Counting our mistakes. Passive resistance: the origin of defeat. People write letters. Five people on guard at gate number two. The fall of a symbol. The techniques of pacification. The strikes are over.

FRASYNIUK I.2

On the night of December 12–13, Frasyniuk returned to his region with a group of activists from Wrocław. On the way they had to change trains. They learned about the imposition of martial law from a waitress in the station restaurant in Poznań.

Of course, we thought this was simply a sign of the panic sown by government propaganda. Later on, a policeman came over to us and told us that martial law had been imposed. Now, he said, pointedly, the police were going to have the chance to really "clean up." To which one of us replied, "Shit, we'll have to clean up, too, in the end." The policeman didn't react and left the restaurant. But later they took that guy who'd made the remark to the internment camp and cleaned *him* up.

We moved off with the feeling that ominous events had, after all, begun. When the conductor looked in on our compartment (we were sitting comfortably in first class, although we only had second-class tickets), we immediately offered our apologies and money for the extra fare. "Gentlemen," he said, "at this point nothing matters, tickets don't matter. I know who you are and I've heard they're waiting for you in Wrocław; you'd better get off at the next station."

The next station was Leszno. The chairman of the Leszno region got off there. No one was waiting for him, everything seemed quiet and peaceful. Anyway, he got off and during the first days of the "war" he gave an interview in which he stated that he was in favor of socialism, whatever it took.

Before we got to Oborniki, the conductor came back to tell us that this was the last stop before Wrocław and our last chance to get off. We told him we'd go as near to Wrocław as possible and then try to jump out before we got to the station, since the train was bound to stop somewhere. The conductor shook his head but didn't argue. A few kilometers outside the city, the train began to slow down. I jumped off while we were still moving, but the others got off without difficulty because the train came to a halt. It's impossible to say whether the driver stopped on purpose, but for the sake of the story let's say he did.

Who was on the train apart from me? Let's see if I can remember. Janek Winnik, one of the deputy chairmen, Jan Seń, the members of the National Commission from our region, the whole Lower Silesia contingent who'd gone to the meeting, Jan Sobczyk, the journalist, the guys from Opole together with their chairman, Jałowiecki, and then that guy from Leszno. Modzelewski? Modzelewski stayed behind with Kuroń to discuss who should be included in the provisional government.

Initial conditions under the crackdown varied wildly. In Wrocław the "war" was vicious. In Poznań the Army Security Service went around unarmed, there were buses and taxis on the streets, and at the station an exhibition devoted to Katyń was on display, complete with candles.[1] And here in Wrocław—one patrol after the other, everywhere there were troops with machine guns, and there was no public transportation.

We didn't yet know whether the city transportation was at a standstill because it had broken down or because of martial law. At the depot on Słowiańska Street we were greeted joyfully, well . . . some people greeted us joyfully and some (women whose husbands had been carted off in the night) greeted us with tears. I said a few words, I reminded them of the resolution passed at Radom, but it turned out that people already knew exactly what needed to be done. Crowds of people were gathering outside the gates (it was Sunday), and the workers were answering questions, showing them the resolution, issuing instructions. There was a workers' guard, flags were flying— a solid strike, no doubt about it.

In this situation we decided to move to depot number seven on Grabiszyńska Street—the center of the August strike. It was likely that representatives from the factories would turn up there, because some people had gone to work even though it was Sunday. It was these people who rescued documents and ran up flags and banners with slogans like "Strike," "General Strike," "Universal Strike." There were flags flying everywhere—at large factories like FAT, Fadroma, Cuprum, Dolmel, Pafawag, Elwro, at small plants, design bureaus, at the university, the Agricultural Academy, the polytechnic, the Higher School of Fine Arts, the Economics Academy. There wasn't a single store, no matter how small, without a red-and-white flag. The streets were full of people with backpacks and sleeping bags, people walking around quite openly with a blanket under their arm. Everyone was getting ready to occupy the factories.

On Saturday night, the ZOMO occupied regional headquarters. They sealed all the doors, secured everything with chains, and surrounded it with radio vans and trucks. Nevertheless, some of our printers got through the fence in order to run off some communiques and conceal some equipment. Others also rescued what they could. The ZOMO caught a guy who worked with the factory radio system just as he was carting off the receivers, tape recorders, and tapes. They took him off to police headquarters, where there was a long line of people waiting to be interrogated. There was a man who'd just had his ID returned to him and was leaving. The quick-thinking radio operator—still with the bag in his possession—handed it to him saying, "Take this and hang on to it until the 'war' is over."

Even now, we have no idea where that electronic equipment ended up, but thank God something was rescued. At least it's helping people to hear Radio Free Europe.

As for the Swedish printing equipment—large machinery that was bolted down—the ZOMO smashed it up when they realized that we were using it right under their nose. They broke down the doors, smashed up the printshop with crowbars, and then went on to the rooms that they hadn't touched before and destroyed everything— cupboards, desks, telephones, radios, tape recorders. . . . In the heat of the battle they went up to the fourth floor, where they also smashed all the equipment belonging to the branch [government] unions.

In depot number seven, the Regional Strike Committee (RSC) was formed. Its members included Frasyniuk and others from the Regional Board who had escaped arrest.

At seven o'clock in the evening, the pacification of the City Transportation Authority (CTA) began. We had already arranged with the drivers that if the ZOMO showed up, they were to leave by another exit without putting up any resistance. The CTA was just a fenced-in area—fuel tanks, buses, and not many people—so there was no point in defending it. The strikers would have been condemned to a heavy beating, if not certain death. Even before the pacification got under way, we decided to move to the Dolmel and Pafawag factories, which were next door to each other.

On Monday morning a general strike began in Wrocław. At this point it's difficult to establish how particular enterprises reacted, because a whole mythology has arisen, and everyone adds something to it, so I don't want to say anything about the factories I didn't go to. People adopted various tactics, but the basics were the same everywhere: every factory established a strike committee and every factory had workers on guard.

Every single worker on the first shift, as well as many from the second and the night shifts, turned up at Pafawag and Dolmel in the morning. At about three in the afternoon some people lost their nerve and began to leave; there was even some jostling and name-calling at the gates. But it seemed that most of them came back between six and seven, bringing food for those who'd stayed behind. At Pafawag, where we stayed on Monday, the typists typed up documents, students distributed posters in the town, and discussions took place in the workshops. Everyone kept going over and over the same question: What to do? Our people repaired the factory radio system, which had been demolished on the order of the director, and broadcast communiqués, played strike songs, and read out leaflets. Of course, the workers immediately hung a photograph of the Pope and a picture of the Virgin Mary over the gate. There were flowers and a red-and-white banner. The atmosphere was fairly militant. Some workers seemed to be extremely hyped up, as though they were actually spoiling for a fight. Others seemed tense and horrified at what was going on, but

21

despite their great fear for their own lives, they felt that they had to do what they were doing (this was moving and somehow disarming). That's why they came back.

RSC representatives informed two of the directors that the workers had occupied the factory. At the same time, they demanded that the *voivod* [regional administrator] and military commander of the city come to the factory. Instead of the voivod and the general, some really elite company showed up: a couple of colonels and majors—both military and Security. They shuffled and shifted around, talked about "the noble, class-conscious working class of Wrocław," about "troublemakers," "antisocialist elements," and "inciters of unrest." One of the colonels made a speech to the effect that he was a patriot and would never agree to shoot at Polish workers, and if he received such an order, he'd rather shoot himself in the head. All in all, though, they were all fairly alarmed at the situation and so agitated by their own propaganda that they forgot whom they were talking to. During this chat, another column of tanks and transport trucks arrived, and the conversation came to an end.

These early days of the "war" were characterized by intense discussions. Workers invited members of the RSC to their clubs, canteens, and workshops and asked one question after another. The main issue was: What did the National Commission do that the other side had resorted to armed force? They talked about economic reform, about justice, about the impossibility of totalitarian dictatorship coexisting with democratic structures . . .

Everyone was waiting for information from other parts of the country. People were convinced that at least sixty percent of factories were on strike, and when we got news on Monday of the strike in the Gdańsk Shipyard, it raised everyone's spirits.

It was only then, however, that people began asking themselves an obvious question: Supposing the enemy gets inside, what do we do? In shops where the majority of workers were young, some people wanted to erect barricades and fight. Frasyniuk called on people not to fight but to do everything they could to hinder an attack. He said that if the ZOMO got into the plant we would leave peacefully, without defending ourselves or provoking them. Even if that happened, the other factories would still be on strike. If they pacified the others, we'd come here, rebuild our structures, and get ready to support other factories.

Privately, however, everyone was hoping that the ZOMO and the tanks were nothing but a show of strength—that the whole country was on strike and that it would be enough to last out honorably for three days for the authorities to give in and begin negotiations.

BORUSEWICZ I.3

It looked as if an unprepared Solidarity was being attacked by an equally unprepared opponent. The campaign that the authorities presented as organized and super-efficient was, in reality, a chaotic struggle. The lists of those to be detained had, it is true, been drawn up in advance, but perhaps too far in advance, because they contained the names of many people who had died or who had long been abroad. In Gdańsk there were cases where two students on the list shared a room, and a police unit came for one of them at two in the morning and another unit for the second one at six—of course, he'd long since made his escape. They didn't arrest anyone from the Port of Gdańsk, and afterward, during the strike, it was one of the toughest centers of resistance.

If people hadn't been so surprised by raids in the middle of the night that they opened their doors immediately, the ZOMO (who didn't always turn up in large groups) would have had to spend another ten minutes breaking doors down with crowbars; everyone else in the apartment building would have been woken up, and the ZOMO would have fulfilled perhaps only eighty percent of their plan. Even though they caught nearly everyone, the small percentage who escaped was enough. But what would have happened if, say, out of ten thousand people to be arrested, two thousand had got away?

This operation, which was the most important of all from the authorities' point of view, was carried out inefficiently; it was effective only because our side made even more mistakes. In this respect they were competing with each other. For example, every few kilometers or so along the road stood tanks that had broken down on the way from the barracks into town. If the armies of the Warsaw Pact are dependent on such dilapidated equipment, how are we ever going to beat the Americans? Nevertheless, Bujak, who has spent some time behind the wheel of these things, declares that if they really have to get somewhere they usually manage it, so I guess they broke down because the troops weren't too enthusiastic about the battle. Apparently neither the rank and file nor their officers would have taken the risk of openly defying an order. If only, though, they'd used the army in the front line . . .

The authorities didn't attempt to overplay their hand and the army was essentially kept in reserve. The successive waves of hardware that rolled through the streets were mostly for decoration. The attack on the Gdańsk Shipyard was carried out with the aid of two tanks. Only two! One of them broke down the gate. Its crew must have been fairly determined (particularly their commander, who was driving it himself), but despite this, and although it didn't look as though people were going to stand in its path, the tank came to a halt before the first collision, giving the shipyard workers time to scatter. Bogdan Borusewicz talked to the crew of the second tank, which dragged off a truck that was blocking the road leading to the neighboring Northern Shipyard. He clearly saw that the tank crew (who must have been specially selected from their unit) had tears in their eyes, even though nothing had really happened so far and they hadn't yet had to shoot at anyone.

Attacks on the factories were carried out mainly by specially selected ZOMO forces (actually, Special Battalions). When the "regular" ZOMO learned that they were going to the Gdańsk Shipyard, many of them suddenly started complaining, "I don't have any gas," "Maybe someone else could go?" Security guys were assigned to these units, but in the end they too got lost somewhere or went off to hide.

BUJAK I.4

The mistakes made by Solidarity had more serious consequences, however. The cardinal error, which hastened the disaster and perhaps even tipped the scales, was our reliance on passive resistance. Bujak considers that the roots of this error are to be found in the period preceding martial law.

The business with the Fire Fighter Officers' School in Warsaw was a litmus test. If the students had defended themselves, if they'd barricaded themselves in, thrown some bricks, if they had engaged in some kind of active resistance, the authorities would have had more to fear on December 13. But the School simply engaged in passive resistance, and people allowed themselves to be taken off.[2] In December, this was used as a model.

24

*Since the business at the Fire Fighters' School, the Mazowsze region
had theoretically been on strike alert, and the whole incident inevitably
influenced further developments in Warsaw. After talking to Bujak on
the phone during the meeting of the National Commission, Wiktor
Kulerski decided to go and see what was going on. He didn't trust the
Reds, so the first thing he thought of was to take some warm shoes with
him. Outside his apartment, a taxi was waiting for him with the news
from regional headquarters that the telephone lines had been cut. So
this was it, then. Now virtually certain, he stuffed various extra items
into his bag alongside the shoes. At headquarters, any remaining
doubts were dispelled. The building was surrounded by ZOMO—this
was no place for Kulerski. He continued on his way. At the City Transportation Authority they were calling all the buses back to the depots.
The Rosa Luxemburg Factory was empty; there was no sign of either the
ZOMO or Solidarity members. It was the same at the Kasprzak Plant.
In the meantime, Kulerski had changed cars and he was driven to the
Warsaw Steel Works in a Fiat station wagon belonging to the City Soli-
durity Commission. It was already early in the morning of the thir-
teenth. The steel works were surrounded by ZOMO. The driver of the
Fiat reversed rapidly, the car rolled into a ditch full of water, the
wheels sank into mud up to the axle, and the wheels lost all grip.
The ZOMO began to look suspiciously in their direction and then some
of them began running toward the car. They didn't make it in time.
Workers leaving the plant were quicker; in a flash, they lifted the car
out of the ditch and set it on the road. The car roared off, carrying
Kulerski and his two companions to a safe apartment where, after an
eventful night, they were finally able to sit quietly and think: what
should they do now?*

*The more they thought, the less clear things became. People were
scattered all over without any way of contacting each other or coordinating resistance. On Monday, one division of Ursus went on strike,
and the rest of the workers went home. On Tuesday those who had gone
home returned to join those who had gone on strike, but the strike was
already over. There were no new organizers, there was no will to resist.*

BORUSEWICZ I.4

*Borusewicz's opinion concerning the fatal consequences of the slogan of
passive resistance is even more radical than that of Bujak.*

Passive resistance brought about the death throes of Solidarity. On the whole, the storm troopers from ZOMO won easily (Upper and Lower Silesia were exceptions), without haste, after having surveyed the situation for a week in order to avoid a head-on confrontation. The worst thing was that they even entered the Gdańsk Shipyard. Everyone saw the shipyard as a fortress, as a symbol, and yet it was clear that the shipyard committee was weak, the weakest of all the committees in large enterprises—in both intellectual and organizational terms, not to mention courage. Proclaiming passive resistance simply encouraged the authorities to crush the strike by force. They should have done just the opposite—they should have given the appearance of determination to fight to the bitter end. Moreover, the slogan of passive resistance gave rise to an unbearable psychological situation, since the strikers were just sitting there waiting when the other side came in and laid into them.

In the shipyard there was a kind of dual power system. On the one hand, there were the activists from the National Commission (to be honest, some of the second string), who tried to rectify the situation and, on the other hand, the shipyard committee. The former had only recently been elected to the union leadership; they didn't know the area or the people; they came from regions that didn't have any great strike traditions. They were here, they signed various things, they pretended to be doing something, but they didn't have the slightest influence on what went on in the shipyard.

SZUMIEJKO I.2

The National Strike Committee, made up of members of the National Commission who had escaped arrest, was not actually formed in the shipyard but in the Port of Gdańsk. Early on Sunday morning, there was no one in the shipyard apart from the janitor. At a meeting at the docks, Eugeniusz Szumiejko spoke.

It was quiet as the grave in the cafeteria, and I thought to myself there wasn't going to be any response, that this was the end of any support, that we were strangers there. I sat down to a bowl of soup next to three dock workers; I stirred my soup and asked them a banal question, "Well, what's going to happen now?" One of them, also stirring his soup, replied, "What do you think is going to happen? We'll fuck the bastards, and that's that." Suddenly my spirits rose. I real-

26

ized that, as far as they were concerned, everything was obvious, and their silence meant simply that they were thinking how to go about it.

On Sunday we printed some communiques and set up an organization. On Monday there were rallies in four of the docks. I was at the Northern Docks. In the meantime, the National Strike Committee moved to the shipyard but, as you know, the strike in the shipyard was broken at six o'clock on Wednesday morning; several people were arrested, and I returned to the docks. There was already a crush at the monument.[3] Someone said that if we could send a hundred lads with sticks, the crowd would simply crush the ZOMO. Staszek Jarosz, head of the docks committee, seized on the idea and began to organize groups, which were to set off by bus. Since I knew there was little point in staying at the docks (Staszek was a bit worked up and said, "You guys from the National Commission, you've screwed up so many things already, at least don't interfere with us!"), and since I knew that this was really the end and that we had to establish contact with those who were still in the city, I told Jarosz I was going to the monument and that we'd somehow find each other later. I got two dock workers as bodyguards and I battled in the front line for about three hours. These two guys finally pulled me out of there and took me to someone's apartment. There was no point in going back to the shipyard either. All that remained there was a broken-down gate.

BORUSEWICZ I.5

During this whole time the shipyard was in the hands of the shipyard committee, although—in Borusewicz's opinion—there was no one among its members capable of directing the struggle.

People said, for example, that there was an agent transmitting information from the shipyard bunker. Nonsense. Who would have shut himself up in a concrete structure with only one way out in order to transmit information? But no matter. When a few guys went off to check, the chairman [of the shipyard committee] said, "It's OK, it's OK, let him carry on transmitting."

Whether or not an agent was transmitting information, the management's radio network was certainly broadcasting the whole time, with the authorities threatening us and calling on people to leave the plant. Just when the wildest rumors were circulating about what was going on in the rest of the country, when we were surrounded by tanks and troop carriers, when people thought they were among their own, the enemy blasted them right in the ear. Nevertheless, no one seized the radio network, because the chairman absolutely forbade it. We, he said, were good men who weren't going to commit any crimes or misdemeanors. This chairman had previously been an excellent treasurer, but he wasn't up to his last role. But, after all, he was chosen and anointed by the Supreme Chairman [Wałęsa] himself.

The workers sitting in the shipyard were frightened, and seeing that their leaders were also afraid, they lost all desire to put up a fight. And this is to say nothing about activists from other enterprises who had joined the shipyard strike and for whom the shipyard became a trap instead of an asylum.

BUJAK 1.5

Bujak was sure that the shipyard would fall. He was staying nearby, and he knew, and saw, what was going on. After his meeting with Janas, who was going to Warsaw (and whom the courier recognized by the fact that he'd shaved off his mustache), he decided to stay in Gdańsk a few more days. During this time he wrote several pieces in which he set out the kind of outcomes that might be expected and when, how to react, and what to do.

In the first piece, which I sent by courier, I demanded that when the shipyard fell it should proclaim a general strike for the spring, on the anniversary of Bydgoszcz. I got a reply—from Szumiejko or Konarski, I think—saying that I was sitting on my backside somewhere and didn't have the faintest idea of the people's state of mind, and for that reason my idea was a sheer fantasy. This attitude made me mad, because they didn't have any ideas of their own, and proclaiming a strike for the spring might at least have seriously alarmed the authorities. Even without this, Rakowski[4] went to talk to Lech when he was locked up. The authorities were taking some precautions just in case everything came apart at the seams and they had to discuss an accord with Solidarity. Of course we were fucked, but there was a real possibility of turning some things around. It was wasted, though.

In the second piece, I wrote about how we should organize. I suggested we create small groups of three to five people, which would concentrate on collecting dues from people they knew and would send them higher up, to a kind of joint account. From the very beginning I thought that any possibility of underground activity (which I was already considering) would depend on whether we managed to support people thrown out of work. This meant that if a hundred lost their jobs, we had to support a hundred; if it was a thousand, we had to support a thousand. The less support we could offer those who were dismissed, the less effective and the smaller in scope the underground would be.

I didn't go to the shipyard because I didn't want to make any silly mistakes. In Ursus[5] I would have known how and where to lie low if we lost out, but in the shipyard I would have had no idea. And in any case, I was convinced that activists at the national level who'd gone into hiding ought to do everything they could to survive the first few weeks. Władek Frasyniuk behaved differently and, like Janosik, ran around from one factory to another inciting strikes. But he was more directly a workers' leader. I don't think the outcome of December 1981 depended on whether or not I was at the shipyard. The course of history is determined by many sociological, psychological, and economic factors over which the individual has no influence. Apart from this, a society's worth is measured in terms of the extent to which its members manage to take responsibility for themselves, to react collectively. For example, during World War II no one had to remind the British to reduce their consumption of water, to turn out their lights, to use less electricity, and so on. They organized themselves, even though they had no enormously charismatic leaders; and no matter how many killed they would have sustained, they would still have known what to do.

LIS I.3

On the third day of the strike in the shipyard, Bujak first made contact, in writing, with Lis, who—as it turned out—had safely reached a hiding place. There he was able finally to rest and think up a litany of things that could be done. His hosts organized a courier, thanks to which he was able to make contact with the shipyard.

In that apartment, where I stayed until January 2, I issued, among other things, two statements that were immediately duplicated by a secret printshop run by students. My courier made contact with Waszkiewicz in the shipyard and gave him a cassette on which I'd recorded a speech to the shipyard workers—just in case it might be useful. The next day, however, the courier brought no answer to my question as to whether I should show up at the shipyard (Bujak asked the same question and got no reply either). Instead, I was informed that the shipyard was in chaos because there was a works strike committee and a regional committee and even a national committee; that out of several thousand people only a hundred or two remained; and that the strike didn't stand a chance of lasting out. This was already Tuesday, December 15, after the first attack on the shipyard.

BORUSEWICZ 1.6

In the afternoon of the same day, Borusewicz went to the shipyard without either asking anyone's permission or waiting for a reply.

I didn't feel obliged to hurry unduly, since I was no longer part of the union leadership. In addition, the works commission wasn't particularly crazy about me—because of the so-called struggle against Wałęsa and because I'd been in KOR;[6] maybe I was a Jew, who knows, definitely a liberal, not a worker. I knew that nothing I said would carry any weight with this group, so I didn't rush there with offers of help.

I wanted to sit quietly for a bit, and I had a place to do this because I hadn't been so stupid during the time of Solidarity as to reveal all my old, oppositionist haunts to the Security Service. So I was warm and comfortable, and it was only when I heard what was going on at the shipyard that my hair stood on end. When I got there, I was absolutely horrified. I asked a guy standing in the guard box by gate number two, "How many of you are there?" "Well, this many," he replied. "How many?" I asked again. "This many." And at gate number two there were exactly five people. I couldn't believe my eyes. I went to the workshops—empty! Just the doors standing open. I found only one person wandering about in total confusion.

There weren't even enough people for them to stand singly along the fence, let alone form groups to guard the most sensitive spots. The Gdańsk Shipyard covers several acres, so anyone who broke through the fence at any given point was immediately in no man's land. Honestly, we didn't stand a chance, particularly as the strike committee in the Repair Yard ignored my suggestion that they send their people to the shipyard. After all, we had to defend a symbol; it wasn't a question of the Gdańsk Shipyard or the Repair Yard or even Gdańsk itself but of Poland as a whole. If we'd managed to draw out the strike in the shipyard, it might have been possible to hold back the authorities on all fronts. On the other hand, I was certain that if the strike in the shipyard collapsed, the fact that a coal mine or steel works was on strike wouldn't make any difference, because people think in terms of symbols and would hang on as long as the shipyard hung on. That's why I tried desperately to defend the shipyard, although we should have got the hell out of there before the curfew.

The strikers were terrified and rendered defenseless by the slogan of passive resistance. It got to the point where we almost had to drag people out of the cafeteria by force before they'd take over from their colleagues who'd been freezing on watch for four or five hours. And then, if you pressed something into their hands (a crowbar or something), telling them to hold it so that *they* [the police] could see it, after an hour or so it turned out that nobody was holding anything and they were all standing empty-handed under the lampposts, where they could be seen from miles away. And this, because some "leader" had suddenly appeared and explained that holding something in your hand constituted a provocation because the authorities were filming the whole thing and the workers would be finished if the pictures showed that they were armed. Only when tanks started to roll were they to pick up their sticks. I explained to people that it ought to be the other way round: first we take up our sticks, and then, when the tanks start rolling and it's clear they're going to attack, we put them down. But until they attack, we have to display the maximum determination, make a lot of noise and look active, everyone with a stick, a crowbar.

When the ZOMO finally struck, there was absolutely no hope of defending anything with our men. The storm troops broke in at several places, and you know how things went after that. . . . It could have been worse, because they didn't beat anyone up. But it was a terrible loss of face.

FRASYNIUK I.3

The techniques of pacification were the same everywhere. Under cover of tanks that broke down the gates or walls, the ZOMO rushed in, using flares at night to light up the surroundings. They broke down the doors to the workshops with axes or crowbars and herded people out. Often they put their truncheons to work and used tear gas. They then took all the detainees to some open space and picked out those whose names were on a list that had been drawn up earlier. They also arrested people for a variety of other reasons. At the FAT Plant in Wrocław, for example, a red-and-white flag was flying over the cafeteria, and because the carpenters refused to take it down, they were all locked up.

During the first attack, on Wednesday, December 16, some forty to sixty strikers were arrested in every factory where the strike was broken. However, the police carted off more people (often in their overalls, sometimes barefoot), lined them up in the courtyard of the detention center or prison, and "checked them out." If someone had a pass to the factory and no one had informed against him, he was usually released after several hours. In this way, they sifted through several thousand people.

During the pacification there was a marked difference in the ZOMO's approach to equipment used by workers versus that of white-collar personnel. On the whole, the ZOMO didn't destroy any industrial machinery but demolished offices in which they found typewriters, calculators, and so on.

In Wrocław the first big attack began at 4 A.M. on Tuesday. The target was the Pafawag plant, one of the two plants where Frasyniuk and a group of RSC activists had established their base.

The ZOMO launched their attack from the side of the factory where there was a lot of open ground surrounded by a chainlink fence. They cut the fence and attacked the building where the Strike Committee had spent the night in March 1981. The second offensive was launched from the street, but the tank didn't break down the gate itself because the workers had hung on it a picture of the Virgin Mary that was lit up at night. The tank knocked out a fair stretch of wall and a couple of cars parked behind it. A moment later, they began the attack on the Dolmel plant. We decided that Piotr Bednarz, Józef Pinior, and I would move to another factory and that the other members of the RSC would make their way to the city to organize underground resistance.

We went to the Hutmen plant. The people there were terrified. They had no idea where the members of the factory commission were, they hadn't mounted guards on the walls, they hadn't mounted a watch at the gate. On the other hand, the factory security guards were still patrolling the plant. It turned out that Hutmen had adopted the tactics of an absentee strike.

So we moved to the FAT plant, where people already knew exactly what was going on at Pafawag. They also knew where their factory commission was (some thirty to fifty people who had stayed to safeguard the factory). A representative of the commission came up to us. "It's fine that you're here," he told us, "We'll organize a car to take you into the city." Our reply was simple: "No car. We're staying till the morning. We'll organize a meeting of all the workers and carry on with the strike." And that's what happened.

From FAT we went to mass meetings in Hutmen and Fadroma. It was only then that we decided that the large factories had to go on strike in such a way that the smaller ones would know. We were told that the entire Elwro factory was on strike. There had already been three attempts to crush the strike, but the women had come out, clung to the gate, and said, "No way. Over our dead bodies." They'd tried to scare them out with tear gas and threats, but they were standing firm. Just imagine, women as the workers' guards. And they didn't let the tanks in.

As you know, Elwro is a precision-engineering plant; it produces computers. The workers' council worried that if the ZOMO gained entry they'd smash up all that delicate equipment, virtually the kind you find in scientific laboratories, and that's why the women were blocking the gate. They were simply afraid that the ZOMO would destroy their work tools. Then some lieutenant gave his word of honor that if the workers vacated the plant, they wouldn't destroy anything or arrest anyone. Two days later they replaced this lieutenant and arrested lots of people; they replaced him so that an officer of the people's army wouldn't have to break his word.

At about two in the afternoon we heard that the workers at Fadroma wanted to abandon the factory. So we rushed over, and as soon as people saw us, they—these two plants, Fadroma and FAT—became so determined that the authorities had to pacify them twice. And finally they simply sacked all the workers and started hiring from scratch.

On the way back to Fadroma, Józef Pinior and I dropped in at the Dolmel factory. The workers there told us how the ZOMO had gone through the workshops waving their pistols, threatening people, beating them, putting their guns to people's heads. We asked one man on the factory commission what they intended to do, and he said they were going to let people go home. But they were supposed to come back the next day and carry on refusing to work.

33

We went back to FAT. It was already Wednesday. At seven in the morning the ZOMO broke into the factory grounds and began an attack that lasted four hours. They didn't manage to catch us, because we'd been given a couple of people whose job it was to protect us. They found an ingenious way to hide us and spread the rumor that there was no one from the RSC still in the factory.

When the strikes in FAT, Hutmen, and Fadroma had been crushed, Frasyniuk called for people to engage in passive resistance. It turned out, however, that even in Pafawag and Dolmel it was impossible to keep the strike going, because every flag that was raised, every attempt to open your mouth, every movement away from the shop floor was met with repressive measures, dismissal from work, arrest. People no longer wanted to lay themselves open to danger, so the RSC had no alternative but, with the aid of the workers, to slip away from this area crawling with ZOMO.
The strikes were over.[7]

NOTES

1. The Katyń Forest near Smolensk is the site of a mass grave of thousands of Polish officers who were captured by Soviet forces in 1939. The Soviet authorities have claimed that they were shot by the Germans, although all the evidence indicates that it was Stalin who ordered their execution.

2. A long and peaceful strike of the students of the Fire Fighters School in Warsaw ended at the beginning of December 1981 with a military takeover by the authorities. The very efficient military operation is considered by many to have been a "dress rehearsal" for the soon-to-come full-scale military imposition of martial law.

3. A reference to the monument erected under Solidarity's auspices in 1981. It commemorated the people killed in Gdańsk and Gdynia by government troops during worker protests against price increases in 1970. On December 16, 1981, a crowd gathered at the monument to honor the anniversary of the shootings and to protest the imposition of martial law. Riot police attempted to disperse the demonstration. According to official sources, during the subsequent fighting, one person was killed, and 164 civilians and 160 policemen were injured.

4. Mieczysław F. Rakowski, chief Party negotiator with Solidarity before martial law, appointed Poland's prime minister in September 1988.

5. Ursus—the district on the outskirts of Warsaw where Bujak lived and the name of the factory where he worked.

6. KOR is an acronym for the Workers Defense Committee, a pre-Solidarity opposition movement founded in 1976 by Jacek Kuroń, Antoni Macierewicz, and

others. It ceased to exist in 1981, dissolved by its members who considered its objectives realized.

7. *Because of lack of information, the rapid course of events, the partial nature of the accounts available to us, and the flaws of memory, our account of the first days of the "war" is somewhat distorted. There are many blank spaces within the broad outlines of the story. And time after time, the course of events gets lost in commentary. The dramatic resistance, for example, of Upper Silesia, and the "war" in Kraków, Szczecin, Łódź, and other cities, remains outside of our story.*

3

**The Pyrrhic victory of the generals. The spontaneous be-
ginnings of conspiracy. Attempts to make contact: Gdańsk,
Wrocław, Warsaw.**

BORUSEWICZ I.7

*On December 12 hardly a single member of Solidarity imagined that
the authorities were in a position to truly cripple the powerful, ten-
million strong union. By a week later, however, almost everyone agreed
that the authorities could do whatever they wanted. The myths had exploded. Nevertheless, Bogdan Borusewicz termed the December exploits
of the generals a "Pyrrhic victory."*

After all, it isn't possible to destroy an organization ten-million
strong with just one piece of paper. Perhaps the Jaruzelski group
thought that six months would be long enough to exhaust society, capture all the activists, infiltrate various groups, then do a U-turn toward
liberalization, and then . . . new foreign credits, normalization, re-
newal. Perhaps the military assumed that the West would take fright,
that its governments would voice only half-hearted protest, that the
issue would simply disappear after six months. Hence the outrage at
the West expressed by Rakowski: "After all," he might complain,
"you yourselves said things couldn't continue like this, that the Poles
had to put their house in order themselves . . . , and now that we've
done so, what appreciation do we get? After all, I Rakowski, am a

liberal, Jaruzelski is a good Pole, so let's agree that we have acted in the interests of Poland."

Yet somehow the issue wouldn't go away. There was deep-rooted mass resistance on the part of most groups of the population. Thus the authorities were unable to make an about-turn that would have lessened social pressure, meaning some civil-rights relaxations and a simultaneous improvement in the economic situation. Instead the "war" entered a new stage.

SZUMIEJKO I.3

Before the "war," Szumiejko had spent only six days in Gdańsk during his term as a member of the presidium of the National Commission (he replaced Janusz Onyszkiewicz), so he didn't know the city or anyone there. He knew, however, that of the people known to him, Lis, Bujak, perhaps Borusewicz (whom he'd met during the strike at the shipyard), and Konarski had gone into hiding. It made sense to try to contact them, but luck wasn't on Szumiejko's side, because he soon learned that Bujak had already left the city. Nor did he manage to make contact with the others.

Whenever I had some kind of tip, I went myself to the address concerned, and because it was usually after the curfew, I generally spent the night there. In this way I stayed in five or six different apartments during the first two weeks. I didn't have any couriers, but that didn't worry me particularly because I wasn't known in Gdańsk and I didn't have to change my appearance. In any case, from the very beginning of the "war," I had false papers: they hadn't arrested me at the hotel, at regional headquarters, at Lech's place, or at the shipyard, and I'd survived several hours of scuffling at the monument, so what did I have to fear? Apart from anything else, I'd been lucky enough to make contact with the right people, the dock workers who'd fought alongside me. For them it was perfectly natural that I'd walk around on the streets; they didn't pull any stupid numbers about how I couldn't go out because I'd get arrested. Finally, I have to confess that for the entire time I functioned under the illusion that the struggle would last only a couple of months and that we'd be victorious. Even in my worst imaginings, I still told myself, "The spring will be ours." Although my hosts were disheartened by what had happened in December, most of them hadn't lost hope either. They welcomed me warmly and offered me what help they could. In only a couple of cases did I encounter a different attitude. At the very beginning, when my first guardians were hunting up other places for me to stay, they made contact with a few groups that they were certain would help—for example, former Home Army people. But these old warriors with such exotic pseudonyms as "Storm" or "Gale" who used to drink vodka together before martial law and talk about how it was high time to crush the Bolsheviks once and for all, sometimes turned a deaf ear and made apologies for not being able to help. On the whole, though, things went well. I beat a few paths in various directions, usually taking my current hosts as a starting point. If someone took me in, he generally surveyed the field and sounded out his acquaintances, not just to find me a new place to stay but also to help me make more contacts. Day by day my position got stronger and I felt increasingly safe. I didn't have any problems with finding somewhere to live, food, clothes, or money.

I found Konarski quite quickly. He was somehow subdued. He would have liked to lie low a bit longer, to have looked around, waited to see if Lech had something to suggest. I was sorry that Jan Waszkiewicz had been arrested when they broke the strike at the shipyard. Later I made contact with other people from the National Commission. No one had heard anything about Lis. It was during midnight mass on Christmas Eve that I discovered that Bogdan Borusewicz was active. Someone had left a lot of leaflets in the church signed by him.

LIS I.4

On December 24 more than thirty thousand leaflets were distributed in Gdańsk churches. This spectacular feat was intended to let people know that resistance to military dictatorship continued. At the beginning of January Bogdan Lis and a small group of trusted people planned an even more spectacular feat—the freeing of Solidarity vice-president Mirosław Krupiński, who had been arrested at the shipyard and was being held in a clinic belonging to the Gdańsk Medical Academy.

After reconnoitering the area, we drew up a detailed diagram showing the location of the Security Service forces. There was a police car parked outside on the corner, and two Security guys were always on duty in Krupiński's room. We made contact with someone on the hospital staff, who was to tell Krupiński what to do on his end to ensure success. Without going into details, Krupiński was to walk calmly out of the hospital one evening; we would be waiting for him with a couple of sleighs (it was forbidden to drive cars at that hour) and we'd carry him off through the forest to a safe place. Unfortunately, Krupiński twice refused to take part in the scheme because he was afraid for his heart. Later, a man who'd been interned at Strzebielinek was transferred to the hospital. He was on the floor below Krupiński, so the Security Service simply moved downstairs. And that was it. After a month, Krupiński agreed.

BORUSEWICZ I.8

Solidarity's easy defeat in December made activists feel pressured to come up with spectacular actions, frequently modeled on examples to be found in literature about the Second World War. Some activists initially thought that only such sensational acts would arouse popular resistance on a broad scale. But already at the beginning of January there was a mass of spontaneous initiatives, mostly concentrated around the distribution of leaflets and information bulletins, as well as agitation in the factories. It was probably Borusewicz who at this time most clearly realized the limited value of anonymous leaders.

If we'd got involved in these structures and groups, we would soon have been arrested. Each of us wanted to do something, but we didn't really know what. Our threesome (Lis, Hall, and I) couldn't cover all the bases. In any case, it wasn't clear that it made sense to try to contain everything within some kind of framework. Resistance was concentrated in numerous demonstrations in December, January, and February, and we had absolutely no influence over their emergence or the course they took.

At that time we were already confronted by the problem of the internal dynamics of the future underground organization: on the one hand, a mass movement; on the other hand, the need for secrecy. Gradually we began trying to coordinate the activities of various groups, particularly those involved in printing and distribution—obviously, without any intention of monopolizing this activity. The dominant view was that the more broadly based the underground, the better for Solidarity. By the spring we could have created a single, enormous

39

organization, only what would have been the point? From the security point of view also this would have been a bad idea.

Quite early on I saw a need to coordinate activities at the regional level, and later on a national level. In order to set up the appropriate structures, though, we had to make contacts, and this was fairly difficult at the beginning. The number of military and police patrols on the streets was overwhelming, and none of us yet had any false identity papers.

LIS I.5

Bogdan Lis, who was already in touch with a number of factories in the Tri-city area[1] in January, was also looking for contacts—above all, with other sections of the Gdańsk region. One day he even walked through the woods in the snow toward the Tri-city ring road to check whether it would be possible to send people that way to Kartuza, Kościerzyna, Starogard, Pruszcz and eventually . . . to Bujak, Frasyniuk, and the wide world.

It was dreadfully deserted, not a car in sight, everything looked strange. Suddenly, right in the middle of the woods, I came across a group of ZOMO and only just managed to escape.

It was not until the beginning of February that Borusewicz, Lis, and Hall met together. Each of them already had their own group of couriers, and a network of safe apartments and mail drops where messages could be left. They'd got together some money collected in the factories, and an underground press distribution network was starting up. They could now start work on building a regional structure.

FRASYNIUK I.4

In Wrocław the embryo of such a structure had been in existence since the very beginning of the "war" in the form of the Regional Strike Committee established on December 13. Its members survived the crushing of the strikes on Grabiszyńska Street and then . . .

After the collapse of the last of the big factory strikes, Frasyniuk, Bednarz, and Pinior were alone on the street. Instead of workers with red armbands, instead of their own people, they were surrounded by

40

anonymous passers-by, perhaps friendly, perhaps enemies, but most often simply indifferent strangers. None of the three activists knew where to find the people who had left the factories under siege on December 14 in order to find safe apartments, make contacts, and start up the underground printshops. At that time, people had been thinking not about organizing a conspiracy but about transferring resistance from factories to the city. On Wednesday, December 16, it was clear, however, that the will to fight was fading and that it would take time to rekindle it. Reality thwarted initial intentions and decreed that they be adapted to the new conditions. The first task was to rebuild union cells in the factories and maintain their readiness to protest, which meant, of course, a general strike. Frasyniuk didn't then envisage any other model of the underground than building from below, from the factories. But the organization of the factories forced the RSC to establish new, broader structures, to occupy themselves with the region, with a distribution network, and with communications. This, however, was all in the future.

For the time being, the threesome went to an apartment where, sooner or later, couriers dispatched by two of them were bound to turn up. They turned up on that very day.

Initially there were a dozen or so people in hiding in Wrocław. At the first meeting they compiled a ten-point ABC of resistance. Its first instructions were: rebuild factory organizations, organize aid for the victims of repression, identify and condemn collaborators . . .

In addition to this appeal to union members, the RSC wrote two open letters to the authorities. The first was addressed to the voivod and the military commander of the Wrocław voivodship and charged both of them with responsibility for all acts of violence and lawlessness. The second, addressed to the director of a bank in Wrocław, dealt with the alleged misappropriation of eighty million złoties by Lower Silesia Solidarity activists. This letter provoked an unexpected although indirect reply. The bank director's response, in the pages of the official Gazeta Robotnicza (Workers' Gazette), quoted extracts from the RSC's letter but was unable, despite tortuous explanations, to refute the idea that every organization has the right to take money out of its own bank account and that to do so does not conflict with any legal regulations, not even those of martial law.

Painstakingly, day by day, the activists living in hiding established a network of resistance. Often they slept five or six to a room, often they went hungry. They contacted the outside world through

41

workers who acted as couriers and who gradually located other "illegals," checked out old apartments, found new ones, tracked down printing equipment. After a few days, however, the couriers gave up, apologizing but explaining they would not be able to help any more because of the terror in the factories; people were too afraid. And because no one from the RSC thought to ask these people for the address of a safe "drop," contacts and cooperation with the factories were disrupted for a short time. In the meantime, some polytechnic students appeared; they were efficient, well organized, and courageous. They had their own information service, their own radio tuned to the Security Service, their own contacts with factory workers. They remained active for quite a long time, but suddenly they too stopped, because they learned through a leak from the Security Service that they were about to be arrested; they ceased work and went into hiding. Then they returned to their families, and the Security really did arrest them.

December—what with Christmas and New Year, tanks on the streets and patrols checking identity cards, spies in the factories and housing projects—was exceptionally difficult for the conspirators. In addition, RSC activists were under unceasing pressure, from churches and factories, from friends and acquaintances, and from other members of the Regional Board in hiding, to do nothing, to wait out the terror, to hide in a monastery, in a cellar, under the floor. And they were left pacing the floor, depressed that they had no news from the city; they beat their heads against the wall, trying to convince people that communications, meetings, and organization were all absolutely vital.

Among those who did not succumb to the mood of discouragement were two Wrocław schools: the Agricultural Academy, where many members of the strike committee were hiding, and the university, whose students and staff provided a whole team in the service of Solidarity, from advisers to couriers and printers. These last included a number of docents and doctors, whose academic titles did not prevent them from doing their turn at the silk-screens. Printers from the university later trained people from the large factories, so that they could do their own printing independently.

The first, most difficult period lasted until January 10. On that day, members of the RSC met with the editors of Z Dnia na Dzień (From Day to Day) and divided the tasks between themselves. Z Dnia na Dzień had been appearing since almost the very beginning of the "war." On Monday, December 14, Frasyniuk had written to "Andrzej"

42

suggesting that he start a Solidarity paper. Distributors got in touch with the factories and renewed their old contacts. This was not easy at the beginning, because they usually made contact with people who occupied fairly low positions, and it sometimes took a couple of weeks to get in touch with someone who actually made decisions.

Distribution was probably the most risky area of underground activity. The danger lay not so much in the severity of any eventual sentence as in the likelihood of getting caught. At the beginning, distributors were being arrested one after another, but they were usually just fined. In one well-known case, twenty-five people were arrested in three days in Wrocław and later freed for a pay-off of four or five thousand złoties. In another, someone who didn't have contact with the RSC paid twenty-five thousand złoties out of his own pocket to free several people who'd been arrested.

The mood of the population went up and down; apathy alternated with the desire to resist. A month after the imposition of martial law, the first protest action was organized in Wrocław factories. The strike lasted one minute—just long enough to observe the occasion. The silence, though, was deafening; not only was every machine turned off, but even the air conditioners. Two weeks later there was a repeat performance, but this time it was a half-hour strike against the price increases.[2] This time the authorities reacted in a decisive fashion: hundreds of people were dismissed from work and arrested.

But even without strikes, work went at a sluggish pace. In Frasyniuk's opinion, passive resistance was initially very popular in the factories.

In any case, however, it would have made no difference if we'd called for a "go-slow." The economy was already tottering. Every measure the regime dreamed up to get it going again had its teeth knocked out, and people behaved in a principled fashion. The women at Chemitex, who were on piece rates, earned eight hundred, thirteen hundred, or a maximum fifteen hundred złoties in February—just enough to keep them in sodas, less than half of the biologically necessary minimum. But they stood firm. We had to write to them, asking them to give up, because such methods of struggle don't work when you're dealing with gangsters and just kill off the population.

Repression and pitiful wages took their toll. In February and March morale gradually declined. In January people had still entertained hope that they might successfully protest against something, that they might

43

win something. Then it became increasingly clear that the struggle would last months, perhaps years. During the strike on February 13, machines were left running but only at idle. People didn't work, but they tried to safeguard themselves against charges of striking. They ate lunch, queued up to buy a newspaper, oiled their machines.

The external effects of underground activity were not perhaps as spectacular as before; on the other hand, the underground press increased its circulation, the number of titles grew, as did the number of readers in all social groups. Conspiratorial structures took root in the factories, thanks to the perseverance of distributors, but also as a result of the training for printers provided by the university network. Other training sessions were organized alongside these: how to organize underground groups, how to defend oneself against repressive measures, how to take advantage of those legal regulations that had not yet been suspended. Sometimes several dozen people attended the meetings, which unnerved the speakers. During this whole period, threads were woven and broken, they disappeared only to reappear elsewhere. Couriers were arrested or gave up. It was necessary to find new people, to persuade acquaintances, to re-create a sense of purpose and to inspire people.

BUJAK I.6

Bujak spent the first week of the "war" in his Gdańsk hiding place.

Maybe I wouldn't have made it back to Warsaw it if hadn't been for the enormous activity that began here. I realized at the beginning that a lot depended on the West, on the information and assessment that we managed to transmit abroad. I wanted to get back to the capital as quickly as possible to make sure I didn't miss anything. Exactly a week after the imposition of martial law, I set off by train. I was helped by the railroad workers, who gave me a uniform: top coat, trousers, cap, good boots. I also donned some spectacles I'd obtained at my first hiding place, but that was a bit stupid because railroad workers are supposed to have good eyesight. As soon as I was on the train and wanted to buy a ticket, the conductors realized that something fishy was going on. But when I asked if they were checking the trains, the chief conductor hastened to tell me that no, the army and police had no jurisdiction over the railways. "If they did," he said, "half the passengers would jump out the windows."

While trying to squeeze into my compartment, one of the Solidarity advisers bumped into me in the corridor, but he simply apologized and continued on his way; he didn't recognize me! It wasn't until we were just outside Warsaw that I went to look for him, and we exchanged a few words.

I sat in my coat the whole journey because the train was freezing. I dozed in a corner, thinking about the union, about my family, about my stay in Gdańsk. I had promised my hosts in the first place I'd stayed a large bar of chocolate with nuts, and the kids in the second place—an enormous pineapple. I still remember their address and one day I'll fulfill my obligations.

The day after I arrived, I met Wiktor Kulerski outside Warsaw—quite by accident, in fact. I'd altered my appearance so much that Wiktor didn't recognize me at first. He told me a little about what had been going on in Warsaw during the past week. What he had to say wasn't at all encouraging. In the large factories most of the people had given up, as they had in the Gdańsk Shipyard, and only a handful of the most determined workers had carried on with the strike. On the other hand, a lot of activists had avoided arrest, including some from the old opposition. NOWa had also rescued its printing equipment.

I went around in the railroad uniform until January because it gave me a feeling of security. During this time I had a series of conversations with Wiktor, and we came to the conclusion that, in order to mobilize a large number of people, we had to adopt the following principle: if people got themselves organized, we would help them as much as we could; at the same time, they should concentrate on starting up just the most basic publications, collecting information, and organizing a distribution network. For the time being, we decided not to set up a regional body (although several people were in favor of it) because we didn't want people to sit on their behinds, waiting for someone else to make all the decisions on their behalf. We agreed, though, that we would sign joint appeals or communiques.

Around January 10, leading Warsaw activists held a lengthy meeting. They reviewed their losses in terms of personnel, agreed that the Romaszewskis would start up Radio Solidarity, and discussed the publication of Tygodnik Mazowsze *(Mazowsze Weekly). As the first campaign of mass resistance, they decided to call on people to boycott the official press and turn out their lights (and to light candles) on the thirteenth of every month.*

A second meeting, which took place about two weeks later, nearly ended in catastrophe. More than a dozen people were running around Warsaw in temperatures of minus twenty degrees as a result of completely unforeseen circumstances. Some very helpful person had rented for the use of the underground an apartment belonging to neighbors who were currently in the Soviet Union. As luck would have it, the owners returned without warning that very day. The many people who suddenly turned up at their door with passwords and pseudonyms were all turned away, at first with amazement and then with increasing annoyance. It wasn't until just before the curfew that one of the couriers found a place where the whole group could finally sit all night and talk. Bujak didn't arrive until the last minute, so he didn't freeze like the others. In any case, he was still wearing his warm railroad uniform.

In no time at all people in Warsaw were telling each other that I was going around in this uniform, so I had to find some other clothes. I was given some regular clothing and an ID card that someone had "found" somewhere, and I altered my appearance in the attempt to match the photograph. This was fairly disastrous, because anyone could see that I'd dyed my hair. As well as the ID, I got a card identifying my place of work. This didn't come out too well; the stamp on it looked completely amateurish even though it was absolutely genuine. On the other hand, the forged ones that I got later didn't arouse any suspicions.

At this time we already had someone who organized apartments— not only as mail drops or meeting places but also as editorial offices, places to store documents, and so on. We changed apartments about once a month or every two weeks if there was a lot of traffic in and out. It was then that we started using the ten million złoties that we'd hidden away before the "war," although it wasn't long before union dues started flowing in. In any case, our expenditures were still minimal, mostly bus fares and taxis. Nobody was earning any wages, and it was only later that we had to help the families of those who were in hiding.

I guess this first period of mobilization in Warsaw, when we were getting various initiatives under way, making contact, and so on, came to an end with the publication of the first issue of *Tygodnik Mazowsze*. Actually, it was the second issue, because material for the first issue had been left in the apartment of Jerzy Zieliński, a journalist who became editor-in-chief of the paper in November 1981 and who committed suicide on the day they imposed martial law by jumping out of a window in the hospital where he was being treated.

We'd set up the printing presses and organized a distribution network. Communication channels, mail drops, who was responsible for what—all this was sewn up. We sent the copy to seven separate print-shops, which produced the first (second) issue on about February 10.

The underground press in Warsaw had its beginnings, though, in the very first days of martial law. The people who retrieved a fair amount of equipment from Mazowsze headquarters and then put together the first information bulletins (aimed chiefly at the West) were former employees of the Solidarity Information Agency, known as AS for short. A group of people spent days writing out information in tiny letters on sheets of onionskin paper. These were then rolled up tightly and stuck in the washrooms of trains going to the West. Despite this method, which had been thought out to the last detail, not one of these rolls reached its addressee. It was just that no one bothered to pick them up. As far as periodicals are concerned, the first regular publications to appear were *Wiadomości* [News], *Wola*, and *Tygodnik Wojenny* [Wartime Weekly].

The large print run of Tygodnik Mazowsze *made broader cooperation with the factories possible. Bujak rightly anticipated that the press would stimulate many initiatives, including the organization of secret factory commissions.*

I would even risk the assertion that the history of the beginnings of the Warsaw underground is the history of the underground press. By this, I don't mean that there weren't independent groups of activists from the very outbreak of the "war," but simply that until they had a network of distributors in the factories, they were nothing more than groups of activists. Only when the networks began to function and could be used to solicit answers to questions or to send out instructions was it possible to begin organizing enterprises on a broad scale. We have been told by many people that it was when we finally began publishing a weekly that many other organizational details improved, including the payment of union dues and the creation of several factory papers.

LIS 1.5

The February meeting between Lis, Hall, and Borusewicz focused on the creation of a Gdańsk Solidarity bulletin (which was all the more important given that, so far, there was no other focus around which opposition in the region could crystalize) together with the formation of a distribution network, which would make it possible to disseminate the underground press and collect money and information.

The activities they proposed were too much for three people, so they recruited two activists from the Gdańsk docks who were in hiding: Marian Świtek and Stanisław Jarosz. They initially divided the tasks as follows: contacts with factories, the printshop, the distribution network, editorial responsibility, and communications with the rest of the country and abroad. All this was highly provisional, since, in practice, many areas of work overlapped one another. At the same time, all five of these people were "illegals," thus any kind of contact with someone "on the surface" demanded additional security measures, which hindered activity. Bogdan Lis still maintains (contrary to the general view) that contacts with people who are not in hiding are the riskiest of all.

The police don't have any information about those who are in hiding. Rarely are "illegals" under surveillance, since they are arrested as soon as they become known to the police. On the other hand, those who are aboveground are frequently subject to an excess of attention on the part of the Security Service. Not everyone has sufficient experience to be able to tell when he is under surveillance. I've developed a certain intuition in this respect. Whenever anything is going on, I can sense it before I even get on the street. For example, once I was going to meet a courier (I'd met him several times before, both at the place where I was staying and in the open), but just before I left home I felt that something was wrong. I took a different route from the one I normally followed and, of course, I noticed the stake-out. The Security guy was sitting low down in his car, but I saw him before he saw me.

BORUSEWICZ I.9

During the first few months, the underground developed in two directions. On the one hand, there was the future "leadership," people with experience of opposition activity, who cautiously established a network of contacts with the intention of forming conspiratorial structures over the long term; on the other hand, there emerged innumerable groups and subgroups, often ephemeral, which functioned without any preparation.

Groups based on ties of friendship operate in greater security even if they don't pay much attention to conspiratorial principles. It's only when they begin joining up with others in order to achieve a higher level of organization that it's easy for the Security Service to

48

infiltrate them. There was a case in Gdańsk when one Security agent brought about the arrest of twenty people—three or four groups at the same time. For this reason, independent conspiratorial groups, which had functioned very effectively at first, ceased to fulfill their role during the second half of 1982. The brunt of the struggle then fell to us.

Nevertheless, it wasn't until the autumn that we began to play a key role—not only as a symbol of resistance in the Tri-city area, but as a regional organizer and main publisher. At the end of 1982 and the beginning of 1983 the Security Service liquidated the last remaining independent group (which was, by the way, exceedingly ambitious)—the so-called Second National Commission. Before that we had twice tried to make contact with them, and nothing came of it on either occasion, which was their fault entirely. Apparently they thought that since they'd adopted the title of "Second National Commission," every regional initiative ought to subordinate itself to them. They were the epigones of the first period of carefree underground creativity.

This first period, however, saw the emergence, blossoming, and death of an organization whose principles of activity differed sharply from those that governed the functioning of illegal groups based on ties of friendship. We are referring, of course, to the All-Poland Committee of Resistance (OKO).[3] The specifics of OKO were based on two factors: although regional structures did not yet exist or were barely in the stage of formation, OKO took upon itself "the duty to direct the union's conspiratorial activity throughout the country" and, as the union's "leading organ," called on Solidarity members to organize underground union cells at all levels. OKO thus proposed that the underground be constructed from the top down, an approach that differed sharply from the majority of proposals put forward in the regions.

NOTES

1. The Tri-city area is made up of Gdańsk, Gdynia, and Sopot.

2. In February 1982 the Polish government introduced the largest increase in retail prices since the end of the war.

3. Ogólnopolski Komitet Oporu, whose acronym OKO means "eye" in Polish. It was organized without the support of the main leaders-in-hiding and was severely criticized for the anonymity of its own leadership. Solidarity's principle was that the leaders had to be clearly identified.

49

4

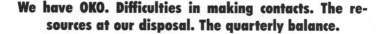

**We have OKO. Difficulties in making contacts. The re-
sources at our disposal. The quarterly balance.**

SZUMIEJKO I.4

At the beginning of January, I, Eugeniusz Szumiejko, having arrived
from the other end of Poland, from Wrocław, was already on a firm
footing in the Tri-city area. This may sound exaggerated, but that's
how I felt at the time, because I'd found several dozen committed
people, and you have to understand that several dozen was a large
number during those first few weeks.

In January 1982, those members of the National Strike Committee
who'd survived the pacification of the shipyard met with a few others
who could be trusted and who had some possibility of action. Without
consulting the other regions, we then published our first document,
which announced the unfortunate change of name from the National
Strike Committee to the EYE-All-Poland Committee of Resistance
(although we could have operated under the old name, since some of
the people were the same). We announced the formation of OKO for
the following reasons: first, there was a need for such an organization;
people wanted to hear that Solidarity, or at least the leadership, had
recovered from the shock. Second, we were afraid that some national-
level activists might be persuaded to represent Solidarity in negotiations with the government behind the backs of those who'd been interned and imprisoned (and such a danger did exist). Third, we

50

thought that the formation of OKO would speed up the consolidation of the regions, even if only because the formation of a national organization would hinder the emergence of other national bodies. Fourth, we actually had some right to do this. Two of us were members of the National Commission's presidium, others had fulfilled important functions in the union, including four of us who'd been members of the National Strike Committee. But more than the right, we had the duty to establish a national body. This we expressed in the last Strike Committee communiques, issued just before the ZOMO attacked the shipyard. We committed those of us from the National Commission who escaped to do everything we could to establish ties with the underground throughout the country. Fifth, we had the people to set up an organization, particularly people who were able to travel around.

We informed Lech about everything. Subsequently (this was two months later) he sent us a written statement empowering us to sign his name to OKO appeals and communiques. Actually, we never took advantage of this, although we did, on several occasions, consult him on the text of our statements.

Let me get back to the main thread. The first OKO document was signed with the pseudonym "Mieszko,"[1] since our own names didn't yet mean much to many people. At the same time, we didn't want the great figures of the movement, such as Zbyszek Bujak, to feel that they had to jump on an already moving train. They too could be cofounders. And that's how OKO was formed. We got hold of a duplicating machine and found some Gdańsk University students who knew how to use it. Other people turned up who were able to do silk-screen printing. Most of the people who helped us worked at the polytechnic, the university, the ferry service, the Port of Gdańsk, the Lenin Shipyard, in the health service, or in education. As a rule, none of them had been opposition activists or active in the union above the workplace level. They simply wanted, and were able, to do something.

We had a bad time, however, trying to make contact with groups around the country. In addition, during this whole period we didn't have any contact with the two Bogdans, Lis and Borusewicz, so we felt that we couldn't really speak in the name of Gdańsk. At the end of January we made contact with Wrocław, and at the end of February— with Kraków. We knew that Handzlik, Hardek and others were in Kraków, but by mistake we wrote to an activist called Piekarz. This was the result of a suggestion from Zbyszek Bujak, from whom we fi-

51

nally heard at the end of February. Actually—this was a bit strange—his courier came to the people with whom I was staying and said she had a letter from Warsaw. I read the letter, which turned out to be a proposal addressed to the two Bogdans, suggesting they make contact with Kraków, where Bujak knew an activist by the name of Piekarz (a member of the Małopolska Regional Board). Zbyszek went on to ask, "What are you up to in Gdańsk? Who are the people from the National Commission who have set up OKO or whatever it is?" He'd heard something, but he was indignant: "Who do they think they are. . . ?"[2] In light of this, I too wrote to Piekarz, but when the courier returned from Kraków, he said that Handzlik and Hardek were members of the Regional Executive Committee and the name of Piekarz was not to be mentioned [in our communiques], because he wasn't in hiding but was walking around quite freely.

In March, we made contact with the West (Milewski).[3] We were already in constant contact (once a week) with Kraków and Wrocław, and were in touch as often as twice a week with Szczecin. Communication with Warsaw broke down after the letter from Bujak, although, of course, I replied speedily. In Gdańsk I was still unable to make contact with either of the two Bogdans. All in all, things weren't going too well. In addition, I received a letter from Władek Frasyniuk, in which he wrote, "Gienek, it's great that you're carrying on the work, but straighten things out in Gdańsk, get in touch with Bogdan Lis to avoid any paranoia." Well, Władek knew me very well, but he also realized that Gdańsk means Lis rather than Szumiejko. A separate problem was the division in Wrocław between Kornel Morawiecki's group and the Regional Strike Committee lead by Frasyniuk. All my letters went, unfortunately, via Morawiecki, who usually gave them to Władek at the last minute, just before the courier was leaving for Gdańsk. Morawiecki applauded the formation of OKO, but this applause by no means meant that Wrocław considered itself part of the organization.

Because things were at a standstill, in the middle of March I got on a train, in a railroad uniform and with a pass valid for any station in the country, and traveled around Poland, beginning with Wrocław. I didn't have any problems along the way, except for people asking me whether they'd make the connection for Częstochowa and other such things I didn't have the faintest idea about. Things went best in Kraków, where I discussed the future of OKO with Hardek and his people. They went worst in Warsaw, where I learned that Bujak was opposed to any kind of national organization, especially OKO, and that he was already dealing with Bogdan Lis on certain issues. I didn't actually talk with Bujak, just with Kulerski.

My travels were, then, only partly successful. At the beginning of April, we published the OKO declaration, a good and substantial document. In the meantime, we had been involved in consultations with Szczecin, Kraków, Jastrzębie, Wrocław, and Warsaw concerning demonstrations on April 13 (the four-month anniversary of the outbreak of the "war"). Warsaw decreed that, if the appeal for demonstrations wasn't signed by OKO or any other organization, they would join in, and Bujak would add his name to ours.

What were our resources at this time? Kraków brought all its groups under the OKO umbrella and was printing a lot of stuff. It's true that Wrocław wasn't yet signing OKO documents, but I knew that I only had to sort out the issue of Bogdan Lis and they would be with us. Szczecin, which was weak from the point of view of printing, had joined us completely. Publishing was also weak in Gdańsk, but under the patronage of OKO we had begun to publish *Solidarność Północna* [Northern Solidarity]. It was called *Northern Solidarity*, because I then had the idea of dividing the country into five regions: the north, with Gdańsk as its center; the east, with Warsaw; the south, with Kraków; the west, with Wrocław; and Upper Silesia. Apart from this, we also published several issues of *WIPS* [Solidarity Martial Law Press Information Bulletin], which was designed for activists.

People from Bydgoszcz, Elbląg, Gorzów, and I don't remember where else announced their membership in OKO. But this was clearly a misunderstanding: it was not our aim to collect courageous names and pseudonyms but to coordinate the work of those regions that were already organizing themselves. After all, we hadn't got hold of just anyone in Kraków and told him that because he lived in Kraków he was going to represent the Małopolska region in OKO and that he now had to set up a regional organization.

In April I received a letter from Frasyniuk, telling me that he was now urging Bujak to set up a national organization and that he hoped I wouldn't insist on the name OKO. I replied that the name was of no importance. Władek Hardek was so irritated by Zbyszek's attitude that he sent him a completely hysterical letter (he sent me a copy, because we then had a craze for sending each other copies of our correspondence to other people), in which he declared, "If you don't make up your mind, I'll screw up the whole mining industry for you and set up a typical branch or interfactory organization."[4] In the last resort, this would have been feasible; for example, the Szczecin members of OKO were drawn largely from the Warski Shipyard, Hardek came from the Lenin Steel Works, and the Jastrzębie people were mostly from the July Manifesto coal mine.

I started to be in good spirits; the organization was growing slowly. I had nearly a hundred people active in interregional communications, publishing, contacts with advisers, in organizing housing, and there were so many who were willing to help that I was beginning to lose control. When I now try to figure out how it was that Security found my location and suddenly broke down my door, I find it almost impossible to say; I can only speculate.

A week before the Security guys came to visit, I got a letter from Bogdan Borusewicz,[5] with whom I rarely exchanged letters, warning me that the Security was watching one of the OKO apartments. Also, my courier realized, after leaving Konarski's place, that he was being followed, but he somehow managed to lose them. Since they were keeping an eye on Konarski, others could well be under surveillance, so I suggested that the section heads be changed. I got a new apartment from someone who was totally "clean," but in order not to "burn" him, I had one last meeting with Konarski and "Konrad" in my old place. That evening they were supposed to disguise themselves—I don't know how, maybe as women—and take off for new apartments. At the same time, I warned him that if they didn't take my warnings seriously, I'd break off contact with them.

They left, I had supper, smoked a cigarette, and then it started. But not the way that Broniewski wrote; they didn't come "in the night and batter the door with the butts of their rifles." Our opponents have made progress, for one thing. For another, the doors aren't so well made these days. So, after they'd rung the bell a couple of times and knocked gently on the door (and someone had nearly opened it to them), they gave it a hefty whack and half of it fell apart. Luckily the door opened outward, so they couldn't kick it in but had to break it down with an axe. The door from the living room into the hallway had a frosted-glass panel, through which I could see how one guy was already trying to scramble through the broken top half, but someone else was holding him back, urging him to wait while they had to go at the rest of it. I threw everything I could lay my hands on into a briefcase and rushed to the balcony. I opened the balcony door carefully, so it wouldn't make a noise scraping on the bottom, as it usually did, and closed it tight. I think it was this that saved me. I climbed from the balcony, which was on the seventh floor, onto the roof and looked around: there were four cars, and police all over the place. One police truck was going round and round the apartment building. I felt a bit humiliated that I had to run away, so I went about everything calmly, as though out of resentment. I rushed off along the roof and down a lightning conductor on a blind wall (my training as a paratrooper was a great help). Nobody was watching this side, everyone was standing by the staircase, behind the entrance to the coal cellar. When I made it to the ground, I hid behind the piles of dirt left by some construction workers. I looked around, and there were some policemen coming in my direction! I thought I was finished, but to my amazement, they simply surrounded the building. I got the hell out of there.

I think what must have happened was this: after they'd scrambled through the broken-down door, it took them a couple of seconds to find the light switch. The curtains were drawn, so they couldn't see the door to the balcony and they decided to search the apartment first. In the meantime, someone probably noticed the hot bulb in the bedside lamp and smelled the cigarette smoke, so they decided to surround the building.

Unfortunately, I didn't have time to take my notebook with all my addresses—not the latest conspiratorial addresses, but the old ones going back a few years. I later learned that the Security had tramped mercilessly from one address to another, including the apartments of people I'd known in high school twenty years ago.

The guy who lived in the apartment I'd run away from happened to be away on business. When he got back, he found a completely new door and a note telling him to collect the key from the local police station. He went, but before doing so, he picked up a few handy items from the neighbors; it was a good thing he did, because they sent him to Strzebielinek and didn't let him out for five months. Actually, quite a lot of people were interned there at that time, some of them without any reason whatsoever. You could see that the Security Service wasn't too sure what it was doing.

After all this, and after sending out a few warnings, I hid myself in a safe place and waited for my hands, which I'd injured coming down the lightning rod, to heal. After a couple of days I heard on the radio that the Interim Coordinating Commission (ICC) had been formed and that its members were Bujak, Frasyniuk, Hardek, and Lis. I couldn't imagine what was going on! One day, out of the blue, the doctor who came to look at my hands every evening brought me a letter from Lis. Actually, it wasn't really from him but from all four of them. It was addressed to me and Andrzej Konarski and had been written by Frasyniuk. It went more or less as follows: You didn't take part in the founding meeting of the ICC only because the courier, who was sent with a message to you, came back with news of your troubles with the Security. Please consider yourselves full members of the ICC.[6]

Konarski had just arrived in Wrocław. He was terribly offended (he hadn't yet seen the letter). He thought they'd screwed us and that everything would be OK if we simply carried on as an alternative organization. I decided to join the ICC, however, I thought we needed a single organization, not a dozen of them, and that, in addition, we had to face facts: Wrocław, which already had one foot in OKO, belonged to the ICC, as did Kraków, the mainstay of OKO. If we had insisted on carrying on, Gdańsk would have been divided: Lis on one side and us on the other. I wrote all this to Konarski, and then I finally met with Lis. Because I wasn't sure why I'd been raided, I cut all contacts with my previous collaborators, with the exception of Konarski, although our communication was completely one-sided, from me to him.

At the meeting, I formally declared my membership in the ICC, and because OKO was already known abroad (after all, it was I who'd started exchanging information with Milewski), I wrote to Milewski, telling him that I was joining the ICC and that someone else would take over contacts with him. I also told him that I was happy that the ICC had chosen him to head the Solidarity office abroad, since OKO had done so much earlier.

As far as Konarski is concerned, I was told at the end of May that he might be an agent for the Security Service. This I couldn't believe, and at the July meeting of the ICC I suggested we write to him. I drew up a letter along the lines of: Listen, old man, we're not saying that you *are* an agent, but for the good of the cause you're to sit quietly for a while, and time will tell. . . . I read it to everyone, and they agreed to send it. Somehow this letter never reached Konarski; the guy who'd agreed to let his place be used as a drop simply got scared and threw the courier out. Afterward, in late autumn, I wrote again, but I already knew that Konarski had joined forces with the Inter-Regional Commission in Defense of Solidarity. (In Kraków their journal was distributed by a network that was more or less associated with the Security, by Zawada and his people, for example.) After this letter, I broke off our one-sided contacts.

It's time to sum up briefly. OKO was an organization that—if the "big guys" had treated it seriously—might have become what the ICC is today. In many places it had achieved the organizational level that the ICC achieved only a year later.[7] It is true, on the other hand, that it was a kind of truncated organization, because neither Warsaw nor Gdańsk, under the two Bogdans, was included. We can only ask why it was that for so long there was no contact between us. They are justified if we're talking about the later period, when they knew about the infiltration, but between December 1980 and April 1981 they had plenty of time to arrange a meeting. If we'd met, everything would have got off the ground more quickly. If we'd made contact at the beginning, we would probably have been able to avoid the anxiety and the lack of security we had at the end.

And there's one more thing—and here I'm talking as the leader of OKO. I really was the leader, although only at the beginning, up to the time that we reached an agreement with Kraków, Szczecin, and Wrocław, when we decided that OKO was to have no directing body or big chief; our statements were to be agreed on jointly, and that was all. The period during which I used the pseudonym "Micszko" didn't last long. Later, when we were in touch with Zbyszek Bujak and others, we said, "Don't get irritated by the signature; after all, it could be a collective pseudonym." In any case, we quickly abandoned "Mieszko."

There's a book called *The Political Underground*, which has been published officially, which defines OKO as "yet another dummy underground organization." No, it wasn't a dummy organization. It was simply an organization with this, and not another, name.

NOTES

1. The first king of Poland.

2. *Bujak: Our courier screwed up the whole thing; because she couldn't get there herself on the given day, she sent a stupid, irresponsible friend of hers. Instead of Bogdan Lis, this idiot got in touch with Szumiejko and Konarski, in other words, with OKO. We were furious, because it wasn't clear what this OKO was or who its members were. When it later turned out that Szumiejko and Konarski were involved, we all breathed a sigh of relief that it wasn't a Security front.*

3. A reference to Solidarity's official representative in the West, Jerzy Milewski, head of the Brussels-based Coordinating Office of Solidarity Abroad.

4. Solidarity derived its strength from the fact that it was a single union repre-

senting all workers, who were organized by region rather than by industry. If Hardek had gone ahead with his threat to organize the miners in their own branch union, he would have disrupted efforts to recreate Solidarity's regional structure underground.

5. *Borusewicz: We rarely wrote to each other because I considered such letters to be an important matter. It looked as though these people were using conspiratorial techniques of the kind used during the occupation, but without any real substance to them; they didn't look like professionals. Apart from this, their organization didn't look too encouraging; the business with OKO and "Mieszko" seemed bizarre. Of course, its members included people who now play a useful role, but I wasn't very optimistic about the venture.*

6. *Lis: At the first meeting of the ICC, we discussed, among other things, the question of OKO; above all, the fact that OKO maintained contact with Wrocław and Kraków. We wrote to Szumiejko, suggesting that he and Konarski join the ICC on the following condition: OKO would cease to exist without issuing any document to that effect, in order not to give grounds for any speculation. OKO would simply cease issuing communiques, statements, and appeals, while Szumiejko's name would start appearing on ICC documents.*

7. *(Note made by Władysław Frasyniuk while reading the manuscript of* Konspira:*) I completely disagree with Eugeniusz Szumiejko's view that OKO had achieved the level of organization that the ICC achieved only a year later. In practice, OKO barely existed, it hadn't formed any organizational structures, it had no regional base, it had no organizational (print shops, for example) or propaganda (its own newspaper) base, and it didn't even have any supporters apart from, of course, those who signed OKO statements and possibly a few people who collaborated with them.*

December 15, 1981—two days after the imposition of martial law—
in the Gdansk Shipyard. Bogdan Borusewicz (with the outstretched
hand) debates with striking shipyard workers. The man on the left
(taking notes) is Marcin Moskit (Zbigniew Gach).

On the other side of the Gdansk Shipyard Gate, taken on the same
day.

Also on December 15, tank crew and passersby reading Solidarity leaflets in front of the Gdansk Shipyard.

Warsaw, May 3, 1982.

The monument to the shipyard workers killed in 1970. It was built in 1981, is sixty-feet tall, and stands in front of the Gdansk Shipyard.

Independent May Day Parade, Gdansk, 1982. The image of Our Lady from Czestochowa is carried in the front row.

Gdansk, October 1982.

Warsaw, October 1982. The banner calls for "Freedom for the Internees."

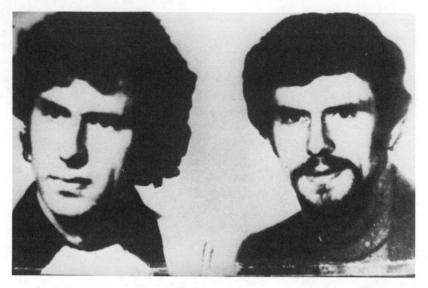

Bogdan Lis on police-search photographs; one with beard, another without (1982).

Eugeniusz Szumiejko in front of the Gdansk Monument (1983).

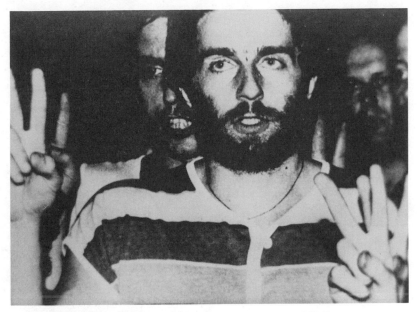

Wladyslaw Frasyniuk after his release from prison (1983).

Aleksander Hall, 1983.

Bogdan Borusewicz on a
police-search photograph
(1983).

Zbigniew Bujak in disguise
while being interviewed for
French television (1984).

All Saints Day in 1984. Candles at the base of the Gdansk Monument commemorate the shipyard workers.

Constructing the foundations: factory organizations. Conflicts in Lower Silesia and Mazowsze: "extremists" on the attack. The beginnings of regional structures: history, specifics, organization. The ICC: a centralized structure or a federation?

LIS 1.6

From the bottom up, not the top down: this was the demand of the ubiquitous "wall art," and it was this organizational principle that won the most adherents. Yet "the bottom" was conceived of in many different ways. One region saw the workplaces as the basis of the new structures; another region thought that activity should be organized by independent groups based on common interests, neighborhoods, or generational ties. All other bodies, from regional committees up to an eventual national leadership, would come only later. Opinion was divided as to the potential usefulness of these last.

As a result, therefore, the organizational shape of the underground in a given region stemmed from the vision of that region's leading activists. Bujak and Kulerski, opting for the old conceptions of the democratic opposition, chose the broad-based "societal" model of resistance. Frasyniuk, however, insofar as he was preparing Lower Silesia for a general strike, had no choice but to focus on organizing resistance in the factories. It was the same in Gdańsk.

In our region, large enterprises account for only ten percent of the total workforce, while medium- and small-sized enterprises make up ninety percent. Yet because the large enterprises play such a key role, we decided to devote most of our energies to them—all the more so since they were definitely *not* the best organized. On the contrary, it was the medium-sized plants that took the lead and still do, maybe because there the people know each other better, have more confidence in each other. In the "middle" enterprises you also don't have the problem with interdepartmental contacts that you do in the large plants, where they have special people supervising these contacts, people usually connected with the Security Service. The best enterprises in the Tri-city area are the Port of Gdańsk, the "Nauta" Ship Repair Yards in Gdynia, and the refinery. The weakest, without doubt, is the Paris Commune Shipyard where, after the first crushing round of arrests, the workers just couldn't get it together for a long time.

From the very beginning, conspiratorial work in the factories consisted chiefly in printing leaflets. In order to help the middle-level activists, we worked out special instructions for the formation of clandestine factory commissions. We stressed that the most important tasks were collecting dues, protecting the persecuted, and printing and distributing newsletters. It was this last matter that seemed absolutely crucial to us, for a factory newsletter is the most visible sign that something's going on, and it can inspire others to action.

By April we had contacts with thirty enterprises, which in turn had contacts with others. And we didn't communicate just by letter. I personally met with people from the Lenin Shipyard, "Nauta," the Marine Radio Service, and others. Meetings of this kind were necessary, because things our intermediaries couldn't work out were usually settled easily in direct conversation.

FRASYNIUK I.5

The organization of Wrocław enterprises was planned on a very broad scale, and it is probably for that very reason that there were complications. March brought a series of painful arrests of people working closely with the Regional Strike Committee. They arrested the new editorial board, several couriers, and, most painfully, the person responsible for conspiratorial work in the factories. They also seized several people whose address books were filled with names and addresses. In January, not all conspirators had made up their own secret codes yet,

*but even those who had, didn't use them everyday. That carefree atti-
tude cost us dearly.*

Luckily, the arrest of this one person who did such great work for
us didn't lead to a break in contacts with the factories. This guy had
been relying almost exclusively on the old Solidarity activists. His followers, however, approached matters more "scientifically": they de-
livered the underground press to the factories by one channel while
using a different channel to consult with the factory commissions,
which were usually led by new people, still unknown to the police.
Each channel was fully independent of the other. This duplicate factory network enabled us to organize direct meetings between the
RSC's contact person and the people making the decisions in the enterprises. At these meetings we'd discuss tactics and strategy, and coordinate our basic affairs. After careful verification of these channels
of communication, members of the regional leadership also began to
take part in the meetings. This was a major turning point, as the factory commissions now became considerably more active. Another
consequence was the flood of correspondence that now began flowing
to the Regional Committee. We started receiving up to twenty letters a
day. These would usually describe the situation in the respective factories or emphasize the workers' high level of organization (something
we looked at very cautiously, because we knew we were getting some
letters from wishful thinkers). Or people might write to ask questions
like, "Can we start our own factory newsletter?" Or they'd ask if we
could set up drop-off points where they could pick up materials, or
whether we could send them some experienced printers. We also got
letters from outside Wrocław. I once read with great satisfaction a
letter from Oława, where residents had begun to reprint and distribute
a reproduction of the Wrocław paper *Z Dnia na Dzień*, without asking
for assistance from anybody.

From the beginning we mainly sought access to the large factories. But when our network began to get along, it became clear to us
that there were just too many factories for us to work with. So we
chose six to focus on, all of them concentrated in one industrial district: Pafawag, Dolmel, Elwro, Hutmen, FAT, and Fadroma. We began by working out forms of collaboration with the first three. The factory commissions got their own direct drop-off points for contacts with
the Regional Committee and began receiving all our materials, documents, analyses, and program proposals. They made use of them in
various ways, publishing some of the material, commenting on others.

61

Elwro, for example, would systematically assess the activities of the Regional Committee. These evaluations were full and honest, and they were drawn up not by professional activists from former Solidarity commissions but by regular workers.

In April we were planning to expand the size of the Regional Committee to include representatives of all six factories. But at that very moment the police made a direct hit on our organization at Pafawag (certainly due to an informer) and succeeded in almost completely destroying it. We were warned at the very last minute, just as we were going to a meeting there. We were practically already at the gate, when a group of workers from a different plant called out to us that there was a "sting" at Pafawag, and that lots of people had already been arrested.

The first conflicts within the underground began at about the same time. Many organizers were calling for long strikes and street demonstrations. (There were personal ambitions at work here, too.) But when we called a meeting to explain our strategy, it became clear that the authentic factory representatives had completely different ideas from those of the factional "organizers." Unfortunately, the conflict was reflected in *Z Dnia na Dzień*, which drifted along without any clear line, representing neither the views of the RSC nor those of the faction that wanted to take to the streets. Kornel Morawiecki, writing under the pseudonym "Andrzej," spoke out rather sharply in favor of taking to the streets, but the rest of the editorial board tried to stay loyal to the Regional Committee. "Andrzej" also impeded us somewhat in our contacts with the factories, and this helped delay organizing the RSC according to the new formula.

BUJAK I.7

There were differences of opinions, sometimes radical differences, in other regions, too. In the period between the publication of the first issue of Tygodnik Mazowsze *in January 1982 and the end of April, there was a sharp conflict in the Warsaw underground: Bujak and Kulerski on one side, and Zofia and Zbigniew Romaszewski on the other.*

I deeply regretted the clash with the Romaszewskis because, thanks to their work with KOR, both had earned a great deal of authority. Nevertheless, I do believe that the Regional Executive Committee would have been formed much earlier if it hadn't been for their radical program. Why? Simple: Zbigniew Romaszewski, as an elected member of the Warsaw Solidarity Presidium who was now in hiding, would have had to be part of the Committee, and, in that case, his wife, too. So if by any chance both Wiktor and I were knocked off, the Romaszewskis could have become the leaders of the Regional Committee—and it was precisely this that I was afraid of. At that time, the spring of 1982, I thought that if I, and only I, were directly responsible for our resistance strategy, I would put off all the more aggressive actions until 1985. I was convinced that that year would be a turning point in the military, and therefore political, balance of power in the world. I thought it would come either to war, or to the weakening of Russia to such an extent that it would be possible to present it with an ultimatum. And if the Poles then stepped out onto the international scene, the superpowers would have to take account of this. Later, however, it turned out that things were much more complicated than that.

After the conflict with Bujak, the Romaszewskis joined up with the Interfactory Workers Committee of Solidarity, which was formed at the end of April. The Committee brought together sixty-three Warsaw enterprises and published two significant journals; CDN (To Be Continued) and Głos Wolnego Robotnika (The Free Worker's Voice). Romaszewski now proclaimed publicly his own program of resistance. The Interfactory Committee regarded itself as an advisory body to the long-awaited Regional Executive Committee to be headed by Bujak and only later agreed to subordinate itself to some extent to the Executive Committee. It organized several spectacular actions—most notably, the successful attempt to free Jan Narożniak from the hospital where he was recuperating after being shot by the police. The organization was short-lived, nevertheless. August saw the arrest of virtually all of its activists, including Zbigniew Romaszewski. His wife had already been arrested. For Warsaw, this was a great loss.

Apart from the conflict with the Romaszewskis, Bujak had yet another reason for his initial opposition to the creation of a regional underground structure.

Warsaw very quickly decided on a long-term perspective—at

least a couple of years—for the underground. And for this reason neither Wiktor nor I was prepared for the immediate formation of a central leadership. We first needed to work out a means for formulating and transmitting directives, not to mention a system for executing them, and all this required time. The Warsaw Regional Committee was formed only after we had a whole network of interregional and interfactory contacts, after we'd worked out agreements with various social and professional groups and independent cultural circles, and after there were a number of different newsletters: then we had something to base ourselves on. That structural mosaic filled us with optimism. Because there's this law of nature, you see, that says that structures rich in form last the longest. The Brazilian jungle can survive anything, but the taiga is more vulnerable. And this rule holds true for everything. A democratic society, with abundant forms of social life and activity, can defend itself against various defeats, while a totalitarian society is very frail, and every setback threatens its viability.

FRASYNIUK I.6

The Wrocław Regional Strike Committee already had a pretty solid base, but its further expansion was accompanied, to Frasyniuk's chagrin, by some rather impassioned discussion.

At a meeting between the original Regional Committee (still made up of Bednarz, Pinior, and me) and the leaders of the Committee's various departments, half of them pressed hard to be admitted to the Committee itself, hoping in this way to obtain a dominating influence. The other half, together with the three of us, argued that such a decision could be made only after the representatives from the six largest factories had been admitted. At the next meeting, the six were added to the Committee without any problem, but the "factionalists" from the departments were admitted only after a big fight. The factory representatives, already fed up with the discussions, finally just asked whether it was really so important to the "factionalists" that they be part of the leadership, and when the latter answered yes, the factory reps went along for the sake of peace and quiet. In the end, a new Regional Committee was elected, consisting of the original three (using our own names), the six factory representatives, and leaders of the five most important departments.

In fact, there are more than five departments. Starting from the center, there's the administrative office, through which all contacts are supposed to be handled. Then there's a department for coordinating work with the factories, one for coordinating work with the region, an information bureau (a sort of counterintelligence), a propaganda department (for press, publishing, and leaflets), a printing department, a bureau for interregional communication, an organizational section, a financial council, and others.

This high level of organization applied chiefly to Wrocław. The other areas of Lower Silesia were still groping around. We brought them newsletters and printing equipment, but the situation was pretty bad there when it came to rebuilding union locals. Of course one shouldn't treat all these other cities the same. It's one thing to organize factory commissions in Wałbrzych or Legnica, but something very different to do so in a place like Wołów, where the largest enterprise is the local prison. In order to stimulate activity outside of Wrocław, we organized meetings with representatives from these other areas. People came not only from Legnica, Wałbrzych, Lubin, Głogów, and Dzierżoniów, but even from Kalisz, Opole, and Gorzów.

LIS I.7

In late April and early May, a Regional Coordinating Committee was formed in Gdańsk. Its members were Bogdan Lis, Bogdan Borusewicz, Aleksander Hall, Stanisław Jarosz, and Marian Świtek.

In drawing up the list of names we took two things into account: the fact that we were already working together, and the need for mutual trust. The five of us made the decision on our own, not worrying about whether anybody liked it or not. And it was accepted by many people who were working with us but who, for various reasons, didn't want their names to be known. Of course, there were also some people who were hoping very much to sign their own names to Regional Committee documents, but these people we didn't particularly want.

The effectiveness of underground activities largely depends on the existence of specialized departments. Because many of these are still active today, I'll discuss the Committee's internal structure only in very general terms, so as not to make the work of the Security Service any easier.

In the first place, there's a network for communication between

Committee members. This department relies on couriers who know our actual hiding places and meet with us directly. Next, there's a department for contacts with the outside world. This consists of a group of people who can represent us in meetings either with Gdańsk enterprises or with representatives from other regions. (One Committee member in particular is responsible for contacts with local enterprises.) Every region must also possess its own "line" to the West, though in actual fact this department is pretty much centralized.

Next comes the publishing department. This is a rather extensive structure consisting of three sections: editorial, printing, and distribution. In Gdańsk this department has never been very well developed, and Warsaw often makes fun of us: "You people in Gdańsk can mobilize a strike but you can't produce any books!"

The next unit we call the "legalization" department. It's responsible for providing us with bogus documents and authorizations of all kinds.

The finance department, and the economic branch connected with it, get half their operating funds from the West. (I'm counting here the printing, radio, and other equipment that we get, all of which is necessary for our underground work.) The other half we get from domestic sources. Dues, however, we leave to the disposition of the factory commissions. The dues are used mostly to help persecuted workers and their families. As to our economic activities, well, given the recent arrest of the two greenhouse owners who were working with the underground in Wrocław, it wouldn't be too wise to talk about this at all.

Two other teams we have are the radio group and the technical shop. The latter produces broadcasting equipment, automatic leaflet dispensers, and other items of this kind—part of the technical expertise unique to the underground.

Each one of these departments should in principle have its own security unit, but in reality that's not possible: there's just never enough experts in that field. So we have a security unit only at the regional level, which serves all. It's the Regional Committee, however, which decides what information gets sent where. We have to consider the organization's security on the one hand (the Security Service is never far away), and the relative importance of the information on the other.

And that would be all. Of course, many Security functionaries are going to be reading this book only because . . .[1]

BUJAK I.8

The formation of the Regional Committee in Warsaw did not in any way limit the hundreds of underground initiatives already underway there. On the contrary, it facilitated more of them. This was the case also for those structures—or, as Bujak calls them, "teams"—most closely affiliated with the Committee.

We have a lot of teams in the capital, and so I'll only name the most important. The first one, very crucial, is the apartment team, functioning since the very beginning of the "war." At first this consisted of only one trusted person, but later it became a specialized group (and so it remains today) providing safe locations for all needs. Of course there's still one main coordinator, whose job it is to check out each apartment before we use it. Naturally, there's a periodic turnover of the apartment team: after someone's exhausted the homes of all his or her friends and finding new ones becomes risky, the person simply moves on to some other work. In this way, at least, we're not condemned to move forever within the same circle.

At the start of the "war" the apartment team had it easy, since there were plenty of "untainted" apartments. Now people have to look hard to find some place where nothing's happened so far. Then there's the problem that sometimes an apartment may be "clean" but it turns out that half the occupants of the building are in the underground, which makes it easy to be caught by accident.

One of the greatest dangers for someone in hiding is indiscretion on the part of the host. We've had cases, although not many, where we had to evacuate suddenly an apartment because one woman has whispered something to another—"in absolute confidence." On the other hand, most of the younger kids have been just great. They don't want to know too much and in general are very discrete.

The next team is the so-called financial council, which monitors the underground's expenses making sure everything is properly accounted for. (After the "war," this council will go public and present our accounts for open inspection.) A treasurer keeps track of expenditures in the region, monitors cash flow and savings, etc. Actually, our bookkeeping is extremely simple: a cell receives money according to a budget estimate and disposes of the money according to its needs. Later, the cell leader provides a verbal account of the group's expenditures for the financial controllers. All notes and receipts are then destroyed. Only a few general statements are drawn up: for example, something stating that such and such a sum was spent on transportation. Actually, even papers like this shouldn't be preserved, since they provide information on the frequency with which we use cars.

During the first six months of the state of war we distributed in Warsaw about 700,000 złoties a month. Later, these sums rose considerably, as there were more things to finance, more people to help, more initiatives, and more underground groupings. Interregional contacts alone cost us about 80,000 a month, and besides that there's the press, publications, special actions, and so forth. We subsidize *Tygodnik Mazowsze*, including the editors' salaries, although they do raise a lot of money on their own (with the greatest amounts coming from private-sector people). Besides this, we finance the Regional Committee's bureau, the leafleting teams, the supplies department, and the broadcasting department. People pressure us: "Do some spectacular actions!" But they don't seem to realize that all this stuff costs a hell of a lot of money. We once installed a giant speaker at a cemetery. It broadcast loudly for a while, and that was that—end of action. Our expenditures, when you count everything, are extraordinarily high. In the courts after August 31, 1982, we paid out over a half-million złoties in fines for people arrested, and that's just about how much it costs us for one well-organized action. Of course, we also get some much-needed financial help from abroad, but we take from this kitty rather rarely.

Printing. Here we've relied mostly on NOWa and other independent publishers. But their machines often break down, so, when we get hold of an offset or copier, we often hand it over to them as compensation for worn-out equipment.

Our problems, however, are not so much with printing the material as with distributing it. Every so often a large group of distributors gets caught. The head of the distribution network, who had contacts with the majority of drop-off points, was arrested just a few months into the "war." They had been observing him for a while, checking out his routes, and then they grabbed him and a few others. A group arrest of distributors is always a big blow, since rebuilding such a network requires long and tedious work. Moreover, while at the beginning of martial law we literally had crowds of people clamoring to be distributors, over time this began to come to a halt. If you put something in someone's hands, they'd still pass it along, but people stopped coming to us on their own. The optimal solution was to cut back the numbers of *Tygodnik Mazowsze* we printed at the center, while at the same time producing stencils that local union groups could use to make their own copies of the journal.

Besides printing presses, we have a studio where we produce cassettes and radio shows. At first, "Radio Solidarity" was run by Zbyszek Romaszewski, but after he was arrested others took it over. Zbyszek, after all, was rather impatient. After our first broadcast he seemed to get a bit carried away by success, and he neglected to follow our original plan, according to which our programs were to be broadcast in segments from several different transmitters. After setting up the first transmitter he just kept on using it, not waiting for any others. Meanwhile, out came the homing devices as military spotters went into action looking for the source of the broadcast. They found it pretty easily, and the cops were overjoyed. Zbyszek's successors took the matter more seriously and didn't begin any action until after they had set up a whole network of synchronized transmitters.

I've mentioned our publishing work, our radio and distribution work, but I almost forgot about our press team. This consists of the editors of *Tygodnik Mazowsze*, most importantly, and then an entire network of local correspondents, informants, and couriers.

One of our most important units is the bureau organized and conceptualized by—well, the name's not important. It's the job of this bureau to know, at every time of day and night, exactly where Wiktor Kulerski and I are, where the editorial board is, how to get in touch with our printers and distributors. Contacts between the different teams, or between the teams and Wiktor and me—all of that is arranged through this bureau. It collects money and distributes it to the various groups, organizes meetings with various people, and takes care of all our administrative activities. Two individuals, with a set number of assistants, supervise the bureau, making sure it's functioning effectively.

The department of interregional contacts—everything that we have to send outside of Warsaw is directed to this unit first. It's here, also, that we check out our contacts from elsewhere in Poland. That is, trustworthy people simply travel to the different areas and check out who's who. In other words, this group does the necessary intelligence work before we establish contacts. At the beginning of the "war" many union activists wrote to me presenting their view of the situation and requesting a reply. Sometimes I wrote back, but it often happened that the person didn't have the slightest idea what was going on or what to do, and my letter served only as a kind of screen, protecting him from the charge that he was just an incompetent self-promoter. People from the department called my attention to this and told me that I should first check with them as to what the situation was, then I'd know how to respond.

Alongside the department of interregional contacts we set up a special radio and telecommunications team, responsible for working out a communications system (wireless or not) between the regions, and in particular between regions with representatives in the ICC. Our goal is a system allowing the transmission of any type of information to any part of the country within ten to twelve hours maximum. This information network, organized with great effort, should be effective in times of the greatest political tension, especially in the face of a general strike. Shutting off the telephones and telexes shouldn't really bother us then. Our press team is actually just a kind of annex to this communications team, one working chiefly for the use of our journal.

Then there's the "legalization" department, whose chief task is to provide us with fake official stamps.[2] Right after martial law was declared one guy came to us with this giant suitcase that he'd been keeping since the end of the Occupation. "I got this from my friend," he told us. "I always felt it might come in handy one day!" And inside the suitcase we find this complete set-up for forging stamps and erasing signatures. But that was just one valuable find. Actually, this department got hold of many other technical curiosities besides that one.

Aside from forging stamps, the legalization team also makes bogus documents. This is terribly laborious work. For example, every page of an official pass, or of any number of various ID cards, must first be hand copied on an enlarged scale, then photographed, then reduced, then made into a stencil. Only then can you make an "original." It's the same with some of the more complicated stamps, which are projected on a screen, copied precisely, and so forth. On the other hand, making false internal passports is a completely different matter. It's extremely difficult to produce the counterfeit paper, particularly because of the watermarks. Therefore we usually only reconstruct "lost" passports. By now our people already know that in such and such a year the documents had such and such a characteristic. For example, the photos done in a certain year might have regularly been retouched by the photographers, or they might have been printed on a special type of paper. The legalization team tries to take care of all this.

The information team is a separate group, extremely secret but with wide-reaching contacts. Its job is selecting and preserving all kinds of information that may be useful to the underground. For example, someone comes to us with an idea on how we can set up a wireless communication network that can't be jammed. Someone else says they've got a tapedeck for duplicating cassette tapes that they're willing to give to us. Or somebody tells us of a place where the police have installed equipment tracing radio transmitters. Or someone has an apartment we can use, or can supply us with fifteen gallons of gas a month, or gives us the name of a police agent, or says they've got access to the Council of Ministers' telecommunications studio, or can give us the names of reliable people in television. We get so much information of this kind, too much to store it all on notecards. And so, in a certain place, all this information is written into a computer, with the disks programmed in such a way that if any unauthorized person touches it, everything is erased.

A control team works very closely with the information team, checking out both the information and the people who supply it to us. The control team has direct access to a whole group of experts from very diverse fields. Suppose somebody says they can help us build electronic transmitters. The control people will go to an expert, get him to specify some kind of electronic assignment as a test, and give it to the first person to carry out. The results are then taken back to the expert to evaluate. If the specialist tells us, say, that the transmitter the candidate put together is a piece of junk, we tell the guy, he's not needed—and that's the end of it.

But the control team has other responsibilities, too. For example, a certain group of people might tell us that they have good contacts with several cities. If they really do, then the team has to check everything in detail, often working together with the department for interregional contacts. We've got to check out what kind of circles these contacts are in, to what extent they might be infiltrated, whether they can run a distribution network or gather information. Then, as a test, we give them a consignment of *Tygodnik* and we watch. We watch how they're doing the distribution, who's gossiping, who's being careless, etc. After a few weeks we sum it up for them, "OK, people, this and that guy you've got to get rid of, the rest of you are OK."

We also have a department of supplies that takes care of orders

71

from the Warsaw underground. For example, a leafleting squad may send us an order for a hundred smoke bombs to use as cover, and we've got to take care of it. The task is passed on to some reliable chemists who do some quick experiments, asking only if the smoke is to float along the ground or gush up into the sky as if from a fire. Sometimes the supply department receives typical organizational tasks, too, such as working out a distribution schedule for sending our press to a certain city, although then it works together with the control, communications, and interregional contacts teams.

Besides all these groups I've mentioned, we also have a few other structures. But these I either know little about or would prefer not to talk about.

The safety of all these teams is intrinsically connected with the question of "good conspiracy." This is a very broad topic, so I can only say that our most carefully hidden asset is our technical equipment, particularly our printing presses. Next comes us, members of the Regional Executive Committee. Although we try to stay deep underground in the most imaginative way, we do have to maintain contact with people, and rather broad contact at that. We have no personal protection, except what's offered through our disguises and the anonymity of the crowd. (Luckily for me, I've got a rather ordinary face, don't you think?) Of course, there are certain safety precautions which we're absolutely strict about following, but, as I've said, all it takes is one stupid accident.

Except for the capture of Zbyszek Romaszewski, who managed to get away the first time they came to get him, our other serious arrests were due to coincidence. Wiktor Kulerski once had a dangerous adventure. He noticed that the police were blocking off the whole housing project where he was staying, so he took his host's dog out on a leash and walked her for seven long hours! During that time he kept meeting the same people out on normal dog walks, two or three times! And while *their* dogs were peacefully running around and pissing, Wiktor kept his on a short leash, and the poor mutt began to get terribly hungry and started forcing his way home. Meanwhile, the ZOMO were searching all the buildings one at a time, and seeing Wiktor so frequently, by now they treated him as one of their own people. Finally they left, and Kulerski could go back to the apartment. But the poor dog, who had actually liked him a lot up till then, never wanted Wiktor to take him out for a walk anymore.

I had a similar thing happen to me. I was staying in a building that the police suddenly started searching early in the morning. I wasn't caught only because my host opened the door right away, thinking it was a friend. When he saw the police, he froze, but they just checked his ID and moved on. Later we learned that people who hesitated before opening the door had their apartments searched in full.

But even if they caught me, nothing would change. The regional underground committees have gotten stronger, and they all have two or even three substitute leaderships. If I'm arrested, Kulerski would probably take the helm, and after him Janas or Bieliński. Names don't matter, after all. What's important are the structures and the mechanisms. And thanks to them, we can appoint a responsible person to any function at any time.

BORUSEWICZ I.10

The regional structure of the underground was determined not only by the perceived need for resistance at the local level, but also by the long dispute as to whether or not any sort of center was even necessary. This dispute essentially began as soon as the "war" did, and opinions were so divided that several months had to pass before any kind of position could be agreed upon.

Bogdan Borusewicz perceived the need for a national structure at once, to provide direction for popular resistance as well as a reference point for the West. The significance of this structure would depend on the degree to which it was accepted, meaning, in other words, that it would depend on the authority of the people who belonged to it.

I wrote to Bujak as early as January [1982], saying it was necessary to form a national body. He was very much opposed. "Maybe it *is* necessary," he wrote back, "but without me." By the end of March, Lis and I already knew that Frasyniuk and Hardek supported our position. Together we put pressure on Bujak. An additional argument we used in order to bring Warsaw to reason was the OKO affair. We explained to Bujak that if we didn't set up something serious, other people would keep setting up not-so-serious organizations, and that finally convinced him.[3]

We in Gdańsk sought to avoid a situation where the absence of a national organization meant that our Gdańsk organization began de facto to act like one. This would have created a situation analogous to the origins of Solidarity, when Gdańsk became the trade-union capital of Poland. This most certainly would not have been fortuitous.

BUJAK I.9

Having long resisted the creation even of a regional structure, we also felt for a long time that interregional cooperation could be carried out without creating an Interim Coordinating Commission. We argued that any kind of centralization meant, above all, the centralization of arrests. We were afraid that a possible mass arrest of the ICC would mean the dissolution of the underground, in the same way that the December 13 [1981] arrest of the National Commission was such a crushing blow to Solidarity. Our way of thinking proved to be quite fruitful as the underground grew strong, chiefly because the ICC that was finally created functioned only as a general programmatic body, setting out the general direction of the movement.

LIS I.8

At the first meeting between Lis, Bujak, Hardek, and Frasyniuk, the main topic of discussion was whether the underground's national structure should take the form of a federation that left a large margin of autonomy for the different regions, or of a central organization controlling all forms of social resistance. Like Bujak, Bogdan Lis also feared that a hierarchical organization could be too easily destroyed.

We based this belief on the experience of WiN.[4] And the future proved us right. For despite the frequent arrests of activists in Wrocław, Poznań, Kraków, and Gdańsk, underground Solidarity still managed to survive. The arrest of small circles doesn't carry great consequences precisely because the different regions are connected very loosely—for all practical purposes, only through the members of the ICC. There is, for example, no separate distribution and informational network embracing the entire country.

In January 1982, I admit, I thought otherwise. I then felt that the government was going to try to create some kind of "quasi-Solidarity" out of "softened-up" leaders from the National Commission. For that reason, I was then in favor of creating a single nationwide organization to symbolize the continuity of the union. In this I was wrong, however. For it turned out that the Communists couldn't find any takers, and so we no longer needed to hurry. I therefore changed my mind, and by the beginning of March I was a supporter of the federation model, where the leaders would possess moral authority but not run any grand organizational apparatus. In the second half of April, Bujak, who was from the beginning opposed to the creation of anything, came around to my position. Hardek, meanwhile, and later also Szumiejko, were adherents of the centralist model. Frasyniuk essentially stood in the middle—that is, he recognized the advantages of what Bujak and I were proposing, but at the same time he pointed to the disadvantages, such as the difficulties connected with the achievement of any concrete aims. Later, however, he supported our position.[5]

In forming the ICC, we were concerned with a few key matters. First of all, it was important to us that the Commission articulate the main course of action for all those organizations that had undertaken the struggle with the dictatorship. Agreeing that there were bounds of acceptable social resistance, we wanted to prevent the rise of terrorist organizations, which the authorities might use for various kinds of provocations. In fact, the Security Service had already taken the initiative in this respect, at least in Gdańsk, where someone named Igor Kureń was trying to form an armed group. This guy had a few pistols and rifles—all, of course, defective and probably supplied to him by the police—and was running around looking for contacts. He requested a meeting with me, and even sent me an outline of his organization. The whole thing smelled from the start, and later I learned that Kureń really was an agent.

An equally important matter, which we took up at the founding meeting of the ICC, was the question of Solidarity representation abroad. I sent Milewski a letter informing him that OKO had ceased to exist and therefore he should stop representing them. I presented him our proposals, and at the same time notified Western trade union organizations that the ICC alone would appoint and recall foreign representatives of Solidarity. Such a move seemed absolutely necessary to me, since there were already several different policy groups in the West all claiming the mandate of Solidarity, and with no coordination between them. Moreover, all kinds of quarrels began to emerge between them, based on personal ambitions. That we had to stop right away, and it seemed that the easiest way to do so was to appoint foreign representatives, emphasizing that if others wanted to do something under the banner of "Solidarity," they could do so only through our representatives.

As for the practical functioning of the ICC, we adopted at the very beginning a series of principles that are still in effect today. We agreed, for example, that the ICC could consist of no more than seven people. I won't say how we choose new people, however, since the Security Service might yet infiltrate some region that, in the future, may send its own representative to the ICC. If I say more, they might learn how to smuggle in one of their own!

BUJAK I.10

I'll only add that the composition of the ICC is not automatic. That is, it's not necessarily the case that people are in it because of their status in the underground. Essentially, ICC members are simply recruited. Of course, we remember that people in Solidarity were elected, and so if there are active, democratically elected leaders not in jail who want to get involved in the underground, we try to consider them before we consider anyone else, even someone better and smarter. On the other hand, Hardek from Kraków, who was not a member of Solidarity's National Commission, was brought onto the ICC ahead of several available Commission members. Personal considerations, it's clear, do play a large role.

FRASYNIUK I.7

News of the formation of the ICC was greeted in Lower Silesia with great satisfaction. Opinion in the factories was along the line of the following: "A great step forward." "Now we've got a committee that can coordinate things and prepare the country for a general strike." "Now it won't be just Wrocław or Gdańsk that moves, now all of Poland will be fighting." In a word, there was massive support—not just for the idea of the ICC but also for its personnel. Frasyniuk was greatly pleased with the reaction.

It proved the correctness of our line. Ever since January, when we first made contacts with other regions, we'd been firmly pressing for the formation of a national structure. We felt that the formation of a national committee, one that would embrace the entire country, would galvanize into action those areas where nothing much had been happening so far. The ICC would formulate a general line of action and disseminate an organizational model tested first in a given locale. And finally it seemed to us that the ICC, with the authority it had, could prevent the authorities from provoking uncontrolled resistance in specific enterprises, not to mention in entire regions.

NOTES

1. *Due to the great inquisitiveness of these functionaries, this sentence is cut off. This itself raises some questions: How many of the departments named by Bogdan Lis really exist, and how many have been concealed? Who's playing what, and on whose board? The reader should keep this problem in mind also (and perhaps chiefly) while reading the next statement.*

2. Bujak is talking here about ink-pad stamps used for identification purposes, like notary stamps, not postage stamps.

3. *While reading the manuscript of this book, Zbigniew Bujak at this point added the following: "What convinced me above all was the strength of the underground structures, and the belief that they would be able to manage the now-increasing tasks."*

4. *Wolność i Niepodległość*, or Freedom and Independence, an underground organization fighting against Communist rule immediately after World War II.

5. *Szumiejko's comment upon reading this passage: "With hopes that this book can supply future historiographers with the true facts, I'd like to add the following: In February 1982, in a letter to different regional representatives, I proposed two variants for the organizational structure of OKO—a centralist model and a federation. At the end of March—beginning of April, 1982, I received replies: from Wrocław (written by Kornel Morawiecki, with a supporting note by Władysław Frasyniuk), from Kraków (signed by Władysław Hardek), and from Szczecin (for conspiratorial reasons I won't mention the names). All the responses agreed: only the federation model was at all viable. We talked exclusively about the possibility of federation. Therefore, in the second half of April, neither I nor, I firmly believe, Frasyniuk or Hardek, could have been supporters of centralization. Bogdan Lis might not have known these facts for the simple reason that in February and March he was still 'not around.' Bogdan made his first contact with Frasyniuk only at the end of March or beginning of April; later with Hardek; and with me only at the end of May, beginning of June."*

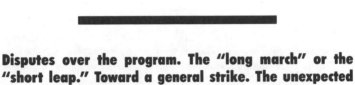

6

Disputes over the program. The "long march" or the "short leap." Toward a general strike. The unexpected third variant: May 1 on the streets.

BUJAK I.11

From the very beginning, the underground's thinking on strategy and tactics revealed sharp differences of opinion that—as has already been mentioned—determined the way in which individual regions organized themselves.

The notion of the underground society was formulated in Warsaw by Zbigniew Bujak and Wiktor Kulerski as an alternative program to that proposed by [then imprisoned] Jacek Kuroń in his "Theses on a Solution to a Situation Without Solution" (February 1981). Kuroń demanded, among other things, that "Polish society prepare itself to liquidate the occupation through collective action," something that Bujak regarded as involving an unacceptable level of risk.

Kuroń's proposals went some way toward satisfying people's aspirations; they held out the possibility of a speedy confrontation and implied the overthrow of our opponents. But Jacek didn't seem to take account of the possible disaster. His main argument was: If you don't want war, prepare yourselves for war. This idea, like his other "theses on a solution," suggested a final showdown.

If you orient activity toward the short run, it becomes impossible to think in terms of a program; it's like a game of poker in which you don't know who's bluffing and on what basis. You don't know what cards your opponent is holding or—even more important—what he has up his sleeve. Of course, I enjoy a bet, but not when people's lives are at stake. Unfortunately, I was drawn into the game in spite of myself, and the only thing I could do was not to bluff (especially since I didn't even know what cards I was holding). If it had turned out I had a full house or a royal flush, then fine. But if I'd put down a couple of sevens. . . . This was why Wiktor and I put forward the program of the underground society. It wasn't a very spectacular proposal, it didn't offer a speedy solution or immediate victory; in addition, it shifted responsibility for the strength and form of opposition from the leadership to society as a whole.

The leading activists of the Warsaw underground placed the main emphasis on mass activity that would take various forms: on the one hand, factory-based struggles, chiefly for the right to continue trade-union activity; on the other hand, various initiatives, such as the creation of aid committees in the parishes (to help victims of repression), an independent press and books, independent education, culture, and research, and a network of Workers' Universities. Only a differentiated opposition movement could, they thought, provide a counterweight to the monopolistic activities of the authorities. At the same time, they felt that every attempt to centralize control over the opposition—which would be necessary to organize a general strike—carried with it the danger of defeat. In a military-police-state, any centralized organization is forced, sooner or later, to adopt the methods of its opponents; in other words, either it becomes enmeshed in escalating terror or it is defeated, leaving behind a lot of "scorched earth." Bujak and Kulerski believed their proposal avoided both these dangers. They based their idea on Gombrowicz's view that society should consciously oppose a totalitarian state by asserting its autonomy rather than by forming an organization that, in the long run, is bound to become infected with the totalitarian virus.

FRASYNIUK I.8

In contrast to the long-term approach adopted in Warsaw, Wrocław favored a more immediate form of struggle. Although Frasyniuk thought that Bujak and Kulerski's proposals were noble in their intent to change and improve people's consciousness, he also considered them something of a capitulation. In Lower Silesia, charitable commissions, education groups, mutual aid, independent culture and research, and so on were considered a fine thing, of course, but unlikely to ensure victory on their own. It was the workers in large factories, in mines and steelworks, who were decisive for the future, not intellectuals organized in small groups of friends. For this reason, Wrocław activists emphasized the formation of factory organizations in order to prepare for a general strike.

Frasyniuk was not, however, satisfied with the results achieved in the first half of 1982.

We adopted the idea, but we had a lot of trouble putting it into practice. It demanded painstaking, unspectacular organizational work of a kind that conflicts with our national character. We prefer fireworks. And here we had to build bit by bit, develop a battle plan, and secure an escape route in case of defeat. We had enormous problems because we couldn't determine in advance when the battle was going to take place. It would be easy to begin the strike when we were best prepared, but what if the authorities were simultaneously best prepared to confront us? Either disaster or victory at too high a price. So we had to wait for that single moment when our chances of success were the greatest and the cost minimal. But in order to choose the right moment, you have to be aware of all the possible consequences of your choice, you have to be organizationally prepared, and you have to be patient. You may have to wait a long time.

In Frasyniuk's opinion, the success of the strike depended also on whether other regions accepted the idea and began preparations. Wrocław stood no chance of victory on its own. Although the Wrocław Regional Committee considered its tactics the best, it knew that if they weren't adopted elsewhere, the level of activity would decline in Lower Silesia too.

You can't keep people in a state of readiness forever; even an athlete is at the height of his form only for short periods and achieves his best results only during the Olympics and not during the intervening four years. Our idea was the most simple one, but that doesn't mean it was the easiest. It demanded that, through the press, through leaflets and publications, we shape political and economic consciousness and maintain morale in the factories. (You have to be careful not to fan the flames too much, otherwise the pot will boil over immediately, and it's not supposed to do that until the right moment—

whenever that turns out to be.) We had to show people the long-term goals and make sure they understood the problems, we had to motivate them and prepare them to make sacrifices, perhaps even to sacrifice their lives. Thus, we just had to undertake the long, slow, painstaking work of forming links within and between enterprises, between cities and regions.

I regret that in April 1982 the ICC didn't announce a specific date by which strike preparations in the regions were to be completed. I'm not talking, obviously, about setting a date for the strike itself, since—as I've already said—that would have been highly foolish. But we could have set a timetable for the creation of factory structures, for the organization of communications, supplies, factory defenses, and so on. Of course, no amount of instructions, regulations, and timetables will move things along if there's no organization at the lowest levels. In such a situation, charismatic leaders are no help either. Even if Lech Wałęsa had evaded internment, in this situation he would have been unable to create a secret organization in the Gdańsk Shipyard. He would have needed to be another kind of activist, to set up a new network and to ready the factory for protest—a "Lech Wałęsa mark II." And the situation demanded hundreds of such people in hundreds of enterprises.

From January onward we proclaimed endlessly: create factory structures, create factory structures. Some people replied, "We've already created them, but we don't know why. Our factory is organized, we've carried out all ten of the RSC recommendations, we're helping the victims of repression, we're collecting union dues, we're printing our own paper and distributing *Z Dnia na Dzień*, and we've organized discussion clubs—and what, in heaven's name, do we do next?" We would meet with them and say, "OK, so everything's organized. Suppose we called a general strike right now, would everyone in your place come out?" "Well, no, not everyone," they'd reply, "because the treasurer is really on his own; he's working actively with twenty others, the rest just pay their dues without being asked." And I'd reply, "I want to know where's the guy who'll lead the defense of the factory gate, where's the group that'll weld the antitank barriers? What kind of system do you have for communications with other factories?" Then they'd shake their heads and say they didn't yet have one, but give them another month and . . .

People had got used to thinking in ways instilled into them by the regime. For example, the authorities used to draw up a five-year plan, they calculated this, that, and the other and then called on people to implement it. From August 1980 until December 13, 1981, people thought in these categories. Everyone was waiting for the National Commission to decide whether they should laugh or cry. Some people are still waiting for directives today, and we have to fight against this. After all, the eventual defense of a factory like Pafawag is going to be different from that of somewhere like Chemitex, and different again in an oil refinery or dockyard. Neither the RSC nor Bujak, Lis, or Frasyniuk is going to come up with fantastic plans without the help of people from individual factories. It is they who must now display the greatest determination and inventiveness. We can only write documents—defeatist or radical, blustering or demagogic—because what else can we do? If there's no initiative from below, if good organizers don't emerge at the lower levels, we can't do anything.

But people are still thinking, unfortunately, in the same terms as they did during those memorable sixteen months: the National Commission must seize the reds by the throat and strangle them, only God forbid that this should disrupt an American movie or a good variety show on TV; God forbid that the blood seeping out of Party headquarters should stain my carpet. Now they're still waiting: there's Bujak; everyone knows him, the whole of Poland knows him, the outside world knows him. Let Bujak tell us how to make a rifle, how to barricade the factory gates, how many people to place as guards round the walls. Maybe I'm just grousing without cause, but I can imagine how things will turn out. A strike will erupt, and the workers will be trying to decide whether or not to wear red-and-white armbands. Aha, there's the head of the RSC, they'll say, let's ask him! But at that point the time for talking will be over.

The organization of a strike was not, in any case, everything. We had to analyze all the possible consequences, particularly the possibility of disaster. As far as the date of the general confrontation was concerned, Frasyniuk remained undecided.

When does a strike have the best chance of success? This year? In August? Shall we build on tradition, proclaim the slogan "August 1980," and charge? In a word, shall we improvise? Improvisation is fine for musicians and poets, but I'm against it. I'm a driver by profession. I can't imagine driving an "improvised" car—one that has an engine but no brakes, or the other way around. Given the current state of preparations, even here, in Wrocław, we're not ready for a strike. Perhaps in a couple of months, if we succeed in mobilizing and concentrating our forces, the situation will change, because the authorities will have begun to soften their stand. If the Reds realize that people are well organized and determined, they may give way in the face of a strike. But we're unlikely to have a strike in the immediate future. So we have to explain to people why the ICC hasn't called a strike, so that they don't start asking, "What are those idiots up to? Are they just hiding somewhere, hoping to sit it out from one winter to the next?"

We have to ask whether, if people's expectations are delayed, they won't start saying, "What the hell have we built this underground for?" We have to ask whether they won't become apathetic, like a boxer who doesn't actually lose any teeth or get himself knocked out, but whose head won't stop ringing after a fight because he's worn himself out fielding and avoiding so many blows.

Another question: Can we manage to survive for a longish period as members of a conspiratorial organization, to protect ourselves from arrest and infiltration, to preserve our ability to act? I think we probably can, because it's not important whether I personally survive; what counts is that we survive. If they arrest me, Bednarz will take my place; if they get Bednarz, Pinior will take over; if Pinior goes, then some Kowalski or other will step in.[1] If we manage to create factory structures, we'll certainly survive.

For this reason, since we haven't managed to prepare ourselves and since the political situation remains unfavorable to us, we should look for a solution next year, in 1983. I think we have some trump cards: August 1980, sixteen months of freedom, and the will to fight under martial law.

Only when the idea of a general strike has had it, by which I mean when such a strike has been broken or doesn't erupt at all, will the time come to implement the ideas of Bujak and Kulerski. In that case, we'll be able to manage without the ICC; all we'll need is a couple of people with some courage. It'll be they who'll introduce the idea of the underground society, because the rest of society will be sitting there quiet like mice—either terrified (if the strike has been broken in a bloody repression) or bored to death and unwilling to do anything (if the strike never took place).

LIS I.9

Gdańsk was also in favor of a general strike. It was clear that the local population had quickly recovered from its post-December state of shock. This was confirmed by the successful fifteen-minute "training strikes." In any case, the coastal area had the strongest tradition of this kind of struggle. The date of a general strike remained, however, an open question. Lis was in favor of June 1982.

I thought it important that a general showdown take place at a time when the students were in town, so that's why I wasn't convinced by the arguments for calling the strike in August or September. My faith in the possible success of a strike was based on my analysis of the events of December 1981. I'd come to the conclusion that the authorities didn't have enough forces to pacify every factory if all of them went on strike at once. This was particularly true since they didn't want to use the army. I was thinking largely about a strike in those regions where there's a lot of large industry. After all, in December the police had to ride around from one town to another in order to deal with the strikes. If we could hold out for three days, the authorities would be forced to use the army, and that might be their downfall. If some of the soldiers went over to the workers, Soviet intervention might become a possibility, and our homegrown Reds greatly fear the Reds from across the border.

At the same time, it was clear to me that, alongside preparations for a general strike, we had to create organizational structures that would play no part in the confrontation and which would, in the event of a defeat, encourage renewed resistance.

With hindsight, I can see that we made a mistake by not making a firm decision on a date for a general strike. The absence of such a decision meant that the whole business remained somehow confined to the realm of fantasy. It was wishful thinking and nothing more.

BORUSEWICZ II.1

In Borusewicz's opinion, the underground leadership was paralyzed by the fear of taking on itself the responsibility for a possible defeat.

The power of the generals could have been broken only by a general strike that, however, carried with it the danger of a confrontation on the scale of 1956 in Hungary. The members of the ICC were faced with a dilemma: on the one hand, the expectations of the population, who believed the junta could be defeated; on the other hand, their own awareness of the price that would have to be paid for even victory, not to mention defeat. The absence of a clear-cut decision, the constant wavering on the part of the ICC as regards the choice of methods (a general strike or long-term activity), the fear of responsibility—all this allowed the military authorities to break the will to resist and to move ahead.

BUJAK I.12

Jacek Kuroń's article articulated two approaches to underground activity: the first might be called the Wrocław–Gdańsk version; the second, the Kraków–Warsaw version. Generally speaking, the program that won out was the one that proposed a struggle to save what we could. To the question, "Are we to be a trade union, a political party, or a national liberation movement?" came a clear answer. We were to be a trade union. Jacek Kuroń's proposal was seen to be unrealistic almost immediately. Only one Warsaw activist—Zbigniew Romaszewski—supported it. The Wrocław–Gdańsk version, which assumed that a general strike would be called in the near future, could not be implemented. All that remained, then, was the Kraków–Warsaw proposal for long-term mass resistance.

HALL I.2

The members of the Gdańsk Solidarity Regional Committee were not, however, in agreement. Aleksander Hall, who joined in the polemics between Bujak, Frasyniuk, and Kulerski in April 1982, put forward proposals that were close to those of the Warsaw-based activists.

Until February 1982, despite some wavering and numerous reservations, I considered a general strike to be a feasible solution. By March, however, I realized there was no point in counting on that dream. After all, if the strike were successful, the authorities (and I don't mean just a specific group at the center but all those who were part of the Communist power structure) would be finished in Poland; all that would be left for them would be to announce the collapse of the system, the greatest defeat for communism ever. For this reason,

85

they would pay any price to avoid this disaster. Of course, they would prefer to avoid bloodshed and carnage. There was thus a possibility that we could exert pressure on the authorities and force them to make concessions. On the other hand, there was no possibility at all of overthrowing the generals in a confrontation, given the conditions that prevailed during 1982.

Each day I became increasingly convinced that there was no way we could repeat the events of August 1980 (even if all the talk about a general strike implied the possibility), because the rules of the game had changed. In August 1980 the authorities had agreed to let us form independent trade unions while we had agreed to recognize the leading role of the Party, and so on. But after December 1981 any such pretense had become impossible because the authorities used their weapon of last resort—force.

I thus became increasingly skeptical about a general strike. I found myself in an unpleasant situation, because at that time the majority of people in our group were in favor of a strike. In other words, they discussed what form the strike should take and when it should be called, but they no longer discussed whether or not it should take place at all. I was absolutely opposed to any proposals, like those that Jacek Kuroń issued from his internment in Białołęka, which linked a general strike with a national uprising.

At the beginning of April 1982, the first "war-time" issue of the Gdańsk paper *Solidarność* appeared. It contained our statement, "Compromise without Capitulation," which, despite everything, was far more realistic. It expressed our readiness to reach a compromise, although one that recognized the existence of the union. I didn't deceive myself that the authorities would jump at the offer. They hadn't decided to undertake a massive military operation in order to hand over the loot afterward. I had no illusions, then. Poland after December was bound to be different from Poland after August—although I didn't exclude the possibility that there would be a place for Solidarity, weakened but still independent. We therefore had to propose a compromise, because it is important who comes forward with an offer and who rejects it.

Some proponents of a general strike considered that it wasn't an end in itself; quite the opposite: it was supposed to lead to a compromise, to force the authorities to the bargaining table. I disagreed completely with this view. You can't use revolutionary means to achieve a more limited goal. Revolution has its own internal dynamic. There's no way you can tell the Communists, "We don't want to throw you on the garbage heap because you might come in useful in dealing with the Russians."

The only choice that remained was long-term activity.

FRASYNIUK I.9

Alongside these two basic approaches, each of which had a number of variants, there emerged a third. It was, perhaps, not very clearly articulated by its proponents, but it was strongly condemned by its opponents. To Frasyniuk, it was a program for an uprising ("let's take to the streets, just as we are, let's improvise, we'll fight, we'll all die together, and even if we lose, which is highly probable, as we did during the January Uprising,[2] we'll be able to call on the memory of the victims, the bloodshed will bind us together and motivate us to further struggle") and a recipe for disaster. Fortunately, however, for the time being at least, there was no possibility of implementing this "third option." In Wrocław, the likelihood of such an uprising was soon seen to be quite small. Elsewhere, on the other hand . . .

BUJAK I.13

When the members of the ICC discussed, at their first meeting on April 22, how May 1 should be celebrated, various ideas were floating around: people should stay at home and not go out; they should go to church; they should lay wreaths. There was little enthusiasm for the idea of counterdemonstrations. And yet the nation chose this version spontaneously. With the exception of Wrocław, where the RSC called on people to stay home, the streets were swarming with demonstrators.

BORUSEWICZ I.11

In Gdańsk, the spontaneous demonstration exceeded all expectations. While the official parade consisted of ten thousand silent and somewhat nervous marchers, the counterdemonstration was more than five times that size. People were fired up, chanting slogans. They proudly carried national flags above their heads; some women wrote "Solidarity" or a large "V" in lipstick on the flag's white half. Every few yards, some young people with buckets of paint would leap out from the end of the demonstration and splatter slogans on the walls. At many windows along the route, people were standing in tears, holding symbols of Solidarity or religious symbols, or blessing the crowd from on high, in a state of ecstasy. The counterdemonstration met with expressions of support everywhere. Taxi drivers blew their horns and streetcar drivers rang their bells in greeting. The parade ended up outside Wałęsa's apartment, where we all sang the national anthem and God Bless Poland.

The counterdemonstration in Warsaw was equally spontaneous. The authorities were quite upset because the Security Service had spared no effort in the attempt to make the official parade look the larger of the two. They brought several thousand Party members in from all over the region, and the formal parade went on forever. In addition, every delegation had to lay a wreath at the Tomb of the Unknown Soldier.

In neither Warsaw nor Gdańsk did the ZOMO intervene, although long lines of ZOMO forces watched the countermarchers. The authorities did not, however, forgive society's display of insubordination, and decided to strike back two days later, even at the price of a provocation. On May 3, police battled demonstrators for five to ten hours in sixteen towns and cities, displaying unprecedented brutality.[3] Above all, they attacked people coming out of churches, dousing them with colored water, throwing canisters of tear gas, and then beating and arresting them. In this way, several thousand "disrupters of law and order" were detained across the whole country.

LIS I.10

As Bogdan Lis readily admits, at this time the members of the ICC were opposed to demonstrations.

I have one response to people who accuse us of being out of tune with the mood of the masses: it is true that we were out of tune, but do we always have to succumb to the prevailing mood? Throughout its entire existence, Solidarity's National Commission gave in under the pressure of public opinion, and where did that lead us? Of course the ICC was formed as a coordinating body, but it was to coordinate activity on which everyone agreed; it wasn't supposed to coordinate people's aspirations, because some wanted one thing, others another, and still others had no opinion at all. Let's take the current elections to the government's People's Councils (June 1984) and the question of whether to vote or not. The issue demands that we take a specific position and tell people that, in our opinion, they should do this and this. Coordination consists precisely in this, and not in succumbing to suggestions that we collect voting cards at the polling stations and hand them over to the Church or in issuing the order for a boycott and organizing it through our structures.

In the first half of 1982 we thought that the struggle should take place in the factories, not in the streets. It's easy to accuse street demonstrators of hooliganism, but not strikers in the factories. However, since the authorities concealed the fact that a fifteen-minute warning strike had taken place (and the strike therefore failed to fulfill its political function), we had to change our approach and agree to demonstrations. In this way we forced the regime to engage in a display of force time and again.

In my opinion, if we had called for street demonstrations on May Day in 1982, the authorities' reaction would not have been so restrained, and the demonstrators would have been beaten as they were on May 3.

BORUSEWICZ II.2

In our situation, a wrong assessment of the possibilities and the mood of the population may result in disaster. And we were wrong on several occasions. The first serious mistake was our assessment of people's willingness to resist on May 1 and 3, 1982. We called on people to stay home, but they took to the streets. They were more radical than we were. It is certain that, had we called for demonstrations, they would have been larger than they were, but they were already large enough to shake the authorities and demonstrate the degree of social solidarity.

NOTES

1. *Władysław Frasyniuk was arrested in October 1982, Piotr Bednarz in November 1982, and Józef Pinior in April 1983. In the meantime, the authors of* Konspira

were also arrested. Nonetheless, "some Kowalski or other" continues in each of their
places.

2. Uprising against the Russian occupation of the Kingdom of Poland, 1863.

3. May 3 was a national holiday in prewar Poland. Not celebrated by the authorities, it was commemorated by solemn masses, sometimes followed by demonstrations.

1

A mass movement or a cadres' organization? Strikes. Demonstrations: the authorities impose a poll tax. The "front of refusal." The independent circulation of information: press and radio. Embassies. Underground intelligence and counterintelligence: "things best left alone." Special campaigns. "People I'd like to smoke out."

BORUSEWICZ I.12

Each of the two approaches to resistance demanded the appropriate weapons. The forms of struggle were determined also by tradition and by people's level of initiative, as well as by the sociopolitical and economic situation. Roughly speaking we can distinguish between two forms, a tendency to adopt exclusively conspiratorial methods, and mass actions, not necessarily inspired by the underground. Both types of struggle were somehow based in necessity, which was itself a product of the intentions and reactions of both the authorities and the population. From the beginning of the "war," activists realized that they had to reach a broad audience, that they had to provide people with information and organize them in joint undertakings. For this reason, they organized the printing and distribution of independent publications and created the beginnings of factory, group, and regional organizations. But this kind of work involved only a relatively small proportion of those who were ready to be active in some way.

The majority of the population also wanted to protest against the dictatorship—hence the widespread boycott of the official media, the ignoring of some official instructions, and the isolation of those regarded as collaborators. The strongest resistance was to be found in the large industrial regions. In Borusewicz's opinion this was particularly painful for the authorities—for both practical and ideological reasons.

What was amazing was that it wasn't only the workers who made clear their readiness for a struggle but also the middle and higher levels of the technical staff, on whom the regime had depended under Gomułka and Gierek. There's no doubt that the level of opposition rose in direct proportion to the size of the town and the enterprise concerned. This alarmed the authorities, since the most powerful plants and regions had considerable clout (which extended to economic issues), and, of course, it was an ideological loss of face. From the very beginning, the Communists had always claimed to represent the large-industrial working class; yet who could they get to endorse them now—the petty bourgeoisie?

For convenience, I've grouped the different approaches to struggle into mass and, let's say, cadres forms, although it would be incorrect to say that we have a clear division between the underground and the mass of the population. Our campaigns are successful and fulfill a purpose only when they arouse widespread response. In addition, the term "underground" includes a variety of groups. Some people are still in hiding, others are living somewhere on the margins, and the majority live and work completely legally while taking part in illegal activity. It is this last group—the aboveground majority willing to resist—who now constitute the core of the underground.

In my opinion, we've developed very few completely new forms of struggle in comparison with the pre-August 1980 period. Innovations include underground radio broadcasts, perhaps the formal establishment of factory cells, and certainly the mass boycott. All the rest are as old as the hills.

Underground structures essentially fulfill a service role. The ICC has absolutely no means of enforcing its recommendations. The same is true of the Regional Coordinating Committee; we thus function according to the principle of old opposition. But the scope of our publishing, informational, organizational, and instructional activity is much broader. How many people do we reach? It's hard to say. Bujak asserts, on the basis of some kind of estimates, that about one million Poles are participating in resistance, even if only paying their dues or reading the underground press. And how many are actively involved in conspiratorial activity? Again, it's hard to say, partly because it's an unreliable indicator (you can be a member of a factory commission and do absolutely nothing; what counts are real organizational activities, collecting dues, printing, distributing, etc.). In the Gdańsk region I estimate there are several thousand people involved, but nearer to three than to ten.

LIS I.11

It was in 1946, in the Gdańsk docks, that the first postwar strike in the Tri-city area broke out. The strike demands were largely economic but also political. It could be said, then, that there is a strong militant tradition among workers on the Baltic coast. Of course it's difficult to calculate exactly how many strikes have taken place during the nearly forty years that have elapsed since this first protest. Nevertheless, Jaruzelski's war against Poland has opened up a new chapter in our history and has accelerated the evolution of strikes. During the legal Solidarity period, participation in strikes did not involve any risk. After December 13, 1981, the cost of such participation was severe repression. For this reason, protest strikes during the first period of martial law were limited to fifteen-minute work stoppages.

The fifteen-minute strikes were intended to demonstrate not only to the authorities but also to the population as a whole that resistance in the factories continued. We counted on the authorities having some common sense that would eventually force them to look at the situation realistically. The strikes took place every month, from January until June 1982. On average, about sixty percent of the work force took part. The authorities reacted in a brutal fashion, often lashing out blindly in all directions. Over a period of six months several hundred people were fired, interned, or arrested. Hardest hit was the Gdańsk Shipyard and, among the smaller enterprises, the ship-repair yard.

Within the ICC and the Regional Committee, we discussed the possibility of other forms of protest—for example, an absentee strike, but we decided not to recommend it for a number of reasons. The strength of a strike depends, among other things, on the fact that people can observe each other and can see that others aren't working, that everyone is in solidarity. If they simply stayed home, they'd be beset by doubts. They'd start wondering if they were the only ones

93

who hadn't gone to work. They'd also start wondering if the police were going to come for them.

An "Italian strike," which involves slowing down the pace of work, was essentially in force the whole time without anyone having to organize it. In fact, we often suggested that people abandon this method, because the authorities were interested only in maintaining their own power and not in improving the economic situation.

The idea of refusing to work because of hazardous working conditions only became practical with the suspension of martial law. We raised this possibility in our program, "Solidarity Today," published in February 1983. As long as the martial law decree with all its executive orders was in force, this road was closed to us, since the regime simply ignored all regulations relating to work safety and hygiene. They simply issued orders and drove people to work. This resulted in the death of the miners in the Dimitrov Mine, forced to go down the shaft even though they'd reported the presence of increased amounts of methane in the tunnels. They were ordered to go down, and several dozen died in the explosion. The authorities either interpreted the safety regulations and Labor Code to their own advantage or ignored them completely. This was bound to affect our strategy concerning strikes during 1982.

In October 1982, after the union had been delegalized, the Gdańsk Shipyard proposed a form of strike that was somewhat new. The shipyard workers would report to work, where they would then proceed to strike for eight hours and then return home; the next day they would repeat the whole process all over again. This made it difficult for the ZOMO to break the strike and, at the same time, gave the strikers a sense of solidarity. The authorities, however, resorted to an expedient by militarizing the shipyard. I think it's possible that they had purposely withheld this step in December 1981 in order to have a weapon in reserve.

FRASYNIUK 1.10

In Wrocław, the first one-minute strike on January 13, 1982, was considered a great success. It helped people overcome the barrier of fear. Subsequent strikes were seen as a way to integrate the work force.

The mistake on our side was to increase the duration of the protest strikes to fifteen minutes, since this gave the authorities enough time to identify organizers, who were then punished in the most exemplary fashion. By April we already found ourselves in a bind: the strikes were fulfilling their purpose, but the cost of each one was too great. As the leaders in this kind of struggle (we had achieved a higher level of organization in the factories than any other region) we had greater expectations. If the four regions making up the ICC had adopted a unified position from the very beginning, we would have had a real chance of a more serious campaign. As it was, unfortunately, during the first six months of the "war," Wrocław bore the brunt of the repression. It's interesting that, from about February onward, administrative personnel began taking part in the strikes. Office workers, who were berated as do-nothings by both official propaganda and by workers, suddenly got militant.

LIS I.12

The severe penalties discouraged people from taking part in strikes. Anonymity is impossible in the factory; it's easy to recognize people and turn them in. At the beginning, the workers would stop working in a mass, but later they began to calculate whether the game was worth the candle. Most came to the conclusion that if they were to strike effectively, it had to be a strike that would break the authorities. Bogdan Lis shared this opinion.

As a result of the regime's brutal revenge, the number of worker–activists declined. We came to the conclusion that, if we wanted to organize a general strike at some point in the future, we had to save our factory structures. Now it's hard for me to say for sure whether the fifteen-minute strikes represented the right tactic. It'll be a couple of years before we can tell. In any event, we had to change our approach. Since, as I've already mentioned, the authorities—from the factory director to the prime minister—concealed the unrest in the enterprises, the workers were terribly angry that their sacrifice was for nothing, from both the political and the propaganda point of view.

HALL I.3

I personally believed the authorities would never retreat from a direct attack, but spectacular actions of limited duration were, I felt, useful.

The cost of the fifteen-minute strikes, in Gdańsk at least, was not very great. Of course people were sacked, but this was nothing in comparison with Lower Silesia, where masses of people were carted off to internment camps after each protest.

On the other hand, the organization of the strikes left much to be desired. There was clearly a considerable gap between the Regional Committee's authority and the actual effect of its activity. The underground sent out signals but had no control over their reception. This is unavoidable under conspiratorial conditions. In other words, things could have been better organized, but only at a price of sacrificing the protection of conspiracy. After all, Lower Silesia, a region that, on the one hand, attributed great weight to the development of an executive apparatus and, on the other, engaged in democratic consultation with factory representatives, lost three leaders in succession in a short space of time. The view that the union could be an effective underground organization with a mass base turned out to be utopian.

FRASYNIUK I.11

Conspiratorial activity has its own unwritten rules and regulations. One of the strangest rules states that the worse the level of underground organization the greater the desire to take to the streets.

And this, hell, is an enormous danger [Frasyniuk is angry]. After all, the Reds can choose the worst-organized region to provoke an outburst, crush it in a bloody fashion, and thus undermine the confidence of those regions that are better organized, which have been slowly but surely building their structures without any fireworks. For this reason, I was, and still am, utterly opposed to sending people onto the streets to confront government forces armed to the teeth and ready to lay into anything that moves. Maybe we'll need to take to the streets at some point, but it should be a last resort. What about peaceful demonstrations? A good idea, only I'm not sure anyone still believes in the possibility.

Some people in Wrocław accused the Regional Committee of cowardice. At the same time, it's easy to tell others to march or throw paving stones at the ZOMO while hiding oneself under the floorboards. If we call for a demonstration, we have to be in the front line. Apart from this, there have been so many, many national uprisings that were unsuccessful, provoked, or ill prepared, that we ought to abandon this idea once and for all.

BORUSEWICZ I.13

If misunderstandings in assessing the significance of the demonstrations arose, it was out of a linguistic confusion. The main issue was the concept of efficacy of such actions. For his part, Borusewicz regarded all mass forms of resistance as effective, since they had an impact on both the population and the regime.

Demonstrations were not, however, effective in the sense that they resulted in the overthrow of the authorities. In order to achieve this goal, the demonstrators would have had to attack regional police headquarters and other regime strongholds, and to occupy and then fortify them. This already implies armed struggle. So far, the demonstrations haven't led to this because they weren't intended to. Their purpose was to show that the nation refuses to recognize the dictatorship.

LIS II.1

It was all the more important to display our determination, given that Jaruzelski was boasting constantly about normalization. The reaction of the underground was, nevertheless, strangely restrained. Shortly after the parades and demonstrations of May 1 and 3, 1982, the ICC proclaimed a unilateral moratorium on all protest actions. No one produced any leaflets or painted any slogans on walls; only newsletters were published. The underground expected a positive gesture from the authorities in connection with the approaching national holiday on July 22: they would rescind martial law, free the internees, proclaim an amnesty, or at least reply to the theses on national reconciliation issued by Primate's Social Council. The underground thus demonstrated its good will; but the hand it extended was left in midair, unanswered. In July we therefore decided that, if the authorities planned to declare that "normalization" would continue as it had so far, we would demonstrate the falsity of this assertion. We thus adopted a new method of rectifying the generals' propaganda. In Lis's opinion, however, this method was adopted without enthusiasm.

If any other possibilities had been open to us, we certainly wouldn't have called for mass demonstrations on the second anniversary of the Gdańsk Agreements. I don't know . . . at that time it was probably the only avenue left. Thanks to this, we introduced yet another day into the calendar of national holidays—Solidarity Day, on August 31. Now, whether the Communists like it or not, this holiday will remain.

The demonstration on August 31, 1982, was the first demonstration organized by the ICC. Did we, however, succeed in directing it? Only up to a point. In Gdańsk, the person delegated to coordinate the whole thing bungled the job (that's why the tape of a speech I'd recorded was never played, among other problems). This man was psychologically incapable of coping with all the responsibility; in fact, he gave up underground activity shortly afterward.

Other organizational elements also broke down. There was no cooperation between the different groups. The nails that were to be used to puncture tires turned out to be too short; they only worked on Security Service cars and were useless against the ZOMO trucks. So, although we had excellent intelligence regarding the routes to be taken by the police, we didn't manage to prevent them from bringing in reinforcements.

In addition, any demonstration is difficult to control. You can only prepare the general framework, announce the date and meeting place, and organize, with the help of the factories, the so-called initiative groups. The core of these groups is made of young people, most of them about twenty years old, workers or students, who attempt to disguise themselves (for example, with stocking masks). In general, the brunt of the struggle, so to speak, falls on the young, although many older people come also—out of interest or to raise their spirits—and the course of events often draws them also into action against the ZOMO.

For our part, we can only try in various ways to initiate mass demonstrations. We have our methods.

BUJAK II.1

The unions' most successful actions were spontaneous demonstrations, mainly those that took place on May 1 and 3, 1982—in other words, demonstrations that were not called by the ICC. It was not until August 31, 1982 that the aspirations of the population and the underground leadership finally intersected. And in Warsaw, states Bujak, it was the intelligentsia rather than the workers who took to the streets.

In 1983, May 1 was not as spectacular as it had been a year before, but it revealed certain organizational achievements on the part of the underground. A committee to coordinate the parades was formed beforehand, and representatives of various conspiratorial structures took part in its work. Thanks to some common guidelines that had been worked out, our propaganda and information campaign worked very well. On the other hand, we weren't completely successful in mobilizing the vanguard. Some factory activists pledged more than they could deliver, although the discrepancy was not great, and the level of chaos was nothing like that of the year before. Having finally acquired confidence in activists from the factories, we soon after appointed some of them as members-at-large of the Regional Executive Committee.

BORUSEWICZ I.14

After several unsuccessful actions, during which an enormous concentration of police forces made it impossible to move about freely, let alone demonstrate, many people were saying that the population had lost the desire to protest publicly. Borusewicz disagrees.

Demonstrations shouldn't be organized too often, and in 1982 we had a demonstration once a month or even every two weeks in Gdańsk. In my opinion, people are still willing to take part in demonstrations. In any case, the underground has no other equally effective mass form of struggle to propose. People who state that in August 1983 we failed to arouse the population to the same degree as the year before are committing the same kind of mistake as Urban.[1] The fact is that in 1983 nobody called on us to demonstrate in the streets! Many people, like the government, don't assess August 1983 in terms of the scale of the transport boycott that we proposed, but in terms of whether or not there were any demonstrations. This is an additional argument in favor of organizing them.

Mass protests certainly haven't lost their supporters, as proof of which we can take the counterdemonstrations of May 1, 1983. In Gdańsk a dense crowd (about thirty thousand people) occupied the whole of Heweliusz Street as far as St. Brygida's Church. The year before, more people took part in the counterdemonstration, because many people joined in when they heard the marchers shouting, "Come

99

with us! Today they're not beating anyone!" The authorities were shaken by May 1, 1983, whereas the previous year they'd simply been caught off guard. The Communists saw that the battle was continuing. Any doubts as to whose holiday May Day had become evaporated.

It's understandable that people get tired of endlessly using the same methods of voicing opposition that don't lead to a final resolution, but we're in no position to continually invent new ones. In any case, even original proposals eventually become hackneyed. In addition, social resistance has reached such a level that people who want to struggle must be allowed to do so not only in secret. There's only one solution—listen to the proposals that people put forward, then concretize them and give them organizational expression. Otherwise, there may emerge a dangerous dissonance between the underground and the rest of the nation.

LIS 1.13

How do I assess the demonstrations we've had so far in Gdańsk? I'm going to repeat something I said earlier in relation to May 1, 1982: it's not the job of the ICC and the Gdańsk Regional Committee to applaud every idea dreamed up by some Solidarity activists and members. We have to implement a certain political line on the basis of our own authority; people will either listen to us or they won't. As far as the demonstrations planned for December 1983 were concerned, we seriously considered the possibility that they'd turn out to be a fiasco: snow, ten degrees of frost—who wants to get drenched by water cannon in that kind of weather? It was no longer December 1981, when people were aroused by anger to battle it out on the streets. But we had to call people out. December 16 is a major symbolic date.

Apart from that, the authorities never know for sure whether or not a demonstration will succeed, so they always have to bring out hordes of ZOMO, sprinkler trucks, and armored troop carriers. Only sometimes can we count on the population's response, but on that of the authorities—always. The very fact of calling for demonstrations constitutes a strong means of pressure in our hands. On the one hand, "normalization" and "democracy," on the other—the ZOMO and military equipment. This spoils the picture painted by Jaruzelski for the benefit of both East and West.

After each demonstration many participants ended up before misde-meanor tribunals, which imposed severe fines with considerable relish (although the police generally provided only the most slender evi-dence). Freedom could be obtained in exchange for a ransom—just like in the olden days, when some unfortunate wretch fell into the hands of brigands.

We buy these people out, partly with our own funds and partly with those provided by various charitable committees that collect funds precisely for this purpose. Of course, there are times when the ransom arrives late, but these are usually cases where we haven't re-ceived the information in time. That's why every case of arrest, deten-tion, or tribunal or court proceeding should be publicized as widely as possible. In the end, this information reaches us. Am I afraid that after this book is published the authorities will think up a cunning scheme to reduce excess purchasing power not by increasing prices or reducing wages but by rounding people up? No, not really. How could such a benevolent regime start imposing a poll tax?

BORUSEWICZ I.15

Participation in mass protest actions involves, however, a certain risk. On the one hand, not all people are willing to take this risk, even if they have declared themselves to be enemies of the regime. On the other hand, everyone can find a place for himself or herself in the widespread front of refusal, which embraces so many areas that it would be difficult to enumerate them all.

The term "front of refusal" was coined by the television evening news, against which, among other things, this front is currently en-gaged in struggle. The term used to be applied to those Arab states that didn't want to have any dealings with Israel and which con-demned Egypt for having signed the Camp David Agreement. We adopted the term because it reflected, and continues to reflect, the essence of the situation. The front is very broad, in fact, it's univer-sal—in terms of both the number of Poles who take part and the vari-ety of forms it takes. It includes various kinds of passive resistance and the boycott of official institutions: the new trade unions, PRON,[2] some of the press. To this we should add campaigns to ostracize col-laborators and those designed to demonstrate solidarity, such as placing lighted candles in windows, wearing union buttons or resistors [electric resistors worn as a symbol of resistance], and similar things. Some of these were suggested by the underground, others emerged spontaneously and simply gained its approval. For example, the actors' refusal to appear on television or in films or plays produced by people whom they considered to be collaborators of the regime wasn't inspired by us (although, obviously, we supported it). On the other hand, we have put a lot of effort into the boycott of the new trade unions and factory-level collaborators. It was simply that the actors organized themselves splendidly, and we have greater access to the shop floor than we do to the stage.

FRASYNIUK I.12

The controversy over what we call "passive resistance" was based on a confusion of cause and effect. The authorities played this for all they were worth in their propaganda, stating that it was the "cause" of their difficulties in overcoming the economic crisis. At the same time, the underground leadership argued that this form of protest was completely successful because the economy was not functioning in any case.

It has to be remembered that passive resistance is used in many different ways, depending on the factory and the kind of wage system in force. If workers are earning piece rates, for example, they demand that safety regulations be observed, that they be given protective clothing and gloves, and that all safety measures be followed (essentially, they bother management the whole time); it's a lot simpler when workers are earning day rates.

We've often stressed the importance of passive resistance, while simultaneously making it clear that it's not so much a question of production, since a boycott of production could be suicidal from society's point of view, but rather of refusing to cooperate with collaborators, of not shaking hands with co-workers who refuse to take part in protest actions, of not signing declarations of loyalty, and other such things. In fact, workers fully understand these nuances, and when someone launched the slogan "turn up late for work," their response was that this kind of appeal only demoralized people. They've also written to us, saying that it's necessary to teach people to work properly, to be disciplined, and to treat their machinery with respect.

The maturity of the workers was also one of the reasons why, in

Wrocław, we had virtually no incidents of sabotage. The few cases that have occurred include such things as a dead locomotive engine in the railroad repair yards.

BORUSEWICZ I.16

Nevertheless, there's another side to the coin. From the factories there emerged some ideas that were completely stupid but which, amazingly, created a great furor. In the summer of 1983, the clandestine Solidarity commission in the Gdańsk Shipyard announced that if the authorities didn't sit down to negotiate with Solidarity, the work force would only pretend to work. Adopting the slogan "Work at a snail's pace," they drew Wałęsa into the action by asking if he approved the position of his own factory committee. What was he supposed to say—no? He said he supported it, which gave a silly proposal a completely new status. These people lacked common sense. First of all, any protest action should be visible to the outside world and its results should be easy to calculate. Secondly, such actions have to be organized in such a way that it's difficult for the opponent to undermine them. The slogan "Work at a snail's pace" might have some meaning in a weapons factory, but in a bakery? For this reason, it was an easy target, and the authorities managed to compromise it without difficulty. I simply don't understand why so much publicity was given to this campaign.

LIS I.14

Should we provide organizational support for the front of refusal? Perhaps, but then every slogan we put forward is either accepted by the population or not. In the first case, it becomes kind of automatic; all you have to do is produce a new idea from time to time and you can carry on almost indefinitely. The boycott of the government trade unions continues, not because the underground is constantly producing new arguments in favor of it but because people are convinced that this is the right thing to do and refuse to allow themselves to be bought off for a few blankets or television sets. In any case, many factories have abandoned these inducements, because when the new unions were putting their seal of approval to the announcement that

103

certain items were available only through them, the goods were actually available in the stores. The welfare departments in the factories have now taken over distribution.

Condemnation of the new unions consists, on the one hand, in refusing to join their ranks and, on the other, in collective ostracism of those collaborators who have already joined. In fact, these people are deathly afraid to own up to their sin. They keep the membership list a secret and they publish only the names of those in the founding group or committee. You can't even get hold of the other names from the finance department, which collects their dues. To avoid being discovered, some of them even continue to pay dues to Solidarity! We have to hunt them out. Otherwise, people will be working alongside these shamefaced types without ever knowing that they're members of the new unions. We have to exert pressure: if you won't publish the names yourselves, the Solidarity factory paper will. Once they lose their anonymity, only self-confessed traitors will join the ranks of the state unions. It's absolutely vital to maintain pressure on collaborators. Even Rakowski has complained about how it pains him that no one wants to talk to him any more.

BORUSEWICZ I.17

Searching for new forms of social protest, the underground called for a boycott of public transportation in the cities on August 31, 1983. What was the response?

Of course, campaigns of this kind aren't very spectacular. Some of the streetcars were jam-packed because no one had announced which stretch was supposed to be traveled on foot. One person could thus walk a kilometer farther than usual and then hop on a bus or a streetcar, while someone else walked the next stretch. Nevertheless, the number of pedestrians on the streets was clearly greater than usual; this was particularly visible in areas near the largest factories. Outside the Gdańsk Shipyard there were such crowds around two in the afternoon that the ZOMO blocked the Błędnik viaduct to prevent pedestrians using it and only allowed streetcars through. People got on the streetcars, went one stop, jumped off and continued walking. Obviously, some of them eventually climbed aboard, but it's difficult to expect people to walk from one side of town to the other.

FRASYNIUK I.13

From the beginning of its activity, the Wrocław Regional Committee was opposed to such actions as lighting candles, putting televisions in the window during the evening news, turning out the lights between seven and eight in the evening, and so on. Actions of this kind were popularized by the underground press, which published information about their results in other parts of the country.

In general, our aim was to consolidate particular groups. This meant, on the one hand, protests in the factories and, on the other, church masses to promote solidarity. Turning out the lights during the evening is often impossible. At that time of day people are busy; they're bathing the kids, putting them to bed. Apart from that, some people turn the lights off, others forget, and it's just a source of irritation. Sometimes, it's true, this kind of protest action was effective in Wrocław too, particularly in workers' hostels and student dormitories, but in my opinion it endangered people unnecessarily. For example, one of the student dorms on Wittig Street was surrounded by ZOMO, who used a loudspeaker to order the students to shut themselves in their rooms. A minute later, the ZOMO troops rushed into the building and beat everyone they found in the corridors. Afterward, all the students were expelled and were readmitted only after a verification and another review of their applications. We had to ask the parish for assistance for many of them.

Similarly, I'm opposed to the apparently harmless walks during the evening television news broadcasts. I'm leaving aside the fact that not everyone may want to give up watching this program because it's often possible to deduce from it where the Reds are going to attack next. Also, these walks often provide an occasion for provocateurs. I'm not saying that such protests aren't successful in Świdnik, but in regions that are better organized there would be enormous repression.

BORUSEWICZ I.18

Does the boycott of the official press, in force since the beginning of the "war," still serve any purpose? It is clear that people want to know what shows are scheduled on television or which movies are showing and they want to read the sports pages. Wouldn't it be more effective to concentrate on a few particularly objectionable publications? When the

Spanish workers' commissions announced the boycott of a particular publication under Franco, the publisher simply went bankrupt.

Well, even under Franco the Spanish press was always highly differentiated. In our situation, though, how are you going to explain why it's OK to buy *Dziennik Bałtycki* [Baltic Daily] but not *Głos Wybrzeża* [Voice of the Coast]? The first is nothing but a cheap tabloid while the second occasionally has bright spots even though it's a Party paper. In addition, there's no point in proclaiming a boycott of rags like *Żołnierz Wolności* [Soldier of Freedom] because nobody reads them anyway. Apart from this, is it possible for a publication to go bankrupt in our system? If it loses money, it gets a subsidy. The Polish United Workers' Party isn't going to go bankrupt either when we call for a boycott of *Trybuna Ludu* [People's Tribune].

The boycott should be coordinated. It's been informally accepted that Wednesday is a day when you don't buy the state's newspapers and magazines. In Warsaw this was proposed by *Tygodnik Mazowsze* or *KOS*.[3] The idea has also been popularized in Gdańsk but with less success because, despite our requests, the regional underground press has rarely spread the slogan "Wednesday, a day without papers." I think that we should have had some kind of statement designating a given day of the week, but, even without this, there's a clear difference between Wednesdays and other days. In any case, state publications—particularly journals—mostly stay on the shelves, even though the print runs have been reduced several times. People just don't want to read lies.

FRASYNIUK I.14

Although people have to be reminded to boycott the official press, they do not have to be encouraged to read the underground press. It has its faithful readers not only among Solidarity members and sympathizers but also within the Party apparatus, the army, and the police (not all police read the independent press solely for professional reasons). Independent publishing constitutes a specific form of struggle with the generals' totalitarian rule; the scope of the free word is simply enormous. It is difficult to calculate the total print run of all independent publications, and, in addition, each copy is read by many people who frequently type many more copies. It is estimated that one million people read the underground press. The organization of printing and distri-

bution is, however, one of the most closely guarded secrets of the underground. Although the underground press is a form of mass struggle—in the sense that it has enormous impact—only a small number of people are involved in writing and editing.

Independent publishing was not initially the strongest point of the Wrocław underground, and for two reasons. The first of these was the conflict between the Regional Committee and its head of information, Kornel Morawiecki; the second—its primitive printing equipment, which consisted entirely of silk-screens. There were about seventy of them, but not all were in use at any given time. For example, if a particular factory had two silk-screens, it saved the second for use only when the first one had been seized by the police or had fallen to pieces.

The main regional paper was a single-sheet information bulletin, Z Dnia na Dzień [From Day to Day], which came out twice a week with a circulation of 30,000 (excluding reprints produced by other groups and individual factories).

Unfortunately, during the first half of 1982 it was a rather poor paper. The information it provided was highly emotional, it concentrated on the bestiality of the ZOMO and the despicable tricks of the Security Service. The whole thing, published on two sides of a single sheet of paper, left the reader with the sense that bloody chaos reigned. In a word, we engaged in gutter journalism instead of publishing a trade union paper. We tried to compensate for the poor legibility of the text by publishing frequently and with a large print-run, but Z Dnia na Dzień was not much liked, particularly in academic circles. The paper played a useful role at the time, nevertheless, and the people involved with it put in a lot of work.

Much more interesting was Biuletyn Wrocławski, a paper put out by students associated with the Regional Committee. Using the same equipment as Z Dnia na Dzień and with the same format, they concentrated on providing accurate information plus putting out one page of interesting commentary. In that extra section you could find advice on how to behave in difficult situations (interrogations, house searches, dismissal from work), discussions of various points of the Penal Code, and so on. All in all, it was less sensational than Z Dnia na Dzień but of more practical use to its readers. It had a circulation of three to four thousand copies.

We've placed our greatest hopes in the ten-page weekly, Dziś i Pojutrze [Today and the Day After Tomorrow], which has a print run of

107

three thousand. It raises issues that are sensitive, unpleasant, or ambiguous—in a word, all the things that we're concerned about. The very first issue contained a very sober, realistic article, but the author was widely attacked on the grounds that he was too conciliatory toward the authorities. I value *Dziś i Pojutrze* above all because it has the courage to voice unpopular opinions.

Our cooperation with factory papers consists largely in sending them information, publications from other regions, and some of the more interesting political articles. [The factories] Dolmel, FAT, Fadroma, Pilmet, as well as Pafawag and Elwro, reprint *Z Dnia na Dzień*, adding a page of their own. These usually provide information about the situation in the factory concerned: they list the names of collaborators, describe the economic situation, unmask abuses, and so on. Their circulation runs anywhere from two hundred to a thousand copies.

BORUSEWICZ I.19

In the Gdańsk region, the independent press reaches several thousand people, although different people have access to different publications. Biuletyn Informacyjny *began appearing almost at the very beginning of martial law and for several weeks was the only underground paper in the Tri-city area. Afterward others got going, among them* Solidarność, *the paper of the Regional Committee, and several dozen factory papers. Borusewicz thinks there are many papers about which the underground leadership has no information.*

[The underground newspapers] either have a tiny circulation or are produced by completely independent groups outside the union structure. The publishing movement is constantly renewing itself. Every so often we get our hands on some new publications, some of them one-page, some of them longer. Often they turn out to be ephemera, but it's the initiative that counts.

We find out about some publications only when the Security Service has closed them down. This was a frequent occurrence in the second half of 1982, when the number of papers increased enormously and many incautious editorial groups were quickly uncovered. Despite everything, nearly every large factory in our region still publishes its own paper more or less regularly. To an outside reader, a lot of the stuff they publish is of little interest: who's currying favor with whom, who pissed in the sink, and what one got a bonus for. On the other hand, such articles provoke a real storm in the factory concerned, particularly as the papers are generally printed on a duplicator, and they can thus respond to particular problems in a few days.

There's some truth in the charge that the Gdańsk Solidarity press has always been a bit neglected. In other towns students do a lot of the work, but we rely on workers, who often have little training. In Warsaw the NOWa publishing house works for the underground. In Wrocław they've invested a lot of energy teaching a large number of people how to use silk-screens. But in Gdańsk the situation is a technical disaster, made worse by the absence of a decent distribution network. All this means that Warsaw's *Tygodnik Mazowsze*, for example, one of the best underground papers, often has more up-to-date information from the Tri-city area than our own papers do.[4]

During the whole period of martial law we didn't have a single political paper; it was only in mid-1983 that *Przegląd Polityczny* [Political Review] began to appear. In Gdańsk we still don't have a single underground literary journal, although the local writers, especially those belonging to the so-called Young Circle, were very radical and made a lot of noise at one time. They had probably grown too used to legal forms of activity, and it never occurred to them to start an independent journal. Apart from this, we shouldn't delude ourselves: this group is fairly colorless—both politically and artistically.

LIS I.15

There's a sense in which the press reflects a region's potential. If a factory bulletin announces that someone is a collaborator, it evokes an enormous response. On such occasions people manage to be quite malicious (they write slogans on the man's car, stink-bomb his apartment), and then the traitor becomes seized by fear. In addition, factory bulletins are sometimes read over the air by Western radio stations. Anyone mentioned by name is exposed to additional antipathy on the part of his workmates, acquaintances, and neighbors.

Of course, papers with a regional focus also have an important role to play. The only paper fully sponsored by the Gdańsk Regional Committee is *Solidarność*, which hasn't actually appeared regularly.

This is largely the fault of the printers, who didn't respond to our reprimands. We eventually took charge of the printshop and found some new people, who—I hope—will behave more responsibly.

BUJAK I.14

Although newspapers, journals, and leaflets are the tried and true conspiratorial methods of influencing public opinion, our use of radio constitutes a complete innovation.

Thanks to the unstinting activity of the Romaszewskis, at nine in the evening on June 12, 1982, the first transmission of Radio Solidarity, lasting eight-and-a-half minutes, took place on the VHF 70.1 wave-band. A month later, Poznań had its first broadcast, and two months later, Gdańsk. The initiative caught on, and Solidarity radio stations were soon established in other large towns, in a variety of forms (in Toruń, for example, the first programs were broadcast from loudspeakers attached to balloons).

BORUSEWICZ I.20

Romaszewski was undoubtedly the pioneer of independent radio. He paved the way for others, although, to be honest, the initial euphoria quickly evaporated. In Gdańsk, people listened to the first broadcasts with bated breath, but they're no longer so popular. You can read a paper several times over, but radio is fleeting. In addition, it's difficult for people to remember that every Monday or twice a month at three o'clock they have to listen to a five-minute program that is often hard to catch. For this reason, if one has printing equipment (and it's always more difficult to get such equipment than a radio transmitter), it should be made full use of. On the other hand, Radio Solidarity in Gdańsk is a fine example of good organization; we've broadcast about forty programs without losing a single transmitter.

LIS I.16

We'll soon be able to increase the number of broadcasts. We're going to establish a large number of transmission points in order to minimize the danger of people and equipment being seized. At the same time, we're taking advantage of the enthusiasm of our electronics specialists to build radio stations for other towns in our region. Both Tczew and Lębork have had transmitters for some time. We also want to help Grudziądz (in the Toruń voivodship). Radio is a less effective means of communication than the press, but it has other virtues: it's a highly emotional experience to listen to an independent broadcast.

BORUSEWICZ I.21

Underground Solidarity's activity abroad has become an effective weapon. Borusewicz considers it of enormous importance that the union far from losing its international prestige actually strengthened it after December 13, 1981.

For the first time in the history of postwar Poland, a delegalized, clandestine organization has acquired widespread recognition in the West. Even Freedom and Independence, which had representatives abroad, never acquired any significance on a world scale. For this reason, I think the political implications are more important than the material support that we've acquired, although this has by no means been insignificant.

LIS I.17

Maintaining Solidarity's influence in the free world demanded new organizational measures. Bogdan Lis considered it vital that all foreign representatives should be subordinate to the national leadership at home.

For the ICC it was obvious that the union's offices abroad should implement our policy. For this reason, we were firmly opposed to the steps taken by Zbigniew Kowalewski, who wanted to make the emigre branch independent. As a result of the sharp reaction of the ICC, Kowalewski was expelled from the Solidarity Committee in Paris.

Activists abroad have much greater possibilities to shape public opinion than we do, above all because they have access to the mass media. This is why we do our best to send them information about the situation in Poland. Nevertheless, they sometimes have to take a stand on particular issues on the basis of instinct alone. For security reasons, we can't tell them everything, since you can never be sure that a particular letter won't be seized at the border. So far, however, neither Milewski nor any of our other colleagues have committed any political errors.

We realize that covert communication isn't enough; after all, things in Poland are constantly changing, and there's a danger that emigre groups will become divorced from the situation at home (as happened in the case of the Polish government-in-exile in London). We therefore plan to keep sending activists to the West and to bring people from various groups over here so that they can familiarize themselves clandestinely with the situation in Poland. The important thing is to bring over not couriers or go-betweens but people who are responsible for the political line of the Brussels and Paris offices.

The chief goal of activity abroad is to acquire and maintain political support. In this we are helped by Western trade unions, which exert pressure on their governments, international organizations, and so on. Support for Solidarity is linked with the controversial issue of economic sanctions. In a statement issued by the ICC in November 1983, we set out our position on Poland's economic situation. We stated that, if the country was to overcome the crisis, economic assistance from the West would be necessary. On the other hand, the lifting of sanctions would itself constitute no more than a gesture of goodwill toward the regime. I'm opposed to economic support for the regime (and this is also the ICC's position) as long as society is unable to control the way in which such aid is used. I personally don't want—and I think the majority of Poles agree with me—dollars from the United States to be used for SS-20s that will simply lead to Pershing and Cruise missiles being aimed at our country. Regardless of which military bloc we happen to be in, the one is linked with the other. And Poland needs other things at this moment—not missiles.

We've also obtained the support of the International Labor Organization, which has set up a special commission to investigate the situation in Poland; they're currently hearing witnesses. The commission's report will probably be presented to the United Nations.

Another success on the part of our representatives abroad is the almost total boycott of the new trade unions. They are regarded as pseudo-organizations; they're not even invited to trade union congresses, which are attended by unionists from the Soviet Union and other People's Democracies.

We enjoy assistance from international bodies like the International Confederation of Free Trade Unions and the World Labor Federation, as well as their member-unions. We've signed a number of regional agreements with the French: between Warsaw Solidarity and the CFDT in Paris, and between Gdańsk and URF and Force Ouvrière in Paris. We were planning a similar agreement involving the Malopolska region but had to postpone it because of Władysław Hardek's arrest. These agreements are enormously important for us because of both the material (printing equipment, foreign currency) and moral support involved. Our French partners have adopted families of people who have been imprisoned, persecuted, or thrown out of work. We're also in the process of organizing agreements between individual factories.

FRASYNIUK I.15

The methods used to combat conspiratorial groups are as old as conspiracy itself. The Communist political police uses all manner of tricks inherited from the tsarist Ochrana and perfected by the Cheka, the NKVD, and the KGB. On December 13, 1981, Solidarity went underground while thousands of agents, provocateurs, and faceless Security Service apparatchiks were milling around aboveground. Frasyniuk emphasizes the "ordinariness" of these people.

They even function in a similar way to us; after all, they have to give the impression that they lead normal lives and have regular jobs. So they live in rented apartments and maintain contact with their superiors through clandestine mail drops. Once a week they get together for a meeting at headquarters. Perhaps they're afraid of being discovered, perhaps they're afraid of underground counterintelligence. . . . They carry out their work with enormous patience and they can follow a lead for weeks in the hope that they'll land someone important. Sometimes, though, they act in the dark, under constant pressure from their boss. "We want results, comrade," the boss tells the agent, "instead of wasting time sticking pins in a map to show where certain suspects are to be found and how often they get together." And the comrade Security officer, feeling pushed to come up with something fast, fingers an apartment he doesn't know much about where an old-age pensioner is selling vodka on the side. If, however, the Security Service has reliable information about someone important, they wade in at once in order not to miss their chance. On these occasions, the officers are tense and react hysterically; one careless gesture is enough for them to start beating you up.

Provocation is one of the Security's favorite weapons. In Wrocław they even organized a clandestine printshop where they printed "genuine" copies of *Z Dnia na Dzień* in the hope of getting some real leads to the underground. I emphasize "genuine" because they also published some fake issues. One of the most interesting of these was an extremely well-done issue of *Z Dnia na Dzień* that contained a lot of genuine information alongside a fake interview with me. In this supposed interview, I attacked a number of people working with the Regional Committee and revealed their names.

The Security Service has been aided by the official press, which has published articles calling on Regional Committee members by name to give themselves up to the authorities, promising a broad-based amnesty, arguing that the Lower Silesia region is known for its moderation, and so on in the same vein. When this didn't work, they began to go on about the super-extremists in the region. One characteristic of the Wrocław area was the large number of arrest warrants issued. In fact, though, these achieved a result quite opposite from that intended: people who were hiding someone sought by the police considered it an honor to help him.

Most of the arrests in our region have resulted from the carelessness of the activists themselves, from meetings either with their wives and families or with someone already under surveillance. Fortunately, we haven't yet had any obvious cases of people being given away by their colleagues, which doesn't mean everyone who's interrogated actually conducts himself according to the principles set out in the pamphlet, "The Citizen and the Security Service" (which was, it should be noted, distributed for sixteen months by all Solidarity organizations). Under interrogation, people seldom "sing" but they do "chatter"—they recount various idiocies, make heroes of themselves, and generally come on as wise guys. During the so-called chats about ideological issues, some people try to convert their interrogator, when the last place you can expect to persuade anyone of anything is police headquarters. Sometimes the interrogator flatters the guy and then he "only" confirms the facts police already have.

On the basis of information obtained by lawyers, it can be said that it's rare for people to refuse to answer every question they're asked by saying "I don't know, I don't remember."

There are some aspects of our activity that are best left unmentioned. Let's agree, then, that I'm only going to talk in the most general terms about some things and others I'm going to leave out completely. Of course, we try to find out as much as we can about our opponent. We have working for us a special group that monitors and decodes police radio communications. I'm referring, of course, to Security Service communications, because the police and ZOMO spend most of their time discussing drunks on the sidewalk and marital disputes. The Security, on the other hand, has the most interesting information service, but only when they're engaged in a particular operation or following someone. In the normal course of events, they rarely communicate with each other.

You don't need any extraordinary technology or super-specialists to work out what the Security Service is up to. You just have to keep your eyes open and think. If they're keeping someone under surveillance, they don't do it like they do in spy movies, having him followed the whole time by the same operative in dark glasses, with his collar turned up and wearing a hat. In reality, the people who keep an eye on us look much like we do, like anyone on the streets; sometimes they pretend to be drunk, often they're women. Mostly, they don't walk but drive around in cars, which they park at intersections or on access roads. This is why you have to take a route that a car can't follow: down steps, alleys, and along roads closed to traffic. Then the Security Service has to have someone follow you on foot, and such people are easy to spot, especially in places where there are few pedestrians. Everyone ought to have an escape route via a staircase, gate, or courtyard, where you can lose your "tail."

We're constantly acquiring experience, but at the same time we're all individualists in this regard. We each have our own methods of transmitting information, of getting rid of a tail, of hiding materials. Some people communicate via a mail drop, others through a courier. Some people deliberately avoid going outdoors as much as possible, others think just the opposite—that it's safest to meet out in the open after having cased a surrounding area . . .

Making a thorough study of one's opponent involves not only a detailed examination of the Security Service's work methods—of how they made particular arrests or how a given escape was conducted—it also in-

volves attempts to influence the repressive apparatus and the army. Lis, however, is largely unwilling to talk about this type of activity.

I can only say that there's an underground paper called *Reduta* [The Fort] that is produced by army officers. It's supposed to be a monthly but it comes out irregularly. I think ten issues have been published so far. The regime considers this highly dangerous; that's why official propaganda tries to make it look totally irrelevant. Nevertheless, it's clear that a large proportion of the officer corps are disillusioned and no longer believe in Jaruzelski or in what they're doing. Some police officers and even some of the Security Service are similarly frustrated. We're not trying to influence them in any way. To be honest, we have very few possibilities to do so.

BORUSEWICZ I.22

Borusewicz is convinced that as long as the authorities are able to demonstrate their power, people working in the army or the police will be obedient, even if they have different opinions.

In the army it's not convictions that count but orders. Things are different when the system begins to disintegrate. Then the repressive apparatus collapses, because it relies on discipline, not ideas. We're far removed from the kind of situation you had on the eve of the revolution in 1917, when the army was one of the active forces. We'd have to have a war with China, and then perhaps our officers would prefer to fight here than in Manchuria. Similarly, we're far removed from a situation like that of Kronstadt in 1921, largely because [he laughs] the people's navy is weaker than that of the prewar Polish Republic and the old Russian navy.

BUJAK I.15

Alongside such broad-based activity as the front of refusal, strikes, demonstrations, and independent publishing, from time to time underground Solidarity sets in motion its own operational sections—to use the terminology of the Security Service. They are active in a number of regions, including Warsaw. For example, the "legalization" group attached to the Warsaw Regional Committee works closely with another special group. Once they sent out a fake letter to people in the Skier-niewice voivodship suggesting that the authorities would soon start req-uisitioning food from the peasantry. This evoked panic, and the head of the local administration was in deep water for a long time. Similarly, people who had set up the new progovernment trade unions and other collaborators were sent summonses to their local police station. The or-ganization of such an action, says Bujak, is extremely time-consuming; first of all, you have to collect names and addresses, obtain official-looking seals and letter-headings, and only then write the whole thing and send it out.

Probably the largest of all our operational sections, and the most youthful, is the leafletting section, which consists almost entirely of students. For reasons not clear to me, workers are absolutely no good at this kind of activity. During the high point of their activism, the leafletters managed to mobilize as many as five hundred people. Later, about seventy remained working. But these are people who manage to be all over the place, even under the nose of the Security. They've mastered sixteen or seventeen different methods of distribut-ing leaflets. The most amusing of these can be used only in winter: you simply take a bundle of leaflets and tie them up somewhere high with string. However, the string itself is held together with strips of bacon fat; birds come along and peck at the bacon, and the leaflets flutter down from out of the sky!

Over time, the group has become technically more sophisticated and they now have clandestine workshops where they make small ex-plosive devices. These devices are attached to a roof, you place a con-tainer with leaflets inside, light the fuse, and run. I've heard about an action involving eighty thousand leaflets, during which only about a quarter of them were initially scattered because leafletters unfamiliar with the technique didn't attach the ejector properly to a roof or lit the string attached to the chimney instead of the one attached to the fuse. Luckily, this action was supervised by another group that corrected the mistakes of their colleagues. We've had far more bitter experi-ences though with factory groups, which screw up far too often.

At the beginning of the "war," several dozen people appeared from various factories saying they wanted to do something, but they weren't prepared to waste their time playing games, it had to be some-thing serious. "Fine," our people said, "what about blowing up the radio-jamming equipment?" "Oh boy," they responded, "absolutely."

117

"Before you do it," our people said, "you have learn about different explosives and detonators, and you have to learn to control your nerves. Perhaps you'd better start by using an explosive device to scatter leaflets. Once you've done this a couple of times, we'll know that you're up to it."

Agreeing, they took the equipment and left. The next day our observers reported that no action had taken place. So we called these people in and asked them why they hadn't done anything. "But we did," they said. "That's not true, our guys have checked." "Oh," they replied, "we scattered the leaflets in Wołomin because there were too many police patrols in Warsaw." Poor Wołomin; it's a place where everything's nice and quiet, and the police haven't the faintest idea where all these leaflets suddenly came from!

We don't really have a special group for small-scale sabotage, although there is a group of people who, from time to time, do such things as using mercaptan to set off a stink-bomb in the Security Service canteen, the office of the city president, or the *Żołnierz Wolności* building. At the opening of a despicable art show someone released several little balloons with "Solidarity" written on them; they rose up to the high ceiling, and desperate officials were running around like crazy because the ladder had disappeared and there was no way to get rid of them. Once or twice we've organized a campaign to pour glue into the locks of cars belonging to collaborators. The boys were going to do something of this kind to the actor Mikulski,[5] but he spotted them through the window and rushed out, shouting at the top of his voice, so they had to defend themselves. It turns out that he's no Captain Kloss, because the moment he got hit, he turned tail and fled.

Several times we've made anonymous phone calls to the police, giving as my address the home of a known collaborator. The ZOMO would turn up there in less than fifteen minutes, break down the door, and start a brutal search, after which they'd have to offer polite and embarrassed apologies. One of our best numbers was to send one of the Warsaw papers the "Przymanowski letter," in which this half-witted guy demanded that the crown be returned to the Polish eagle. The editors published the letter in good faith, and Przymanowski[6] made a terrible row afterward.

I'll mention just two of the actions we've organized out in the open. One of these took place on August 20 at the Ursus Tractor Plant on the second anniversary of the founding of the factory's Workers'

Solidarity Commission. The point was to see whether it was possible to hold up the movement of ZOMO forces. So we organized a demonstration in front of the commemorative plaque and made a couple of speeches while one group monitored the police radio, another waited with special nails to puncture the tires, and a third—with oil, in order to prevent the trucks from getting out of the tunnel. The action wasn't very successful. The ZOMO turned up too late, when the demonstration was coming to an end; the nails were too short to do any damage to the tires; and the oil didn't immobilize the trucks.

The second operation took much longer to prepare. It involved putting up a memorial plaque opposite the Royal Palace on September 27, 1982. This was done in an instant, using quick-drying glue to stick the plaque to a part of the wall that had been rendered smooth in advance. Over the plaque we put a tin plate which stated that it was forbidden to put up posters in this place (the "legalization" group had produced the documentation needed to authenticate this instruction). Three days later we removed the tin plate, a loudspeaker was erected, and the plaque was ceremoniously unveiled. Of course, it only stayed there until dusk, because the Security guys later prized it off with crowbars. But we have a lot of photos of the event.

LIS I.18

Various kinds of operational actions were undertaken also in the Gdańsk region, although not by groups directly associated with the Regional Committee.

Intimidation of the enemy doesn't really fit in with the underlying idea of Solidarity, even if it's just in retaliation. If people want to use this weapon, they can, as long as they don't do so in the name of Solidarity. In addition, they ought to observe an iron rule: one should never choose one's enemies at random. Before you put a smoke bomb in someone's car or apartment, you have to be absolutely certain that the owner deserves it.

I too sometimes feel like getting back at someone or other, but usually I don't take it any further. Perhaps if I were active elsewhere. . . . Whom would I smoke out first of all? Security Service informers deserve something better, so perhaps members of the new trade unions. I also have a couple of personal enemies, but I'm not going to name names, otherwise they won't be able to sleep at night.

Special actions in the prisons? I realize that there's no such thing as an indiscrete question for a journalist, but you must realize that there are indiscrete answers. So, I'll just say this: if the journal *Gryps*, which specializes in prison issues, publishes information from inside, it must have got it from somewhere. If the prison authorities in Potulice find and confiscate a radio, someone must have smuggled it inside. If Staszek Jarosz got ten days in the punishment cell because they found a handcuff key in his Nivea cream, someone must have sent him this cream.

It's easier, however, to smuggle a radio into prison than to organize systematic assistance for the families of those who are inside. This help should be carried out by people who aren't in hiding, who have themselves spent time in prison or in internment, but who currently aren't doing anything—only keeping up a pose as activists, proclaiming the inevitable victory of Solidarity without doing anything to bring it about.

FRASYNIUK I.16

For a number of reasons the underground leadership has never seriously considered the possibility of terrorist struggle. Leaving aside the practical aspects, which render terrorism senseless in a totalitarian system, the most important argument against the use of violence is a moral one. To adopt the violent methods of our opponent would undermine the ethical basis of underground Solidarity. In addition, Frasyniuk has always emphasized the importance of mass resistance, and terrorist struggle can only be waged by a cadres organization operating under the strictest discipline.

At the beginning of the "war" there appeared in our region a paper published by a group calling itself the First Battalion of the Home Army. A couple of issues appeared and that was it. Other fanatics tried to get pyrotechnicians, chemists, and God knows who else involved in the Regional Committee. We soon dissuaded them. Interestingly enough, it was mostly workers who initiated this kind of activity. There was one group of about eighty people, all of them from the same factory. I wrote them an open letter explaining our approach, and they dissolved the group themselves. Ideas of this kind border on provocation; that's why we always react strongly to any attempt at terrorism, no matter how bizarre. For example, some people in one factory in Wrocław made a diving suit. When we asked them what it was for, they said, "Well, when the authorities force us to fight, one of us puts on the suit, dives in the water, puts something on the bottom of the ship, and bang, the ship is gone." But can you really call such a crazy idea terrorism?

LIS I.19

Terrorism would mean the end of Solidarity. If the Communists began to line people up against the wall, the most determined part of society would be in favor of fighting back as hard as possible. But our job is to prevent the underground from deviating into terrorism.

Foreigners familiar with Polish history are sometimes surprised that, despite our tradition of uprisings and our love of armed struggle (even when it's doomed to failure), so far not one shot has been fired by our side in the "war" with the junta. Well, yes, there was the killing of that policeman, Karos, but that was a strange story; I don't know whether the people involved got carried away or whether they were put up to it by the Security.[7] Probably they got carried away and acted out of stupidity or fear.

Terrorism is a last resort for which we have no need at the moment. But if all other forms of resistance fail, if the poverty and repression get worse, then . . . Today the lads who want a fight shave the heads of collaborators or throw smoke bombs into their apartments; tomorrow they may decide to throw grenades. But then we'll already have an uprising on our hands.

BORUSEWICZ I.24

An uprising of the classic kind has absolutely no chance of success in today's Poland. The level of the population's determination to resist is, however, important. The threat of armed resistance may be a crucial psychological factor in forcing the authorities to adopt a more flexible position. If not, sooner or later there will be a confrontation, and civil war would mean a total defeat—a defeat for everyone, regardless of which side they're on.

121

NOTES

1. Jerzy Urban—the government's press spokesman.

2. Acronym for the Patriotic Movement for National Rebirth, an umbrella organization established during martial law and intended to elicit popular support for the authorities.

3. *KOS*—the acronym for the underground Committee for Social Resistance and the name of its journal.

4. *A description of the underground press would demand a separate chapter, or even an entire book. The enormous variety of titles, the importance of the issues they discuss, the significance of clandestine publishing in providing a model for underground Solidarity in Warsaw (which Bujak mentioned several times), the role of independent publishing houses, particularly NOWa and Krąg, and the participation of large numbers of writers and journalists—all this allows us to hope that such a book will be written.*

5. Stanisław Mikulski, star of a 1960s television series about World War II entitled "Captain Kloss" and a supporter of martial law.

6. Janusz Przymanowski, a former officer in the Berling Army, a well-known writer and supporter of martial law.

7. In 1982, a Warsaw policeman, Sergeant Zdzisław Karos, was accidentally killed in a struggle with three students who tried to seize his gun. The three later claimed that they had planned to use the weapon in an attempt to free political detainees from internment camp.

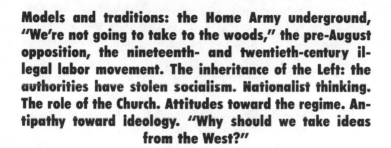

8

Models and traditions: the Home Army underground, "We're not going to take to the woods," the pre-August opposition, the nineteenth- and twentieth-century illegal labor movement. The inheritance of the Left: the authorities have stolen socialism. Nationalist thinking. The role of the Church. Attitudes toward the regime. Antipathy toward ideology. "Why should we take ideas from the West?"

FRASYNIUK I.17

Despite underground Solidarity's decisive rejection of terrorism or, more broadly, of armed struggle or a national uprising, the movement inherited something from the Home Army. Frasyniuk makes no secret of the fact that a number of books about the wartime occupation—particularly Jan Nowak's Kurier z Warszawy *[Courier from Warsaw] and Władysław Bartoszewski's* Państwo podziemne *[The Underground State]—made a great impression on him.*

To a large extent, we hark back to the years 1939–1945, but with one important exception: we've based our resistance movement on the technical aspects only of the Home Army experience; however, we do not—nor do we wish to—resort to force. We've copied some of the Home Army methods that proved successful (involving in underground activity people who aren't in hiding, who are employed in state institutions and whose documents are in order), but we've also tried not to copy its mistakes. And many such mistakes have been immortalized on the pages of numerous books: noisy meetings, birthday parties, frequent meetings with family members, the monopolization of information by one person, and ostentation. As far as we are concerned, you won't find any cavalry boots and British Army trenchcoats. We avoid anything that might make an underground activist conspicuous. We don't even want our female couriers to dress too elegantly.

As for experience drawn from living people as opposed to books, we've had contacts with only one Home Army soldier (who actually held a position high up in the organization) able to offer us truly useful advice; he even gave us the plan according to which his network had been organized. The others gave us advice they didn't take themselves—as a result of which one of them got himself arrested in the most stupid way imaginable.

So, let me repeat, the Home Army tradition is a reference point for us in the technical but not the ideological sense. Nor have we adopted, at least not in the Lower Silesia region, the methods of the Russian dissidents which served as an example for KOR. Although under constant surveillance, they lived openly, "aboveground." We are in hiding, like the Tupamaros, not in order to kill anyone, however, but simply so that we can gradually build an organization that will eventually force the authorities to make concessions.

BUJAK I.16

How many underground activists have sufficient information about social or nationalist clandestine organizations to be able to state firmly that they feel an affinity with a particular tendency?

I myself have only the most general impression of the Home Army underground, and I know almost nothing about any other underground structures. I feel closest to the principles of the pre-August opposition, because that's what I remember best. Even the things that go beyond the formula worked out by KOR (false ID cards, gas canisters, small-scale sabotage) have nothing to do with building on any kind of tradition, but only with our assessment of the current situation. We've received letters telling us how we ought to build the underground according to the best conspiratorial traditions, but they never say precisely what these "best traditions" involve. They don't spell out any organizational principles for even the simplest activities. Nothing apart from the "best traditions," which is a key that's supposed to open every door! The people who write such letters don't understand the first thing about underground activity; their heads are filled with fragments of books, scenes from movies—in other words, a jumble of slogans.

Of course, we have some people with experience from the Home Army, but they don't hold prominent positions. We generally come across them when they offer us the use of their apartments, and we often have reason to admire these old conspirators. I once had the following situation: I arrive at a place together with a courier; we knock at the door, which is opened by an elderly woman who peers at us strangely, as though she hasn't the faintest idea what we're doing there, and looks as though she's about to slam the door in our faces. We ask about the number of the building and the apartment to make sure we're in the right place. She shows no reaction. It's only when the courier remembers that he has to give a password that the old woman smiles and invites us in. A minute later, while we're sitting there, we hear the next guy knock at the door. He, too, has forgotten about the password, so he just mumbles, "I've come to see Maciek," and the woman slams the door in his face. Then the courier rushes out, explains the situation, apologizes. After the meeting was over and we'd thanked our hostess for her hospitality, I told her that this was the first time I'd come across such an attitude and asked her where she'd learned to be so cautious. She told me that for the entire five years of the war she'd run a clandestine school in her apartment.

Another example: a former Home Army guy gave us a handbook devoted to the pruning of apple trees. Only when you read it carefully (skipping part of the text), did it become clear that the real subject was small-scale sabotage. A dozen Security guys could have leafed through it, and not one would have known what it was about. The book caused a sensation, but somehow there weren't any imitations.

Finally, one more thing: people who demand that we implement the principles of conspiracy practiced by the Home Army don't understand that it's simply impossible. The Home Army was an army, and we're not. We don't issue commands and we don't sentence people for failing to obey orders; we don't have power, and this means that we have to build our underground in a different way.

125

At the beginning, in particular, we tried to derive inspiration from the experience of the Occupation, but that model has little relevance to current conditions. First, Solidarity isn't a paramilitary organization. Second, there was a kind of criminal orderliness in the activity of the Germans, so it was possible to predict their reactions. There's nothing orderly about a Communist system; hence you never know what might happen next. Third, infiltration presents a different kind of problem today than it did during the occupation. The Germans were completely isolated from Polish society and they had to make special efforts to recruit their agents. Today we're facing an internal enemy: there's no way you can ignore two million PUWP members. Of course, not all Party members are informers, some have even declared themselves opposed to the regime. On the other hand, you also have a considerable proportion of new trade union members, and there's the Security Service and the army. All these people are part of society.

During the occupation, the moment a German moved into a tenement it was clear that he was an enemy. In any case, they all wore uniforms so it was easy to recognize them. This isn't the case today. And that's why our conspiracy has to be more rigorous, more disciplined, even though we don't possess the means to enforce obedience that the Home Army had. Solidarity is a mass movement, and it's precisely this that is the source of its strength. Of course, the movement contains various political tendencies, but they're united in their struggle against a common enemy, the Communist regime. During World War II, on the other hand, within the Home Army (subordinated to the London government) there were various political parties, each pushing its own program, even though they were subordinate to a single military leadership.

Harking back to the past can be dangerous because of the way in which this past has been portrayed in literature and films. How is the history of the occupation presented to people, particularly young people? Raids on the enemy, blowing up trains, partisans fighting in the woods. The political activity of Sikorski, Stalin, and Mikołajczyk gets lost somewhere, along with the doctrinal disputes between different groups in the underground and the political conflicts between the Home Army and the People's Army. This approach to our recent history might lead people to believe that armed struggle is justified in all circumstances, in other words—the partisan myth. When people forged the slogan, "The winter is yours, but the spring will be ours," in the early days of martial law, some people associated it with taking to the woods.[1]

BORUSEWICZ I.25

There are two basic models of underground activity and organization. The first is based on the Occupation and is the model which many consider to be far and away the most effective; the second is based on the pre-August opposition. In Borusewicz's opinion, it is mainly the Warsaw region that prefers the second of the two.

On the other hand, those regions without a strong tradition of opposition activity in the pre-Solidarity years basically opted for the Occupation model, with some important changes of course. Currently, both models have been adapted to immediate needs—and that's the best thing. If, at the beginning, we'd been organized in the same way as the pre-1980 independent groupings (on the basis of improvisation, goodwill, and so on), we would soon have needed to work out new principles. The dictatorship of the generals created conditions completely different from those of the Gierek era. Similarly, you can't just transfer the Occupation formula to the present day. We have different methods of defending ourselves from infiltration, of dealing with Security agents; our opponents' methods are different too—they don't often shoot us. If the Communists shot at us every day, we too would have to take up arms. As it is, we don't want to aggravate the situation simply in order to compete with veterans of the Home Army.

BUJAK I.17

Our desire to feel ourselves masters of our own country has long been part of our collective national consciousness. Bujak sees certain similarities between the present day and the period of the 1830 November Uprising.

Having read Marian Brandys's five-volume work, *Koniec świata szwoleżerów* [The End of the Light Cavalry Era], I can draw certain analogies. For example, in 1830 the entire population, led by the army, wanted to fight the Russians. Everyone knew that they were confronting the most powerful force in the world at the time, but they rushed to battle. With hindsight, you could say that there was a possibility of a positive outcome. I mean, it wasn't clear how the contest as a whole would turn out, but it was more probable than not that some battles would end in victory. However, this opportunity was wasted. The Polish commanders, who didn't know how to make use of the enormous will to fight, how to forge it into a weapon for military victory, lost all their authority in the eyes of the nation forever. History has condemned them. But was it simply that they were incompetent? Perhaps they were paralyzed by a feeling of responsibility, by a concern to preserve the nation's physical stock.

A hundred-and-fifty years later, I too fear to take the risk, I too, together with other undergraduate activists, fear a Russian intervention. After all, at the beginning of 1982 we knew that an enormous number of people wanted a fight, were aiming at a confrontation. Reading Brandys and following the disputes between historians over the November Uprising, I was afraid that there might be an analogy at the individual level. These disputes may go on a long time yet, and their outcome isn't predetermined, but nothing will salvage the good name of these commanders. Perhaps I too will be viewed in this way some day.

BORUSEWICZ I.26

A model of purely conspiratorial activity that is not based on a cadres organization emerged at the end of the nineteenth century. This model, which is deeply rooted in, and at the same time exerts an influence on, the masses is the one that Solidarity tries most to emulate. It was created by the illegal labor movement. At one extreme you had the flying universities, demonstrations, and strikes; at the other extreme—clandestine activists, the distribution of union papers in the factories, the formation of factory-based structures. But the tradition of the labor movement has no resonance among the hundreds of thousands of Poles who support underground Solidarity. Borusewicz thinks that it simply isn't accepted.

We could even make use of the experience of the Bolsheviks, who were efficient and effective, but we don't draw on their example because of moral as well as pragmatic considerations. What about Waryński?[2] Of course, it's an oversimplification to compare the Great Proletariat with the Bolsheviks, but Waryński has been completely taken over by the Communists. They've stolen this whole tradition and they're welcome to it! I don't think it's worth fighting over. If I had to draw on a tradition of some kind, I'd choose the Polish Socialist Party (PPS). I don't see any other, external models. For example, no one takes as their model the Spanish workers' commissions under Franco. The only time anyone referred to them was after August 1980, when we were deciding what name we should give to union cells in the factories.

LIS II.4

Some efforts to transplant Spanish models were also made before August. I took part in these myself. In any case, as early as 1956, after the June events in Poznań, workers were also making demands of this kind. But the evil resides in the system, in its structural determinants. An entrepreneur in Franco's Spain was interested in the economic results of his enterprise and not in his ideological dependence on the center.

The myth concerning the effectiveness of the workers' commissions also flourished after December 13, 1981, but it didn't bear any fruit. People started to set up clandestine factory commissions as well as Committees of Social Defense, which included not only manual workers but also white-collar employees, scientists, doctors, and students. The factory commissions are probably more effective; in any event, the authorities fear them more. For this reason, our activity in the factories, among workers, has the most importance. This doesn't mean, however, that we see ourselves as a continuation of the illegal labor movement of the late nineteenth century. There has never been a movement quite like ours, and attempts to draw an analogy with any other movement are misleading.

HALL I.4

My opinion may shock some people, but alongside some similarities to the ideas of the PPS (including its independence-oriented wing, personified in Piłsudski), I see the influence of left-wing traditions— and in the most extreme, Trotskyist, form. This can be seen even in the language used in statements issued by the ICC and regional bodies:

129

"We shall advance," "We shall demonstrate," "the masses," "the long march." It can be seen also in the fascination with revolutionary methods of struggle, in other words, a general strike. These issues shouldn't be ignored, although these references are, of course, often unconscious, and people would be indignant if you told them they were following left-wing traditions.

BUJAK I.18

The dominant view among underground Solidarity activists and members is, however, that the movement does not see itself as part of the left. Bujak thinks that this is based not only on hostility but also on ignorance.

When Michnik or Lityński gave lectures on the history of the labor movement, crowds of people came to listen, and they were well received. If there were a real possibility of acquiring unfalsified knowledge of the history of this movement, this psychological barrier based on ignorance would disappear. There is of course another, ideological barrier. The Communists have appropriated virtually the whole of this current, and official propaganda has caused people to identify the labor movement with Bolshevism. I think we have to win back this tradition. This is an enormous task that unfortunately we didn't accomplish before December 13, 1981.

Left-wing thought is difficult, it demands a certain level of maturity, of complex analysis. Other ideological trends are somehow easier, they use phrases that are easy to grasp (God, Honor, the Homeland). Because of this, though, they're superficial. There are very few people who are conscious nationalists, for example. I've met only one— Wiesław Chrzanowski. His views form a coherent and consistent whole and they provide precise criteria for making one choice rather than another. You may not agree with him, but you have to respect his opinions. Other people, on the other hand, just mouth slogans and treat ideas themselves in the most shallow manner. This is characteristic not only of those who consider themselves nationalists but also of those who use the terminology of Christianity. Even our Catholicism is very much on the surface, traditional, based on symbols.

Let's take the period preceding martial law. The Solidarity period gave various people the opportunity for social advancement, and everyone tried to find the political current in which he could swim easily. That's how the group of "True Poles," who used such aggressive phraseology, came to be formed. Actually, this group was isolated from the mainstream, even if it did make a lot of noise. The thinking of KOR had a much stronger basis to it. It's true that people like Michnik, Kuroń, and Lityński were viewed with reserve, but people were also interested in what they had to say, and when they had listened to them, they frequently became enthusiastic about their ideas.

There were other points of reference alongside God, Honor, the Homeland, crosses, the Virgin Mary, and red-and-white buttonholes in your lapel. At meetings, workers shouted, "We're for socialism, but not the kind the authorities have to offer," and there were references to the Swedish model. You need a certain amount of political sophistication to detect the socialist principles at work in Sweden.

LIS II.5

Underground Solidarity contains many political ideas and tendencies—as it did during its legal period. If, by some miraculous turn of events, political pluralism were suddenly to reign in Poland, all these tendencies would find their way to the surface, creating—in Lis's opinion—a mass of complications.

You would have to define the boundaries of the political system, in both quantitative and qualitative terms, and you'd need to use common sense in the event that someone wanted to set up a fascist party.

Looking at the problem from a purely theoretical point of view, I think that the first party to emerge would be a socialist-type party, perhaps the Polish Labor Party proposed by Milewski. Alongside this, there would definitely be a Christian Democratic Party (perhaps with links to the Liberal Democrats), and, I guess, a Communist Party with some kind of modified Marxist-Leninist ideology (after all, there are a fair number of Communists, or rather pseudo-Communists, among us)—although, in my opinion, Communist ideology in general has no credibility, simply discredits its adherents, and only offers privileges to the Party apparatus, the military, and the police.

It's clear how people are recruited to the Party. Some of them join to avoid being thrown out of work for drunkenness, others join to get an apartment, yet others so that they can be promoted faster. But once you join the Party, you have to follow the line. Only a few people managed to take a stand against what went on within the Party. I should know, because I used to be a member. I joined the PUWP when I was in the army. In my case, as well, ideological considerations didn't play any role; I joined because of a conflict with my commanding officer, who was determined to see me in the lockup. Actually, my Party card was a great help later, when I got involved in opposition activity. I wasn't once detained before August 1980, although the Security Service knew perfectly well what I was up to. They just threatened me from time to time.

Getting back to our futurological discussion: during the first period, the strongest party would be a nationalistic one. Before elections are held, however, there ought to be a period of two to three years' provisional, but strong, government. After that, I don't think the National Democrats would win.

HALL I.5

Nationalist thinking doesn't have a strong hold on the underground and has even less of a hold on the population as a whole. This isn't true of ideological values proclaimed by the National Democrats. These values—not all of which, it's true, were associated exclusively with National Democracy—have become widely accepted.

The time for creating political parties hasn't yet come, but I do see a need for political programs that would bring certain groups together. A political party is absolutely necessary once you get to the stage of struggling for power, but we're a long way from free elections. If I had to make a prediction, though, I'd say that the nationalist–Catholic tendency would have the greatest chance of success—with the proviso that this couldn't be a simple continuation of any previous political party. What I'm thinking of is more an organization that would synthesize national and Catholic values. Such an organization would stand the greatest chance of success if it managed to obtain the unofficial support of the Church.

During our most recent history, the Church has played an exceptional role. And although it has made some mistakes, it has fulfilled (thanks mainly to Cardinal Wyszyński), and continues to fulfill, its role as spokesman for the nation's interests. This doesn't mean that it has behaved in an optimal fashion since December 13, but I think that underground criticism of various steps taken by the Church are premature at the very least.

FRASYNIUK I.18

In Lower Silesia, cooperation between underground Solidarity and the Metropolitan Curia worked out well from the very beginning. Perhaps because both sides recognized the other's separate interests. The priests were a great help, even hiding people or taking delivery of special consignments. Frasyniuk emphasizes the enormous role played by the far-sighted and astute policies of Archbishop Gulbinowicz.

Long before December 1981, [Gulbinowicz] was concerned to maintain the right kind of balance in cooperation between us. There was no question of Solidarity using the Church or the other way around. Now, this is paying off. Not everywhere, though, are relations as sound as they are in our region. In any case, there are divisions within the clergy between those at the bottom and those at the top. The parish priests are far more radical, although there are differences of opinion within the Episcopate. Some bishops consider that the Church has to come out strongly on the side of society, others think the situation is hopeless and that we should just salvage what we can. Cardinal Glemp is probably somewhere in the middle. He doesn't want any bloodshed or clashes on the streets; that's why he reacts so strongly against calls for demonstrations. At the same time, in order to break the deadlock, he ought to put a lot of pressure on Jaruzelski.

SZUMIEJKO I.5

It's not up to us to assess whether the Polish Episcopate is good or bad. In the last analysis, the Church thinks in terms of millennia, so it's hard to criticize it for not coming out clearly on the side of the underground. The mistakes that we ourselves have made in our contacts with the Church hierarchy have also, no doubt, played a role. In those regions where we haven't made mistakes (like Lower Silesia or Małopolska), things are working out as well as they possibly could. On the other hand, in Warsaw, for example, attempts at cooperation have been made by people who were unsuited to the task. Instead of closer ties, there were some nasty incidents from time to time, as I heard from Zbyszek Bujak; and Glemp let fly some invectives about Jews and Masons and so on. Both sides bear the blame for the bad relations.

LIS II.6

The Church is society's ally. Regardless of what it had to say about Solidarity, it has never come out against the nation. Here I'm thinking largely of the hierarchy, because Solidarity has always enjoyed a great deal of support from the parish clergy. The priests are most helpful in shaping social consciousness among believers. People often go to church because they regard it as the last oasis of freedom in a country occupied by the Communists. Those churches whose priests show genuine concern about the events taking place around us have the largest congregations.

The future will show how far Cardinal Glemp's current policies are correct. They are based, I guess, on his belief that the authorities are willing to conduct an honest dialogue with the Church. I personally don't think they are. If it turns out that I'm wrong, I'll go and confess, but it's unlikely that I'll have to do this any time soon. In my opinion, as soon as other social forces have become weakened, the authorities will attack the Church. It's true that new churches are springing up all over the place at the moment, but you have to remember that in a totalitarian country they can be closed down or transformed into museums of atheism (as in the USSR) at any moment.

BORUSEWICZ I.27

Underground Solidarity is much more secular than Solidarity was before December 13—and this has nothing to do with the influence of the old opposition. Borusewicz thinks that elements of anticlericalism are to be found among factory activists, who often refuse to accept the need for tactical gestures or silence on certain issues.

The term "anticlericalism" isn't really appropriate, because it's more a question of antipathy toward Cardinal Glemp. Everyone appreciates the activity and support of the lower levels of the clergy, but because Glemp is the head of the Church, his attitude affects people's assessment of the Church as a whole. His statements are criticized by many priests themselves, who frequently engage in outright sabotage of his policies. The Primate clearly considers Solidarity to be a lost cause and sees no point in returning to the issue. Nevertheless, in hundreds of churches there are what amount to constant demonstrations on behalf of Solidarity.

BUJAK I.19

Whenever I consider the whole issue of a confrontation with the regime, I can't get enthusiastic about discussions between the Church and the authorities. When we talk about attitudes toward the authorities, we're immediately confronted by the basic question: Are we to base our struggle on purely political principles or on moral ones also? Because the Communist system is devoid of any kind of ethics, the moment we adopt political methods we are agreeing to take part in a game without any rules of fair play. The only guarantee of victory (no matter how distant) is if we remain true to our moral principles. If we adopt these principles, then there can be no talk of any compromise, but only a cease-fire—and then only in relation to specific issues.

This is why any possible conflicts within the power apparatus have little importance as far as we are concerned. Of course, they may make interesting gossip, but that's all. It would be a mistake to assign them any importance in terms of our struggle. The same goes for the idea that we could reach an agreement with Moscow over the heads of our native Communists. This idea is so ridiculous that it could only have been suggested by people who haven't the faintest understanding of the Soviet system. I simply don't believe that we could ever squeeze anything out of the Russians. The most we could hope for would be a postponement of the intervention—unless, of course, Solidarity's deputy-chairman became, so to speak, "their" man. All such attempts to establish amicable relations in the Soviet bloc have ended in tragedy, however, so I don't see why it should turn out differently in our case. At the very most, we might get to collaborate with Moscow, which would mean, essentially, working against independent movements in other People's Democracies and against the repressed nations of the Soviet Union itself. And that would be the end of us. Our moral principles would have been replaced by ideology—and by the "leading" ideology, at that!

BORUSEWICZ I.28

I'm hostile to ideologies of all kinds, because they lead to nothing but evil. During its legal period, Solidarity didn't really have any clear-cut doctrine, just a few slogans and a great desire for change—and that was enough. On the other hand, if someone tries to explain the whole world with the aid of a magic formula, it usually ends in disaster.

Differences of opinion in the underground aren't based on differences in ideology. These are a secondary issue. There's no choice to be made in terms of being for or against the Soviets. When someone tells me we have to get ready for complete independence, for withdrawal from the Warsaw Pact, I . . .—my God!—What do we have to get ready for? For a battle with the Red Army? We have to deal with specific questions, with current issues, like how to survive as an organization. We're pragmatists. For us, the current problem isn't how to liberate Lithuania, Latvia, and the Ukraine, but how to bring about the release of political prisoners. It's totally ridiculous to set ourselves a greater goal that we cannot, in any case, achieve. If we succeed in changing the situation in Poland, then we can sit down and talk about how we can help others.

FRASYNIUK I.19

A measure of the Poles' political maturity is the widespread consciousness that none of the colors of the political spectrum—from white to red—is what it's about. There's only a noisy group of KPN[3] members and neo-National Democrats who think otherwise. It seems to me that something new and special is emerging. Our union movement—despite its nationalistic jingoism—is somewhat similar to the alternative political movement in the West. Do you remember the elections for Solidarity chairman? Rulewski had an incredibly nationalistic program, but all he got was a lot of applause and . . . fifty votes (seven percent)—fewer than the number of people who'd signed the statement putting him forward as a candidate. He appealed to people's emotions (the Slav soul, the Ukraine, Katyń, and God knows what else), but people are cautious, they've learned from the experience of their fathers and grandfathers.

Our society is trying to construct a new political model without rigid divisions along party lines. It doesn't want any hand-me-downs from the West. People are afraid of all political colors—brown, red, even pink. But they're also afraid of something else. Even the USA, where there are few socialists and even fewer Communists and fascists, doesn't appeal to us as a model. Here, freedom is restricted by the police, there—by the power of money.

Western Europe hasn't come up with any new ideas, the Communist regimes have had it—even the Africans are no longer interested. So, I repeat, we are building something for which we don't yet have a name, a new consciousness, a concern for the values of truth, freedom, equality, and justice—and, of course, independence, but of a kind different from nationalism.

NOTES

1. *Bogdan Lis's complaint that books about the struggle against the Nazi occupation have created a mythology of partisan activity can also be viewed in the context of the underground that exists in 1984. Two tendencies can be observed among those who set themselves the task of interpreting the nature of this underground: on the one hand, they like to erect shrines, in which there reigns silence and an atmosphere of reverence and exaltation; on the other, they want to undermine the sense of conspiratorial activity, to question the usefulness of underground activists: in a word, to reduce everything to the status of an insignificant dispute on the margins of social life.*

2. Ludwik Waryński, founder of "Proletariat," the first working-class party in nineteenth-century Poland.

3. Confederation for an Independent Poland.

9

The people of the underground. Motivations. Activists' origins: former dissidents, Solidarity activists, new recruits. The younger generation in the underground. Nameless heroines. Landlords. Social life. "In bathing trunks everyone looks the same." How to escape the Security Service. Family tragedies. "I'm abnormal." Loneliness. Underground love. Personality disorders. "We of the first brigade . . ."

BORUSEWICZ I.29

It is hard to give an accurate and complete answer as to why people go underground. The reasons for entering the underground are a personal matter, and it is difficult to pinpoint and analyze them. Generally speaking, the majority of those in the underground support the ethos of Solidarity, the system of values that the union formulated in 1980 and which it tried to follow in practice. Borusewicz suggests that political motivations play only a small part.

There are few people in the underground with a specific political program. I took up underground activity largely for ethical reasons, although self-respect has definitely played a role: the self-respect of someone forced to accept something that he could never, at any price, support, of someone who is appalled at the prospect of being afraid of a piece of paper. The authorities announce a new decree and people curl up in their corners as if August and Solidarity had never happened. To break this paralyzing fear I began signing the first issues of *Biuletyn Informacyjny* with my own name. But I did it also out of pure anger.

HALL I.6

Moral motivations based on opposition to evil are mixed up with political calculations. Of course these calculations vary. For some, they involve faith in a complete victory for the underground; for others—creating a certain mythology for the future. As far as the political sphere is concerned, it seems to me that we all have complete freedom to choose our path. Regardless of your political stance, however, the primacy of moral values means that there are certain things that are forbidden—for instance, no one should leave the underground in a manner that compromises Solidarity. Even if the underground is a worn-out formula and even if there is no apparent reason to remain in it, there are also many important reasons for not giving up.

LIS I.20

Apart from moral or political reasons, or feelings of self-respect, there's one other thing that strengthens my determination to keep going. It's the same if you're a mountain climber. At first, you climb intently to reach the top. Then tiredness sets in, but you still keep climbing, because there's no other way out.

I began my conspiratorial activity out of conviction and a sense of responsibility. Others sat in jail or in internment camps, but I survived. Was I supposed to do nothing? After a short time it became clear that the underground had to exist, because it was needed. Of course, the work's tiring, like mountaineering, but you want to reach the top, to reach the goal. Then again, as the march gets longer, turning back becomes just as difficult as going on. For me, turning back would wipe out two years of work and all the ideals for which I first took up this activity in the first place. People are always in jail; when some are released, others are arrested. They have already been arrested . . .

SZUMIEJKO 1.6

For nearly two hundred years, as soon as a Pole was old enough, he has been forced to decide: how much for himself? how much for Poland? With no hesitation, Eugeniusz Szumiejko decided on December 13, 1981, that the time had come to give more to his country than to his family.

That was the first, most important incentive. I made the decision quickly.

What kind of ideals do I aspire for in our movement? Find a person in Poland who is not permeated with the ideal of independence. There was Kościuszko, the Uprisings: November, January, Warsaw. The reactivation of the union or the freeing of political prisoners are only short-term goals. During Solidarity's legal existence people would tell us: we don't care about money, the most important thing is the fight against the Bolsheviks. The vision of independence outweighed everything else, but it was dressed up for the time being in the words "Independent, Self-Governing Trade Union." These feelings really exploded when the authorities declared "war" on society.

FRASYNIUK 1.20

The underground isn't merely a small group of wanted activists, but thousands of people who help in varying degrees. The majority of these are Solidarity activists who joined the fight against the government after August 1980. The pre-August democratic opposition is represented in underground structures by a small group of activists who escaped arrest in December 1981. (For instance, the Wrocław underground leadership was initially made up of four post-August and two pre-August activists.) Finally, there are new people who, with the imposition of martial law, came to see that the authorities had finally and irrevocably discredited themselves and who responded by taking up active opposition.

BORUSEWICZ 1.30

The decision to undertake conspiratorial activity is always a personal matter. It's true that after the imposition of martial law, the Young

140

Poland Movement published a declaration stating that it was suspend-
ing its activities and putting its activists at Solidarity's disposal. But
Bogdan Borusewicz considers that declarations of this kind remain
mere words.

I don't know of a single group that would go underground as a
whole. The decision is always made by individuals, mainly because of
differences in mentality, but also because none of the opposition
groups was organized on the "Bolshevik" model, with its strict discipline. The union's conspiratorial activity isn't based on political parties but on individuals, most of whom received their political education between August 1980 and December 1981. Not many of the older
oppositionists are left. They played an important organizational and
educational role in the initial stages of the struggle, but the people
who experienced only the Solidarity period now equal them. This
allows for a gradual changing of the guard.

There's also another argument, although in the Gdańsk region it
doesn't carry much weight. Namely, the pre-August activists all bear
some kind of label—KOR or ROPCiO[1]—and the positive or negative
sympathies associated with it. The previous differences of opinion
don't exist among those who are active now but only in those groups
that do little or nothing. For them, the old polemics are still the most
important thing. The new activists, however, already treat the Solidarity period as history, and the pre-August arguments as prehistory.
I, too, concentrate on the present and not, for instance, on where
someone was or what he said in 1979, or what he thinks about Kuroń.
People whose activism is based on arguing with each other don't feel
the weight of the moment. If they did, they would stop splitting hairs.
I'm addressing these remarks, in particular, to the group headed by a
certain lady. The argument about Wałęsa versus Gwiazda now belongs
to history.[2] To look for followers of one or the other when we are all
being trampled on is political stupidity. Personally, I divide people
into those who are active and those who aren't, and perhaps into those
who are honest and those who aren't.

Since December 13, numerous judgments, some more fair than others,
have been passed on the pre-August oppositionists. One extreme ten-
dency has accused them of closing themselves off in their own circle and
excluding others from the more important issues. Others have argued
that, in fact, it is precisely the dissidents who ought to be isolated, espe-
cially if they have come out of internment or prison and want to be

141

active, because they were well known to the police and might easily give others away.

Like all extreme judgments these, too, are unfair. The former opposition can't be accused of blocking initiatives. If this were the case, we wouldn't have built the present functioning structures. The "form," of course, was organized by the pre-August activists, whereas the "content" was provided and is still being provided by people whose activism began during the Solidarity period. And a sprinkling of caution, even distrust, is not indispensable. This didn't exist during the Gierek years, because there was a different model of opposition activity, people then acted openly.

As far as the second problem—in no way related to the first—is concerned, it is created by activists who have only limited experience, who don't know exactly how to analyze their motives or abilities, the dangers, and the level of risk. I must admit that in the beginning we, too, were afraid of former internees, although this fear quickly passed. But among the activists in the factories this fear was stronger. They would rush off when approached by someone who had been released from internment, cursing that some guy was following them around and wanted something from them. This reflected an ignorance of the methods used by the Security Service; they rely on information supplied by agents; they don't keep tabs on every one of the thousands who were interned or imprisoned.

The specific characteristic of dissident circles is based on something different: namely, they have brought to the underground their belief in the correctness of engaging in open and legal activities. This reflects a longing for old times, as well as memories of the relatively small scale of repression during the Gierek years.

LIS 1.21

It is difficult to pinpoint where underground activists come from. There is no way to calculate percentages: so many from KOR, from the Clubs of Catholic Intelligentsia, so many from Solidarity, or so many natural talents who emerged after December 13, 1981. Even if someone wanted to make such calculations, he or she would also have to take into account the specific characteristics of particular regions. For this reason, we can only make estimates, and any opinions based on them must be made cautiously. If Bogdan Lis allows himself such generalizations, this is usually only for his own use.

In the Gdańsk underground there are practically no old oppositionists. Is this because they were, or are, in jail? Probably not, since the Young Poland Movement (YPM), for instance, was not repressed. The number of pre-August activists who continue to work today can be counted on the fingers of one hand: Borusewicz, Hall, and maybe two or three more. I don't include myself in this group because I wasn't part of any opposition structure before August nor did I sign any documents. I was only involved with the Free Trade Unions of the Baltic Coast. But people like me, who maintained occasional contacts with the opposition but didn't belong to it formally, now give the most of themselves.

Now, why didn't the YPM come through? They had an organizational structure and experienced cadres, but beyond Hall and a few other people no one does anything—a surprising fact, but true. Maybe this resulted from their political views. Before August the group concentrated on its own circles and essentially didn't go beyond them. Their publications were also intended only for their organization. Drawing on the nationalist tradition, they functioned in a fairly specific way. With several exceptions they were, in my opinion, even disappointing during the Solidarity period, especially in March 1981, after the Bydgoszcz incident. At the outset of the "war" some of their people quickly came out of hiding and pressured others to join them— a kind of equalizing downward rather than upward. They probably felt guilty and wanted to cure their moral hangover. As an organization they declared their membership in the underground, and soon after— in June 1982—withdrew this declaration.

The situation wasn't any more promising in other opposition groups. Many of those arrested or interned from Kraków, Łódź, and Wrocław didn't take up opposition activity after getting out of jail but emigrated! Maybe they were tired, maybe because of their experiences they couldn't adjust (before August you were locked up for forty-eight hours for political activity, now you could get forty-eight months). At any rate, this is how some people explained their refusal to participate in the underground. But the other lot, those who weren't part of any organizational structure before August, started from a completely different point—without the earlier experiences with the Security Service, and without this comparison.

143

FRASYNIUK I.21

*In Wrocław there is no social group or institution that did not produce
any new activists after December 13, beginning with workers and tech-
nicians, and ending with the universities and colleges, which are particularly rebellious and work closely with the underground.*

There are also people who support us now who didn't belong to
Solidarity before December 13. The imposition of martial law eliminated any residual hope of achieving any kind of socialism with a human face. The Communists did this better than the August strikers.
For instance, there was one person who had a strong aversion to Solidarity during the sixteen months of its activity because he felt that one
union for everybody was an illusion. According to him, academics
like himself should have their own organization like they do in the
West. He would say, "Our interests are specific, because we academics, artists, and creative intelligentsia have specific work." And it was
precisely this man who ran to his place of employment after December
13, in order—to everyone's surprise—to join Solidarity.

Others who didn't belong to the union also help us now. They
didn't belong before because they wanted to remain independent or
because of their jobs, but the situation in the country pushed them
into our arms. We even have contacts with several Party people, but
mostly these are rank-and-file members; we lack contacts with the
higher-ups. Maybe this is because many primary Party organizations
were dissolved after martial law was imposed and democratically
elected factory secretaries were kicked out.

BORUSEWICZ I.31

*Among the many who are able to support the underground, students
make up a special group. Their special qualities are youth, intellectual
productivity, and mobility. But in Gdańsk, to the surprise of Borusewicz,
students have not been equal to the situation.*

The authorities have frightened the universities more than the
factories. For this reason, workers have organized themselves much
better. Students are organized in a mass of small groups, mainly discussion groups; and if they don't already know people in the other
groups, they don't try to contact one another. They haven't even tried
to coordinate activities on a regional level or publish a good paper.

Kret [Mole], of course, is published, but, on the whole, the structures are rickety. Is this because the underground has suggested that students shouldn't organize themselves but should fulfill a service function for workers? No, absolutely not! We neither suggested this nor did we assign other work to the most active students, which would have weakened student opposition circles.

Why, then, does the independent student movement still inch along? Here I think you could draw a certain analogy with the political situation in Africa. Whenever some African nation received its independence from its colonial master as a gift, this nation always had problems with its own government. But when new governmental structures were formed in the course of struggle, the subsequent history of nations or tribal groups was completely different.

The Independent Students' Union (ISU) fell on the students like a gift from the gods. Suddenly students found themselves in a wonderful situation: they were free, they could do what they wanted—influence the rectors, deans, senates, create new organizations, withdraw from the official students' union, and travel overseas. Everything was handed to them on a plate, without struggle and without any risk. No wonder they didn't know what to do.

The Student Solidarity Committees (SSC) that functioned before 1980 didn't create their own structures either. You could argue that this was because they only assisted the "adult" opposition, organizing meetings between KOR and young people, distributing NOWa publications, and helping the Society of Academic Courses. But if we're discussing the pre-August period, you have to remember that students were better represented in the opposition movement than workers. The turning point came only after August, because then the factories had to fight.

The ISU's harking back to the SSC tradition was strictly verbal. At that time there remained very few people connected with the SSCs. And if there is now a single student who used to belong to an SSC, then I congratulate him on a successful university career.

The argument that we don't support the students is ridiculous, and the same goes for the accusations that we don't give them paper, ink, or money. If someone wants to be active, he gets on with it and doesn't run around after money. Then again, how much money does one need to be active? You can even get paper from school notebooks. If someone tells me that he'll do some printing, but only after he gets a new duplicating machine from the West, original stencils, and at least

145

50,000 złoties to start, then I give him nothing, absolutely nothing. I've had a few clients like this who took me in. It's a different story when a person comes with some talent, who's competent organizationally (because he can get paper), intellectually (because he can write), and physically reliable (because he can manage to roll stencils for many hours). This kind of person will always get help.

There's one more point that ought to be mentioned. Young people in universities and schools are worst at observing the rules of conspiratorial work. In Kraków, for example, the Security rounded up thirty people in one go, everyone from the Student Resistance Movement. What's worse, most of them were in one apartment.

Unfortunately, the way students respond to interrogation also leaves much to be desired. Strategists have long known that young people are good on the offensive, but in retreat they break easily. For this reason, good military units are made up of people of different ages and include older people, who are worse on the offensive but better in retreat.

The situation in Gdańsk is specific because the Young Poland Movement has, and continues to have, a large influence on the student elite. The YPM currently feels that underground activity doesn't make sense. It feels that activity ought to be out in the open: self-government councils, independent education circles, and so on. At Gdańsk University there is an old self-government council, but it does nothing. The members probably feel that its very existence is enough.

LIS II.7

Bogdan Lis is not much concerned with the question whether the younger generation has specific concerns or functions, or whether its problems are just one aspect of the fate shared by all Poles.

Young people are keen to take part in conspiratorial activity; in the underground they see the ideals that Solidarity first instilled in them. For obvious reasons, we prefer not to use young, very young people in our activities, but because of the pressure they put on underground structures, we have organized a training program for them. As a prerequisite for further involvement, sixteen- and seventeen-year-olds are required to take part in self-education circles—by the way, there are quite a few of these in the Tri-city area. In any case, we've had to structure, and even limit, their activity a bit, because as well as high school and vocational school students, kids from grade

146

schools were also engaging in opposition activity: organizing demonstrative "moments of silence," distributing leaflets, and even publishing their own newspapers and making radio transmissions. Some also distributed the independent press, and others who couldn't do this copied out dozens of leaflets by hand.

Although I'm full of admiration for these secondary-school students (admiration combined with fear, because seventeen-year-olds can be jailed in Poland), I have my reservations about university students, about young people who are, after all, adults. Repression and infiltration of these structures by the Security Service have taken their toll. In the regional structures there are indeed student activists, but in general there are no university organizations. I could name only about three groups that cooperate with us. Their numbers include some academics as well as students.

Unfortunately, everything good that can be said about young people ends the moment they are arrested. During interrogation, members of youth groups usually break easily and talk. This shows their lack of psychological preparation.

BORUSEWICZ I.32

If you were to base your knowledge about the underground on ICC documents or regional structures, you would probably come to the conclusion that it is something like a monastic order. There is not one woman among the signatories of declarations, communiques, and appeals. But the participation of women is significant, and as Bogdan Borusewicz states, women may be more eager to take up activity than men.

Women aren't as intense and are more talkative in their work; on the other hand, they have very firm views. Now, because of the poor economic situation, women in particular have reacted strongly. You could say that the increasing radicalization of workers is due to their wives. In December 1981, they dragged their husbands home arguing, "Where can you go, why risk it, you might die." Yet today, a man comes home from work with his average 15,000 złoties and all he hears is constant grumbling: "There's not enough money, work overtime, do something on the side, there won't be enough to make it through the month again, you'll be eating black pudding, we can't go on living this way." It's a special incentive for a man when a woman not only doesn't discourage his ambition but actually encourages him to take action.

Women in the underground are more amenable and less demanding than men. They don't have great personal ambitions, and they don't have to be part of the center. They're willing to clean up after the printers or deliver letters. Men, however, are against using women. Traditional views have an influence here, but also the fear that women are weaker and less stable. These fears are justified, however, because women are rarely so strong as to not spill everything during interrogation. Naturally, if they go underground not because of their principles but because of their husbands or boyfriends, they don't break, since this would endanger their loved ones. In general, anyone—male or female—who doesn't have a rational basis for his or her activities sooner or later breaks down.

FRASYNIUK I.22

In Wrocław, it's almost always women—often single, living alone—who provide apartments for underground activists. Men, on the other hand, do this unwillingly. Even in families women are more active and usually take the initiative. They don't regard their activities as being prestigious, they want nothing for themselves, they aren't nosy. It doesn't matter whether a woman is a professor or a cleaning lady, she runs around like a messenger providing food or tea and doesn't ask questions. And she knows what she's risking. Anonymous heroines, that's what I'd call them.

On the other hand, men show more ambition but in a negative sense. They like to do spectacular things, make decisions, be important. If they're delivering a letter, it has to be to Bujak or Frasyniuk, otherwise they won't do it. We've had quite a few guys who declared their willingness to help us at any time, but only if they have direct contact with the boss.

In my opinion, the underground relies to a large extent on the quiet and sacrificial activity of women, whereas men are good in work requiring leadership and organizational skills.

LIS I.22

The life of an underground activist is a constant shuffle from one apartment to another, meeting new people, learning about different world

views, customs, even cuisine. Lis states that he now has a broad knowl-
edge of what people eat in Poland.

There were even places where I had to cook for myself, and
thanks to this I learned something new. I haven't yet counted how
many different places I've lived in. In the beginning, the constant
moves were so draining that I quickly made friends with the people I
was staying with, people who were strangers but who made sacrifices.
When I had to move suddenly, there wasn't always time to grab all my
belongings or remember my ration cards. But this never created problems. Then again, after a while you learn about different personalities
and know what makes people nervous and what doesn't. For instance,
I lived with a woman who, after the second or third day following my
arrival, spent literally seven to eight hours standing by the window. I
felt bad knowing how nervous she was, and quickly moved. After
some time I returned and everything was quiet. She hadn't noticed
any suspicious activity around her house and had become bolder.

Sometimes, when someone brings in a typewriter and starts hit-
ting the keys for the first time, the landlords go crazy. A certain
couple, about thirty-five to forty years old, assumed I wouldn't be
going out at all. It's true they didn't know who I was (usually I don't
tell anyone), but when I left their apartment for the first time they
nearly had a heart attack. They thought I was going to sit quiet as a
mouse under a broom and at the sound of the doorbell make for the
bathroom. Some people think that an underground activist actually
lives underground. A friend once told me that while in hiding he met
his grandmother. The old woman started to cry and said, "I understand how you can do it now (it was nearly autumn), but how will you
make it through the winter in the forest?"

BUJAK I.20

*As to the average age of those who provide housing for activists, there
are both old and young people.*

I remember how some young people wanted to provide us with a
room, but they felt that first they had to talk it over with their father.
With their own money they prepared a special dinner and asked
him if a corner could be found for a conspirator. The head of the family answered, "You have doubts? And what would happen if you
needed help?"

The people who provide us with housing in Warsaw usually come from intellectual circles, but I can't say why. I know, for instance, that activists of underground factory committees (often workers) have great problems in finding a quiet corner for meeting places, somewhere to leave messages, their archives, and so on. Although we never look for housing amongst our family members or friends, this is almost always the case with them.

I always feel best in a relaxed household. I arrive, become a member of the household, and the landlord doesn't get hysterical. Every landlord says at the beginning that he can handle anything except my being caught. (But if this has to happen then not at his place, because he'd feel guilty for the rest of his life.) When someone is too cautious, the situation becomes unbearable. Then I, too, begin to feel unsafe. In one of my first apartments the landlords were so panicky that at the sound of a loud car, one ran to the window, the other to the peephole. They woke me up at two in the morning once for something like this, and they kept guard for another hour. This type of thing has an effect. I, too, looked around for a way to escape: the front door, through the window and down the gutter, or down the lightning-rod. However, when I arrive somewhere and see that the person is relaxed, that we can sit down and talk about how my presence is to be explained, I immediately feel confident.

Practically speaking, I'm prepared to meet with anyone if it's really necessary. However, I'd rather have an inquisitive reporter than, say, an obsessed activist. A Warsaw semiactivist once wanted to meet with me. I wasn't sure about him because during the legal Solidarity period he was constantly scheming against me. He insisted that he had to see me, but I had no desire to see him. I turned him down. When someone becomes hysterical and starts to yell, then he gets nothing from me. There's nothing in the underground that just has to happen. And without our meeting everything continued to function.

LIS I.23

Some feel that activists do nothing but conspire. Others feel that people in the underground have time for everything. Does the truth lie somewhere in the middle, or is one side or the other correct? Maybe they are both correct?

Everything depends on why a person is in hiding. If you're there only to avoid getting caught, then of course there's time for everything. But if you're in the underground with a definite goal, there's never enough time. For me there's little time to do the things I enjoy. In the summer of 1982 I went to the beach a few times. I went to get a tan because I was running around the Tri-city area white as a ghost. And here it was summer with the sun and sea nearby. In bathing trunks everyone looks the same, so I didn't even have to think about a disguise. In any case, from the very beginning I went out often and quickly broke the barrier of fear. Leaving my hiding place the first time was a big moment, the second, not as dramatic. This way I got used to it. (Some people have sat in the same place for half a year and then suddenly would give themselves up.)

Later I even went fishing and mushroom picking. At times funny things happened. In 1983, I almost ran into Wałęsa in the woods. I met his children and had to get away quickly because the police were probably nearby picking mushrooms also. To reduce the chances of being recognized, I always go out of Gdańsk for longer breaks. I've been in the mountains, where I even got close to the border, and I've been on a canoeing expedition.

I conduct a perfectly normal social life in an apartment I am staying in, with people among whom I currently live and with whom I eat breakfast, lunch, and dinner. When the landlord celebrates a name-day and invites guest, I also take part in the festivities (although in disguise). I swear at the Communists and so forth. I had a good laugh once when a guest (who didn't of course, know who I was) told how he'd allegedly recognized Bogdan Lis in disguise—limping, with a cane.

Although 1982 was a year of hard work, after things settled down and went their own course, I had a little free time. I read more: Solidarity and other publications from the West, underground and official press. In addition to this I read books. If I read for pleasure, then most often they're books about nature or animals.

FRASYNIUK I.23

Being in hiding does not always mean attending continuous meetings or organizing something. Sometimes there are lifeless hours between one contact and another, or empty weeks after a big roundup.

Once we sat depressed for two weeks, eating rice and macaroni because there was nothing else in the house.

Despite these dead hours, it's difficult for an underground activist to organize his free time. In the beginning I told myself I would study a foreign language and exercise regularly, but nothing came of the studying, and I exercise only once in a while. In order to cram words or train, you need a daily plan. You can't have that with contacts coming whenever they want—even at one in the morning. An activist has to be available and ready for every contingency, and this wears you out the most. My main diversion is listening to music, which allows me, at least for a moment, to forget about this damned reality.

LIS I.24

Life in the underground generates certain particular personality traits, rarely found in normal conditions of life. But maybe, says Lis, it only sharpens dormant but existent traits.

I once read that a person uses only a certain percentage of his brain. The rest is blocked off, as if useless. The same with the senses. Maybe long ago, when cave men still lived, other senses—not known to people today—functioned. After all, human beings once had instincts, like animals that can smell water or birds that know flight patterns. I think that in many activists a kind of addition to the self-preservation instinct has evolved. With this you can anticipate danger without nervously looking around. I've trusted this feeling several times and I was right, because I avoided several unpleasant surprises.

Instinct, however, doesn't mean you never make mistakes. While changing my hiding place before Christmas 1982, instead of driving up to the front of the apartment building that I was moving to (like any normal person would do), I told the driver to pull up at the back. The driver waited in the car while my contact and I tramped to the front with my belongings. Someone must have been watching the house and regarded our trek as having a special significance. But maybe there was something else to it, because right before the holidays a whole series of manhunts took place in different parts of the city. Anyway, the police checked the apartment I was staying in. The only reason they didn't find me was because I didn't lose my nerve. I watched them as they went through the apartment looking through the closets, beds, even the refrigerator. I had my addresses in my mouth (coded, but . . .), but I didn't swallow straight away because I thought that if they found me I would still have time. And they didn't find me! Where did I hide? I'd rather not say because it might be useful in the future. An hour after the search I felt better, but the landlord got such an upset stomach from the tension that I had to calm him down for some time. I stayed there another week since it's darkest under the light.

BUJAK II.2

Early 1983 was a time of numerous organizational meetings of the Warsaw underground. We were meeting with all kinds of people, changing our meeting places often. Once, in addition to the invited guests, the Security charged into the apartment. They must have had a thousand people from ZOMO surrounding the immediate area. They asked for our identification papers and took us away for questioning. I realized straight away that they didn't know who I was. We were taken to the investigative detention center on Rakowiecka Street and put in the reading room, where I discretely ate what I had to eat. It was all only a routine police investigation, but I decided not to risk anything. After a while they called me in for questioning. A Security guy told me to sit down and asked a lot of routine questions about the information in my identification papers: name, address, date of birth, names of my parents, whether I was married or not, and profession (according to my documents I was a psychiatrist, ha, ha!). And then he really started pestering: with whom had I gone to the apartment, and what for. But here I had to refuse to answer.

The guy was surprised: "What's this, a normal social gathering and you don't want to talk?" I answered, "I'll say one thing, the host will say something else, and I'll be accused of lying." At one point he asked me how many rooms my apartment had. Since I'd never been "home," I had to refuse to answer. He said, "Are you crazy?" I said, "You know, I'm a psychiatrist. I've had patients who answered simple questions like this and we both know what happened to them later." He finally decided that we'd go to "my place" for a search and was clearly furious.

We left at about 9 P.M.; there were four of us. On the way they asked me again how many rooms I had. Apparently, they wanted to know how long the search would take. We went through some twisting narrow streets and finally drove up to a building I didn't know. My chance was approaching. I knew I could count on my legs—in the army I'd run long distances—but I had to gain the advantage with the first step. We got out and I said to them gallantly, "To the stairway, please." They then said, "Oh, no, please, you first." Aha, I took three long steps, then a quick leap to the side, and took off! I slipped off my coat and was gone. The Security guys toppled over after me, clamoring and shouting, "Stop, or we'll shoot." But after sprinting four hundred meters I turned around and saw them jogging back to the car. I had to take advantage of this lucky moment. I stopped a cab almost by force (a man running around in only a shirt; maybe he's just killed someone?) and was taken to where I had to go.

HALL I.7

Continuous tension, daring escapes like the ones in adventure movies, and the risks of mundane daily activities . . . every underground activist has lived through more than one draining physical and mental experience. Hall is no exception.

Despite the constant stress, do those in the underground have common personality traits? These are people with different habits, personalities, and temperaments. It's impossible to find one criterion common to all of them. Some adapt easily to what can only be called abnormal conditions. Others experience something like a breakdown. Intense activism has its cost in enormous psychological exhaustion.

After more than two years of life in the underground I feel pretty good. Not surprisingly, I miss certain things I'm used to: freedom of movement, contacts with others, and normal work conditions. But this is no great sacrifice. I have, though, noticed something unsettling—I'm not tempted to come out "aboveground." Maybe this is because I understand what my life would be like—under constant surveillance. I'm also in good physical condition.

If you're in good shape physically, even a several-year stint in hiding doesn't have to be accompanied by a nervous disorder or ulcers. I also have the luxury of being a bachelor and don't have to be responsible for anyone else. For this reason my stoic attitudes can't be generalized, and, in particular, can't be applied to those who have wives, husbands, or children.

*One of the most difficult experiences is being away from one's family. A
sailor or someone working abroad on contract knows exactly when he'll
be with his family again; usually he sees them at least once every six
months. An underground activist has to be more immune to depression.
In addition, he knows that the shortest road to his family leads to a
guaranteed minimum of several years in jail. For this reason, only a
few want to talk about this.*

I've developed a special self-defense mechanism: weeks and
months go by, and I don't think about my family. I do this because the
days when I long for them are very painful (at the beginning of martial
law my daughters were four and five years old). As I've already mentioned, everyone with a family has to keep in mind the question: how
much for himself, how much for the country? Crossing the dividing line
to one or the other side can have terrible, irreversible consequences.

A healthy mind won't allow itself to be tortured too long and de-
velops a self-defense mechanism. But the problem isn't a matter of,
how shall I say, creating a "surrogate family." Much more troubling
than the lack of a sexual life is your inability to help those closest to
you and to participate in the development of the children, where a
father is needed very much. I'd like to share their new joys and sor-
rows, to guide and advise them.

I see my wife rarely, and only when I hear that she's had it with
everything. I don't take these signals lightly. From the time my underground activity began she's been undergoing psychiatric treatment,
including time spent in a closed ward, and at the moment she's on a
disability pension. She's smart and politically mature. She knows perfectly well why we're suffering, but this doesn't prevent her getting
depressed. So, sometimes she has lost consciousness, lost control and
lashed out, screaming . . . and next to her were two small children.

At the beginning of martial law, the Security Service worked
strenuously. My wife was harassed almost daily and often interrogated. During the interrogations, our place was searched in order to
increase the mental strain. They took this opportunity to install a bugging device. After eight or nine months of the "war," my wife turned
on a tape recording of me playing with the children. After a few
minutes the Security Service was right there. My daughters have also
been affected. At first they cried almost continuously. Later, there was

a period when they would get up in the night (especially the younger one) and go to the bed to check if I was there. It's nothing when we talk about it, but you have to be in the position of a wife and mother who sits alone engulfed by helplessness. The crying of your own child is most oppressive.

In addition, we had little outside help at the beginning. A few times my wife was approached by provocateurs with packages "for Gienek." The ones who really came to help were scared away by the police who watched the building constantly. Despite this, some people helped. One of the neighbors who dropped in only to ask about the family's health had his apartment immediately searched. Once, right before Christmas, my wife wanted to visit my mother with the children, but one of the downstairs neighbors who is a cab driver wouldn't take her no matter how much she offered to pay (it was very cold then).

This went on for some time. Then my wife sought the advice of lawyers on how she should handle her problems. She then became assertive. The children also calmed down. But certain mental processes took place and I don't know what the end result will be.

I haven't seen the children in over two years. Luckily, they have a different sense of time than adults. Then again, from the beginning they knew very well that their father was fighting for Solidarity—so there could be plenty of bread, butter, so that all children could have what they wanted: bikes, dolls and dresses, and fathers—as they always told their friends in the playground. But apparently something recently started to happen that worries me very much. For instance, when their grandmother, who sometimes takes care of them, goes out of the apartment, the girls don't want to let her go, saying that she'll probably go and not come back, like their father. They also ask my wife more often whether their father still has to fight for Solidarity. Maybe this is because of a neighbor who has been wringing her hands over them: "Unlucky babies, poor orphans, and that father of theirs . . ."

I think about my daughters the most during holidays. There was one particularly difficult moment when the children were allowed in the apartment where I had a short meeting with my wife (apparently, there was nowhere to leave them). Of course I couldn't let them see me, because the whole circus of their nighttime experiences would begin all over again. They ran around the house looking in every corner and finally tried to get into the room I was in. And I, their father, had to block the door with my foot. In moments like these it's not very easy.

FRASYNIUK I.24

The notion of "people on the margins" suggests a variety of deviations to which underground activists succumb. A life full of stress results in physical disorders: insomnia, a tendency to put on weight, heart disease, and fatigue. The specific conditions of conspiratorial activity also give birth to complex psychological problems—for instance, the feeling of being different. Frasyniuk verifies this by relating a long discussion with a young married woman. associated with the Wrocław Solidarity regional strike committee.

This woman felt that she could no longer speak to normal people. "I leave the room," she said, "when they start to ask questions that drive me mad. For instance: 'What do Security guys look like?' 'Why do the police surround a building when they come to arrest someone?' 'What will you do when they throw you in jail?' Then questions that are particularly irritating: 'How do you stand it without your family, your children?' Damn it, I only make it because I don't want to think about these things, much less talk about them—this is a taboo topic. We become schizophrenic living in the underground. The normal world (children, a husband or wife, silence, peace, happiness, eating together, the feeling of security) is unknown to us. I don't want to remember this, or long for it! That's why I avoid such discussions, even though I know that the people who ask these questions are perfectly normal. I'm the one who's abnormal. Now I can only talk with illegals—and with them I can discuss anything. I think that even if the underground ceased to exist, I'd continue to live in an atmosphere of conspiracy; it's physically and mentally exhausting, but it's close to me. I don't think this is being an 'outsider,' it's just that I feel a strong attachment to a group for whom certain things are evident without having to ask stupid questions."

She talked this way frequently and I listened to her with a growing sense of discouragement. I'm tired of conversations with activists who don't understand even half the problem. Most activists need detailed answers to the most simple questions, in addition to some maternal care. Because of this, my relations with activists are getting worse,

157

while I relate excellently to the people I stay with and their children. I eagerly tell them what Security guys do, how to recognize them, and what precautions to take. I think I fall into the other extreme.

Next to the feeling of being different is the problem of loneliness. If you sit for twenty-four hours like a stump, and only one contact comes to see you daily, then you practically stop thinking. That is, you think only about organizing conspiratorial activity. You become extremely one-sided. People discuss things in order to revise their own opinions, and loneliness makes this impossible. It increases egocentrism, for instance: I have a toothache or headache, and no one is here, they've forgotten about me, they don't care. This creates a negative attitude toward one's surroundings.

There's also the other side of the coin—the desire to be alone. Many people prefer to live alone. They cook for themselves, wash their own dishes and clean, just to avoid falling into worn-out routines: at 4 P.M. the landlord returns from work, dinner is made, and some chit-chat; at 7 P.M. "Maya the Bee," the kids' show on TV; then tea and typical comments on the evening news. Slogans, nothing but slogans. Yet we conspirators, including me, have our own underground slang. We talk about mail drops and tails, and we have our own words for getting arrested, living in hiding, and so on. It's possible that we're unable to maintain the necessary distance toward our own activities, but any way you look at it, many activists can't bear nonunderground rituals—like that woman I referred to.

The problem of loneliness can be solved by hiding in pairs, but this isn't always possible. Another solution is "underground love"— two people who are both in the underground. It's enough for a female courier to appear on the horizon and you already have someone making moves on her. At the beginning of the war, we often got a laugh out of the fact that in order to find someone who was in hiding, all we had to do was look up his old girlfriends. Our success rate: ten out of ten. People would frequently hide out at their girlfriend's place, because you kept away from your wife for fear of the police and it was relatively quiet at a girlfriend's. A lover is devoted, makes sacrifices, respects you, and you trust her—it becomes a question of mutual understanding and safety. Beyond this, she looks at "her" activist with awe, which he quickly responds to, because it's the only warmth he can find.

We move around a lot and we've noticed that the women we stay with usually admire us and would gladly give themselves to any activist—especially to those known as the Wrocław threesome. It's a question of fascination, a certain myth about heroes. But compliments also have an impact on activists. When someone hears that he's more handsome than Belmondo, he goes a bit crazy. I've discussed this topic several times. People say, "I have a wife whom I love very much, but hell, this girl in the underground—I think I love her too." Or women say, "I have a man outside waiting for me who misses me very much, but there's this printer . . ." One after the other, people who advocate monogamous relationships fall into a new situation and, to their own surprise, admit that they could deeply love two people.

The world is very complicated. A beautiful housewife wants to love, admire, and give herself completely, but on the other hand, this same woman, completely dressed, whispers, "You know, you're a moral authority, an absolute gem . . ." Can such a gem turn out to be a fake? What is he supposed to do in this situation?

BUJAK 1.21

Wiktor Kulerski and I once stayed with a divorcee who had two children. The arrangements weren't so good because the former husband, who liked to drink and talk, would drop by from time to time without warning. Because of this, we arranged to move. Right before we were to move we realized that the street was being watched (this was apparently due to activists from the Ursus factory, who had a meeting place close by). We had to scrap the move and sit tight, although it was high time we moved for another reason. Wiktor helped this woman so much—jumped to help her and kissed her hand—that, how shall I say, she began to look at him seriously. One more week and she wouldn't have wanted to live without him. As it was she already had tears in her eyes. So I said, "Wiktor, let's get out of here, because once she falls into this, it'll be very bad." This finally got him moving. He hadn't noticed anything himself. But to this day he likes to wash the dishes.

LIS 1.25

The pressures of reality bring about gradual but perceptible changes in the mentality of underground activists.

159

In the beginning I used to get very attached to people. Roundups were hard to take, especially if they involved people whom I had enlisted. Other people mattered to me, not myself. I'm prepared for the moment when I have to go to prison. With the passage of time I've got used to the thought, like people become accustomed to death during wartime. I used to get jumpy for others. When Władek Frasyniuk was arrested, I had an upset stomach for some time (I tried to cure myself with pepper vodka, but with little success).

Today, I try to stay away from close emotional ties. This, of course, doesn't only concern love. Partings are burdensome, but, on the other hand, maintaining contacts can be dangerous. Despite everything, I'm not overwhelmed by loneliness, isolation, or feeling different. Walking along the street, I seldom look at women (unless, of course, I've been drinking and the woman is gorgeous). I tend to observe the situation and sometimes think: I wonder who's in the Security Service and who works for the underground?

Mentally, I feel pretty good. I don't have any physical problems either. I don't get sick, although a couple of times I've had a cough or runny nose, but this passed quickly. We do, however, have contacts with doctors. If it's necessary they can even get you into the hospital—which has happened. Luckily, not to me. I have, though, together with several others, gone through complete cardiovascular checkups. These didn't show any great differences compared with my condition before the "war," nor any great deviations from the norm. You can get used to tension, even if it's permanent, and then it goes away. Four months after the imposition of martial law, I quit smoking. I came to the conclusion that it's easier for a nonsmoker in prison.

I've also avoided the dangers of applying a different moral code to myself than to others. Although I take risks, suffer for millions, and am a great fighter—does this mean I have more privileges than the next guy, that it's OK to pick up girls left and right and buy booze with the union's money? I won't say that I don't drink. When I get mad, I like to have a drink. This calms me down. But I have my own money for this. Activists who don't have families get 5,000 złoties a month. I pay practically nothing for food, and, as I said, I don't smoke. I can therefore buy half a liter of pure spirit a month, mix it with water, add some pepper, and drink it with my friends. The problem with finances lies somewhere else. The union's funds have to be honestly accounted for. And I don't like money matters, because the problems only multiply. For instance, how to account for nine dollars that went for some cognac on the occasion of a meeting between Lech Wałęsa and the ICC? True, I spent the money, but he told me to!

SZUMIEJKO I.8

Walking along the streets I don't even think about any danger. Maybe this is a mistake born of routine. But I don't think so, because today, with one quick glance, I subconsciously take in as much as I used to when I looked behind me ten times. But what the hell are we talking about! If Security guys were to follow us—the underground leaders— around, then screw this kind of conspiracy. Let's not pretend that we're heroes. More than anything else, a good organizational structure and intelligent and committed people are needed. The rest falls into place.

One of the greatest mental dangers for an activist is the growing conviction that the Security Service knows everything. I once received news, for instance, that the Security Service in Wrocław had sent addresses of the places I had stayed to the police in Gdańsk, and the police in Gdańsk had sent the same information to Wrocław, but for now they didn't want to make an arrest. If you succumb to this kind of thinking, you can really get the shakes. I remember that someone once brought to a meeting of the ICC a device to monitor the police radio. The atmosphere was terrible, because every other minute you could hear something going on—either voices or some kind of hum. Let our experts fool around with this kind of thing. I've renounced using this kind of junk. I'm in no hurry, I sleep calmly.

FRASYNIUK I.25

Underground activists are divided into those who don't take the repressive apparatus seriously and those who fear it excessively. Falling into one of the extremes is a professional hazard that eliminates certain activists.

There are some illegals who get fits of panic. For no reason at all, one of our friends once started crawling into a small storage space shouting, "They'll be here any minute and there's no fucking hiding place here; the closets are full of clothes. Screw this, I'm not going to jump out of a window." Luckily, this type of obsession, like exaggerated mistrust, doesn't occur very often. On the other hand, there are considerable feelings of distrust related to the self-preservation instinct—but for the organization rather than yourself. Even long-term friendships don't count here. You only say what's necessary, not a word more.

In my opinion distrust is a normal emotion, even though it results from the abnormal situaton in which we function. People have disappointed me many times. Those whom I thought I could count on refused to help. Or they pretend they'd like to help but haven't been able to make contact with us for the past three months. In the meantime they've done literally nothing! I have no respect for people like this. I won't tell a guy anything, even if he's my friend. When someone asks a question, I immediately think: What's he going to do with this information? Does he want to use this against me?

An instrumental way of treating others, and also yourself, creeps into your everyday activity. I'm like a bull that works until it's dead: I'm tired, but I write; I'm beat, but I go to the next meeting. Sometimes I ought to chew someone out, but I praise him, because I know that this is the only way to encourage him.

Distrust and a manipulative approach to others produce a more serious problem—loss of faith in people. At times, the daily, purely technical and organizational matters so overshadow our primary goals (the ideals that inspired us to fight) that we lose sight of them. All around you notice cowardice and mental weakness. You become convinced that there's no one you can rely on except yourself. Crudely, I could say that we're active, we build conspiratorial structures to defend society against the regime. But society is made up of individuals. And here lies the doubt: maybe we're trying to defend people who aren't worth it.

Something that's as old as our conspiracy are the different factional conflicts in the underground. Although everyone wants to fight for an independent Poland, a self-governing society, brotherhood, and so forth, increasingly we're using dubious and underhand methods. Brotherhood becomes a fiction, there's no unity, and ideals get pushed aside. Theoretically, ideals exist, but they're becoming more abstract, because the methods we employ are incompatible with them. For instance, you want to disseminate information, you want to set up a press to educate and inform people, but it turns out that you only really want to get even with X or Y.

Then again, underground Solidarity is threatened not only by the loss of ideals. Activists are prone to various mystifications that threaten to make us lose touch with reality. For instance: the desire to play the hero. In general, this doesn't appear in people who were elected, who have been more or less forced to go underground, but it's typical of poseurs. For instance, a guy brings a bundle of *Z Dnia na Dzień* to work, ostentatiously lays it on his desk, and says "Damn it, I wrote to Frasyniuk yesterday. I really bitched him out and told him what he should do!"

Many people have come into the underground who previously didn't manage to be active. We have activists who, despite strenuous efforts during the sixteen-month legal Solidarity period, were never elected to any union office. Basically their workmates felt these people lacked qualifications or a sense of responsibility. These people, who are now curing their complexes, came into the underground of their own free will. In Wrocław, two of them even became leaders of sections. So you have a young man doing serious work who is simultaneously bluffing to show how important and necessary he is, even though they underestimated him previously. ("They're cowards, but I . . .") In this way he reassures himself. If this continues, people might start to think that we're developing a conspiracy just for its own sake. Art for art's sake.

BORUSEWICZ I.33

The fundamental danger for every illegal organization is to lose touch with reality. This happens when the group stops expressing the ideals, goals, and interests of society and starts expressing only its own. In Polish history there have been underground movements that have gone against the general current, but—as Borusewicz suggests—they were not successful.

Our task is only to give a general form to what major sections of society do, or want to do. We shouldn't impose our own views but should help to articulate ideas that are beginning to develop. The most fatal thing is to forget this. Forcing your own program through only increases the danger of radicalism. The longer you're secluded, the more you lose support, and the easier it is for you to accept extreme and violent methods. Because if you're already going against the current, you might as well go all the way! No one understands us or wants to, but we'll show the indifferent masses our strength. A feeling of superiority grows.

Luckily, we haven't reached the stage where we might sing the old version of, "We are the first brigade . . ."[3] Do you know it? The legionnaires were extremely underrated, and what happened? It didn't take long before they overrated themselves. Then, people again rejected them. All from a feeling of isolation and superiority.

This doesn't threaten us yet, but we have lost touch with reality several times: in May 1982;[4] then after the delegalization of the union— a strike erupted in the Lenin Shipyard in October 1982 and, instead of acting, we just sat around and discussed what to do; and finally a month later on November 10. This was supposed to be a day of almighty national protest against the delegalization, but it turned into a great loss of face for us.[5]

NOTES

1. ROPCiO—Movement for the Defense of Human and Civil Rights, an independent opposition group of the 1970s.

2. Borusewicz talks about Anna Walentynowicz's opposition to Wałęsa.

3. The first line of the song of the First Brigade, a military force organized by Józef Piłsudski during World War I in the effort to regain Poland's independence.

4. On May 1, 1982, spontaneous May Day demonstrations took place alongside the official parades in Warsaw and a number of other cities. These demonstrations took by surprise not only the Polish authorities but also underground Solidarity leaders, who had simply called on people to boycott the official parades and attend church services.

5. On October 8, 1982, the Sejm passed a law that banned Solidarity, as well as the remnants of the pre-Solidarity branch unions, and created the basis for a new, official trade union structure. The underground Solidarity leadership responded to the ban by calling for a general strike on November 10, reasoning that factory activists would need time to mobilize workers. Workers in the Gdańsk Shipyard, however, went on strike immediately and called on others to follow suit. As the next chapter of *Konspira* shows, the ICC was caught offguard by the shipyard strike, which was quickly crushed. Although scattered work stoppages took place on November 10, the strike call went largely unheeded. The ICC's failure to call for an immediate strike to protest the delegalization of Solidarity and its failure to come out in support of the strike in Gdańsk generated a wave of criticism from other underground activists.

August 1982: success or disaster? Delegalization. "They ought to admit their mistakes voluntarily." The strike in the shipyard or a missed opportunity. A day in November.

HALL I.8

The authorities delegalized Solidarity because they reckoned they could afford to bear the costs of this decision. They made this calculation right after what seemed at the time to be the underground's greatest success: the mass demonstrations on the second anniversary of the Gdańsk Agreement. Aleksander Hall also saw the events of August 31, 1982, as an undoubted victory for Solidarity.

Now I have a much more critical attitude toward these events, but at the time it was I who proposed that the Gdańsk Regional Committee organize an anniversary demonstration. I argued consistently in favor of such a demonstration, particularly since I was opposed to the idea of a strike. My position was influenced by the success of the demonstrations on May 1 which had proved that mass forms of protest can be an effective way of exerting pressure on the authorities. Of course, such pressure doesn't bring about a sudden change of course, but it can result in partial shifts. Apart from this, what alternative was there to a demonstration? Given the prevailing state of consciousness, only a general strike. At that time, people viewed the search for other forms of action as doing nothing at all.

165

The view that August 31, 1982, was a victory for Solidarity was, of course, superficial. The authorities saw what we were capable of and came to the conclusion that the balance of profit and loss worked out in their favor. At the same time, the itemization of the costs to society was much more complicated. You can call for demonstrations once or twice, but there's no way you can make them a permanent form of activity. You can't demand that people confront police batons (or worse) without any guarantee of success. And after all our proclamations of victory, Solidarity was delegalized.

I don't think, however, that it would have made a fundamental difference to the subsequent course of events if we hadn't demonstrated. At most there would have been a sense of dissatisfaction if underground Solidarity hadn't once managed to confront the enemy head on. I'm far from presenting the history of the underground as a string of heroic exploits, but I do believe that the battle served a purpose. Once again, people died from police bullets;[1] this fact itself has dramatic significance, but it also means, for example, that the Lenin Steel Works will never be the same as it was under Gomułka or Gierek. What counts is not just the immediate political outcome (this was a failure), but the impact on social consciousness: we tried, we didn't give up without a struggle.

BORUSEWICZ I.34

To me, August 31, 1982, means very little. I don't know why you insist on treating it as crucial. It was just a repetition of something that had happened before. You think the ICC called for a demonstration and the population responded overwhelmingly? The underground isn't just a few guys who sign appeals. In general, it's nonsense to make a distinction between the underground and the mass of the population. Why are we active? Because society wants us to be. When its will to resist weakens or dies out, then we too will stop our work.

LIS II.8

In calling for a demonstration on the second anniversary of the agreement, the members of the ICC did not exclude the possibility of taking it

166

further; they proposed, if participation was on a massive scale and if demonstrations continued on September 1, to consider calling a general strike from September 2 onward. However, in Bogdan Lis's opinion, the response was not as great as had been hoped.

The intensive campaign of intimidation conducted by the authorities had some effect. Before August 31, Zbigniew Romaszewski was arrested in Warsaw and Stanisław Jarosz in Gdańsk. Many small groups that didn't observe proper security measures were caught (the authorities made great use of this in their propaganda at the time). Even so, the Communists felt they didn't have enough successes, so they simply manufactured a few more. For example, they announced the capture of a particular group more than once and they kept showing on television the same "workers" condemning the underground.

In many cities, nevertheless, including Gdańsk, the demonstrations were massive; at the same time, a lot depended on the level of organization in the different regions. In Gdańsk we had an intensive campaign, beginning around August 14, to make people aware of the call for a demonstration; we produced lots of leaflets, factory newspapers came out frequently, and there were special broadcasts of Radio Solidarity. Despite all this, I must repeat, the response was smaller than we'd expected.

BUJAK II.3

It seemed that the way in which the underground proposed to celebrate August 31 coincided with the aspirations of Solidarity members and sympathizers. Everyone applauded the ICC's statement and awaited the anniversary with optimism. Why, then, asks Bujak, did the authorities' propaganda offensive lead to such a decline in enthusiasm, particularly among workers?

Of course, some young workers took part in the Warsaw demonstration, but the majority of people were from the intelligentsia. In general, the largest factories didn't come up to expectations. It was the same in Wrocław and Nowa Huta, although worker turnout there was proportionately better than in the capital. Apart from anything else, Warsaw's urban structure works against demonstrations, because industrial enterprises are scattered on the outskirts of the city. In Nowa Huta, you've got twenty thousand workers in the center of town the moment the first shift ends; in Gdańsk, the shipyard workers step through the gates and they're right at the monument; in Wrocław all the largest plants are on the same street, and demonstrations somehow take off naturally. In Warsaw, you have to show slightly more initiative and make your way to the starting point.

Did we place too little emphasis on propaganda? Did we make other mistakes? Certainly we did, but perhaps we didn't read people's state of mind correctly. After all, from the organizational point of view, we were well prepared. The arrest of Romaszewski made things more difficult for us, but what really thwarted our plans was the fact that there weren't enough demonstrators. The streets were full of ZOMO and Security people, and we didn't have any radio but only couriers to communicate with one another. People are safer in a large crowd, but when the crowd thins out, the Security Service has nothing to do but pick up anyone who's hanging about suspiciously. At one point, one of the groups whose function it was to protect the demonstration had to fight the police, who were trying to take out both the lead marchers and those who were trying to protect them.

We had four alternative plans for the demonstration, depending on the number of people who turned out, their level of determination, and their success in holding off the ZOMO. Everything depended on the mass of demonstrators being able to disperse the police—and this is what we were counting on. I was absolutely convinced that there'd be 50,000 people, and I wouldn't have been surprised at 100,000; I'd have been slightly amazed if 150,000 had turned out. I knew (like the other members of the ICC) that August 31 would decide the fate of Solidarity. In Warsaw the combined forces of law and order reckoned that they could cope with 50,000 but not with more. Unfortunately, barely 15,000 people turned out, far too few to save Solidarity.

We had to implement the least favorable variant, or even worse. We had originally decided that if the crowd numbered less than 30,000, our groups would not join in. Nevertheless, our boys went into action simply because they couldn't bear not to.

Some people said subsequently that we should have played it tactically on August 31 and done nothing, that we should have saved our resources for a big show when Solidarity was delegalized. This wouldn't have yielded much. The authorities would have gained some freedom of maneuver and postponed the decision, and without the cohesion brought about by a confrontation Solidarity would have begun to fall apart.

I went to the ICC meeting feeling frustrated and I even wanted us to issue a statement criticizing the workers, but my colleagues argued against it. In their opinion, things hadn't turned out too badly.

LIS II.9

On September 2, the ICC considered the question of a general strike. The proposal was defeated by a vote of three to two. Who voted for what is not important; the fact is, the decision was "no." In those regions where the demonstrations went well, the mood was heady, even though more people had been killed. It had to be assumed that, in the event of a strike, the authorities would react with the same hysterical brutality, that they wouldn't think in political terms but would simply start shooting immediately out of fear.

SZUMIEJKO I.9

Both the Władeks (Frasyniuk and Hardek) were pressing for a strike. The situation was good, they argued, and in September we had to come out with something bigger. But Bujak and Lis were opposed. Bujak even said we could go ahead but in that case Frasyniuk could take over the leadership of the whole circus (meaning the ICC). If we lost, he'd cease to be the leader and if we won, he'd carry on.

BUJAK II.4

Given that Frasyniuk and Hardek wanted to follow up with another action, I agreed conditionally. I said that it was fine with me, but only if someone else would take charge. I'd sign on and, what's more, I'd accept my share of responsibility, whatever the outcome. But if it didn't work out, we'd change the chairman. It would be a defeat for an individual, not for the ICC as a whole. Well, I suggested that Władek Frasyniuk take over the leadership, but he didn't agree. It was then that (remembering our experience in Warsaw) I voted against a strike. For some reason, so did Bogdan Lis.

SZUMIEJKO I.10

Delegalization was in the air. Everyone was expecting it. The only question was: when?

A week or ten days before the official announcement, some couriers from Małopolska arrived in Warsaw. The message they brought was that we had to move up the next meeting of the ICC and hold it before October 8 because (and this was absolutely reliable information, they said) this was the day on which the authorities were going to dissolve Solidarity. But the guys in Warsaw (Zbyszek Bujak's people) said there was no reason to hurry, because there would have to be a first reading in the Sejm before they could pass the bill. In Gdańsk, Bogdan Lis said he'd received information that they weren't going to delegalize Solidarity until about October 19. It seems as though we didn't really want to keep up with events.

BUJAK II.5

In Bujak's opinion, it is an illusion to think that it's possible to foresee every conceivable course of events and to draw up plans corresponding to every possible alternative. Events make it impossible, for example, for the Interim Coordinating Commission to draw up three different versions of the same statement and to publish only the one that corresponds best to the current situation.

The reason you can't do this is that there's always some important information that only arrives at the last minute, and without it there's no way to decide on the final text of a statement. I'm leaving aside the fact that sometimes you simply do have to make a binding decision. The ICC functions collectively, and this has a paralyzing effect in situations in which urgent decisions are needed.

Of course, we arranged things so that we would meet as soon as the authorities took the decision to delegalize Solidarity and before it was officially announced. We would have received this information in advance, prepared our response, and at zero hour each of us would have been ready with a plan of action for our region. Unfortunately, the well-timed arrest of Frasyniuk thwarted all our plans. In fact, it brought them to a standstill, because we didn't have any information as to how widespread the damage was. This was decisive for the subsequent course of events.

How we came to make the decision about the action we would take is a separate issue. There was a widespread conviction that the union had to reject the scenario imposed by the authorities and seize the initiative. It seemed obvious to me that, if we were to seize the initiative, we should ignore the day of delegalization itself and that we should begin the struggle on a date that suited us. I was supported in my view by detailed information I received concerning ZOMO preparations to crush resistance.

I did my military service in the paratroopers and I know how they train the first storm divisions whose task is to "clean out" the area before the first proper attack. These shock troops are isolated from the outside world for several weeks and engage in nonstop exercises. They're running around the whole time, without a moment's rest, only a few hours' sleep—and that in fits and starts. After two weeks of training, they eliminate those on whom this draconian regimen has not had a dehumanizing effect, because such soldiers may fail to follow a command to shoot people who are unarmed. Those who remain are ready to carry out any command and in the most brutal fashion. When I heard that the ZOMO were engaged in precisely this kind of training, I was absolutely afraid of a fight at a time decided by the authorities. I knew that it was impossible to maintain the maximum level of aggression and readiness over a long period of time and that after a month the animals would become human beings again.

LIS II.10

Apart from the date of the next session of the Sejm, many other factors (including the position of the Church) suggested that delegalization would take place around October 18–20, 1982. Nevertheless, as we now know, the decision was taken on Friday, October 8.

The day after, we learned that the Gdańsk Shipyard would begin a protest strike on Monday. Bogdan Borusewicz, the ICC member responsible for contacts with industrial enterprises, happened to be out of town, which made things very complicated for us. On Sunday, October 10, members of the underground regional authorities (without Borusewicz) met together with Eugeniusz Szumiejko in order to take the necessary operational decisions.

We sent out messages, summoning couriers from other groups to contact us on Monday. They arrived when the strike had already started. The notorious ICC statement about a four-hour strike and demonstrations on November 10, that is, in a month's time, was also published on Monday. On that day, I got a letter from Bujak saying that he was leaving to me the decision as to what to do next; if I thought there was any point in going to the shipyard, he'd go to Ursus, but he needed two days to organize a strike in Warsaw—in other words, the Mazowsze region wouldn't go on strike until Wednesday. Basically, I wanted to go to the shipyard, although I didn't really believe that a strike in Gdańsk or even a possible national general strike would be successful, and as far as the latter was concerned, we hadn't even decided on it yet. The authorities weren't going to back down for any reason, and if they broke a strike by force, they would also break the backbone of society and eliminate Solidarity's underground leadership.

On Monday afternoon Borusewicz finally returned; he too was in favor of going to the shipyard. On Tuesday Frasyniuk's successor, Piotr Bednarz, arrived from Wrocław. From him I wanted to find out if there was any possibility of a general strike in Lower Silesia. Bednarz said that the position of the Wrocław factories was that if the shipyard workers undertook an occupation strike, Lower Silesia would join them. But, even though the couriers were running twice a day, they needed two days to prepare. Only on Thursday, then, would things get underway.

For its part, the shipyard was waiting for someone from the underground leadership to turn up, and they were subsequently very resentful that they hadn't got any support. But that's not absolutely true. We called on other enterprises in the Tri-city area to come out in support in order to check the possibility of a general strike in the region (the shipyard, as I've said, was on strike only for eight hours a day). Bujak issued a similar appeal in Warsaw. On the third day Nowa Huta came out on strike, but it was all over in Gdańsk by then. If the shipyard had held out another day or two, if we'd gone there ourselves, perhaps there would have been a possibility of a breakthrough (although the ZOMO would certainly have attacked). In any event, all this shows that, in order to call a general strike, you have to maintain a high level of excitement for several days, then you come out and wait for the result. But the shipyard strike was broken on the third day, and the authorities announced that the yard had been militarized. Despite this, the shipyard workers later claimed that if only

172

the Regional Committee had moved to the yard, they would have renewed their struggle on Wednesday.

Every evening we broadcast a special radio program (the last one was on Thursday, I think), and the Regional Committee issued communiques twice a day. At the same time, the situation brought to light organizational weaknesses in both our distribution system and contacts with the factories. For example, there came a time when we were no longer able to communicate with the shipyard Solidarity commission at all.

As I said, Bujak empowered me to make a decision on his behalf; Bednarz and Szumiejko were on the spot, and the only person missing was Hardek.[2] So, although we could, in principle, have made a joint decision to extend the fight, in fact it would have been a one-man decision—mine.[3]

BUJAK II.6

What took Warsaw by surprise was not the delegalization of Solidarity but the strike in the shipyard. Bujak blames the Gdańsk activists for the lack of information about the strike.

They ought to admit their mistakes voluntarily. The courier who left the Tri-city area on Sunday evening told me the next morning that nothing was going to happen in Gdańsk. The decision of the shipyard committee didn't reach Bogdan Lis until an hour after the courier had left. So, in the morning I hear that nothing is happening, and in the afternoon, all of a sudden there's a strike! I sent a courier to find out if they thought it would last. The reply was: probably not. OK, so we won't make a decision to join in. But the second day another courier arrives from Bogdan and says it's a strike to the very end! If that's the case, we'll mobilize our forces—all this, only to discover after several hours that it's all over in the shipyard.

Communications between the regions functioned extremely well; the problem was that the Gdańsk Committee had no sense of what was going on. If I had known about the shipyard strike on Monday morning, if I had known that it was a solid strike and the workers were determined to hold out, Ursus would already have been on strike on Tuesday. Zbyszek Janas was all prepared to go to the factory and get things underway. The workers were in the right frame of mind; the day

173

before they'd held a demonstration inside Ursus. My grudges against the people in Gdańsk are all the greater since it was precisely they who had insistently advocated a general strike, and this was the optimal moment. If Bogdan Lis had contacted us and said, "Support us," that would have meant that we were beginning a fight to the end, that he was going to the shipyard on Wednesday to shout, "Let's strike, because in a day or two the whole country will be out!"

Szumiejko I.11

There have been some strange coincidences. How many times before a major event has someone from the underground leadership been arrested? Remember? Before August 31, 1982—Jarosz and Romaszewski; before October 8—Frasyniuk; before November 10—Bednarz. . . . I don't want to create a myth about the all-knowing authorities who seize people only when it suits them, but I want to emphasize our difficulties. The shipyard goes on strike, every minute counts, and suddenly we have no contact at all with Wrocław, one of the best-organized regions. Actually, there's no need to talk about Lower Silesia, since communications didn't work well within the Tri-city region itself. Perhaps if we'd gone to the shipyard, stirring things up, singing the national anthem. . . . But how could we have gone when we didn't know what we'd find there? You understand? We didn't know! Perhaps the Security Service had run up the flags and were waiting for Lis and Borusewicz! I argued that we ought to wait until we were contacted by representatives of the shipyard commission who were the ones who ought to work out all the details, including how we were to get into the shipyard. But then, on the second day, on Tuesday, I realized to my horror that we didn't really have any decision-making contacts with either the shipyard or any other enterprises. I kept asking Bogdan Lis what was going on, and he kept telling me that everything was OK. Whenever I pressed the issue, he told me to mind my own business. It was this state of affairs in the Gdańsk region that determined the course of events in the country as a whole.

But the factory structures in the Mazowsze region weren't functioning too well either. By this, I mean there was no single person in charge. We got the following response from Warsaw: tell us what to do, whether to go on strike or not, because if yes, we'll distribute some leaflets around Ursus (which meant that they'd no doubt find a dozen brave guys who'd go there with some underground publications). What they needed to do, as they did in Lower Silesia, was to bring together the heads of all the largest factory commissions and decide: are we going to fuck the bastards good and proper or not?

I have no doubts about the matter. We lost this battle because in Gdańsk and Warsaw the factories weren't under a single leadership (although it's possible that the interfactory bodies in Mazowsze were functioning at this time). In addition, contacts with Małopolska—which was well organized then—weren't too good. I don't know whether they thought it was too far to send a courier. In the end, someone did turn up, but he went back on Wednedsay, when things were already over. In other words, there were two regions that weren't fully coordinated, where it might have been possible to go to the factories and distribute leaflets. And while we're on the subject of leaflets: the first leaflets issued by the Gdańsk Regional Committee in support of the shipyard workers were distributed in the shipyard on . . . Wednesday.

In general, I detect a certain law at work: those regions that don't have leaders with big names are better organized. Maybe it's easier to give an interview to Western television than to unite ten factory organizations into a single structure. Of course, I'm being ironic, but fame gets in the way of everyday activity. A well-known chief has to conceal himself with care; before anyone gets to meet with him, he has to be checked out a dozen times, and time is passing. Someone who's less well known, on the other hand, can walk around quite freely and has more time for work because he's not bothered by various visitors and hordes of journalists.

HALL I.9

We didn't catch on in time. The whole business was well underway, and we were lagging far behind events because of our organizational ineptitude. The same goes for the ICC as well.

October 1982 was a turning point. It had become clear that if the authorities struck hard and resolutely, we were incapable of counterattacking and couldn't even defend ourselves. Our model of resistance didn't stand the test. The wrong decisions were taken, they were taken too late in the day, and some decisions weren't taken at all.

LIS II.11

The ICC statement about postponing the protest for a month and hold-
ing a demonstration and a strike on November 10 was issued on Sun-
day, October 10—in other words, at the very moment the shipyard
commission was deciding to go on strike. This statement was funda-
mentally at odds with the population's expectations, but the ICC must
have taken some factor or other into account when it issued its declara-
tion. According to Bogdan Lis, the ICC mainly was influenced by pub-
lic opinion polls that had been carried out in industrial enterprises be-
fore October 8.

These polls suggested that there was absolutely no question of a
general strike (in response to the dissolution of Solidarity). However,
public opinion polls aren't always reliable. The ICC in addition was
unable to come up with a final version of the statement before the
shipyard strike broke out, because every change had to be approved
by all the members, who communicated with one another by courier.
And the changes were significant. The first draft just set out the ICC's
general position without specifying what form the protest should take.
Kraków declared that this was pointless (the statement should call for
demonstrations), whereas Bujak thought that demonstrations without
strikes were a waste of time. Time was passing. A discussion that
takes place on scraps of paper isn't a discussion at all. The ICC statement finally emerged, but as a result of the chaos that ensued with
delegalization.

And here in Gdańsk the shipyard went on strike without regard to
anything or anyone else.

BORUSEWICZ I.35

I personally think that the situation was enormously advantageous.
We only had to expand it to the whole country and, before that, go to
the shipyard with the maximum determination. Unfortunately, most of
my colleagues were unenthusiastic about the shipyard strike because
they didn't believe it was possible to win a confrontation with the authorities. They reasoned thus: since the strike has already broken out,
we're in a tough spot, but since we don't know what to do with the
strike, we'll just leave it to go away on its own. This attitude was

based on the fact that people had no faith in their own strength. It *is* possible to beat the regime—it's just a question of knowing how to. That's why I decided to do something. I really don't understand why some people stay in the underground, when the only thing they think about is crawling out of hiding, working with this group or that, and creating political programs. Similarly, I don't understand why we didn't take advantage of October 1982, even though this was an occasion we should have exploited to the maximum. Any other approach was bound to demoralize people.

The proposal that people postpone their spontaneous anger for a month, until November 10, and the failure to rescind this proposal after the collapse of the shipyard strike, demonstrated the poor qualifications and plain fear of the underground leaders. They were not (nor are they now) capable of making vital decisions, and playing it safe doesn't always pay off. October 1982 constitutes a clinical example of how not to proceed. Contacting people around the country, waiting for couriers to show up, endless deliberations—and all to delay making a decision. Involving Bednarz and Szumiejko was nothing more than an attempt to play it safe, to avoid facing an independent decision of any kind—either to join in the strike at the shipyard or to ask them to call it off. They just waited for . . . it's not clear what. Even in the underground, some people manage to develop certain bureaucratic tendencies. They can't act without the proper documents, without couriers arriving at the appointed time, without contact points, and so on. And when one person is late, a second person gets scared, a third is picked up by the police, and everything falls apart. When you simply have to improvise, when you have to rise to the occasion, you can't afford to wait for couriers. You have to get up from behind your desk, because the only thing you can see when you're sitting on your backside is the blotter.

LIS II.13

After the strike was crushed, morale in the shipyard plummeted. The factory commission felt betrayed: after all, it had protested "legally," in accordance with the ICC's first April statement in which it had declared that a general strike would be called in the event that Solidarity was delegalized. They thus expected—as we now know, in vain—that

*a strike would be proclaimed and that representatives of the under-
ground leadership would go to the shipyard. When Bogdan Lis later
asked the shipyard workers about the prospects of a protest in November,
they simply voiced grievances and resentments. They didn't want to
hear about any further protest actions.*

They responded evasively that they couldn't rally these frustrated
workers into a renewed state of readiness.

I'm not convinced that November 10 was a total washout. In the
end, we did achieve some of our goals: they finally announced the
Pope's visit and Wałęsa's release.[4] Perhaps we should have called off
the November demonstrations. But how? After all, the authorities took
the decision at the last moment, and the union underground isn't a
regular army. You can't pick up the phone and issue an order to retreat.
The ICC couldn't meet until the second half of October. Disturbances
in various localities had only just died down, and we also had to follow
security procedures. Given that we hadn't called a strike straightaway,
November 10 was the earliest possible date. It was the anniversary of
the registration of Solidarity, and the next day was the anniversary of
Poland's regaining independence. If the demonstrations had really
taken off, they could have been extended, and then . . .

But they didn't take off. This whole business had a negative impact on morale, although this was justified only in part. In the end, as
I said, we achieved two goals—the release of Wałęsa and the Pope's
visit. Maybe the latter encouraged Brezhnev's departure to the next
world. Ha, ha, ha!

HALL 1.10

*In Hall's view, the call for protests in November—given the situation
and the overall scenario—was evidence of a complete lack of realism.*

There was no way it could have worked. I feel a certain sense of
bitter satisfaction because I was opposed to it at the time. Of all the
various moves made by underground Solidarity, November 10, 1982,
is the one I'm most critical of. That day showed that a strike won't
take place simply because you call for one (without the necessary
technological and organizational backing). All in all, the whole month
was a disaster. All our hopes that the suspension of martial law and
the release of Wałęsa might signal a change for the better turned out
to be groundless.

BORUSEWICZ II.3

This totally-missed opportunity (this inflated sense of one's own importance, this harking back to the events of the month before, the contempt for public opinion) met with a masterly stroke on the part of the authorities: the release of Wałęsa, following his unfortunate letter,[5] and Glemp's statement condemning, in no uncertain terms, the forthcoming protest action. The prestige of the underground declined, people lost the desire for action; if the authorities had proposed that we all come out of hiding in exchange for the release of all political prisoners, we would probably have done so. I was in favor of this on the grounds that when we win, we're in a good situation, but the moment we lose, we're confronting disaster. Luckily, we didn't experience any more disasters like that of November. One more like that and we'd have had to collect our toys and go home. . . . Go home?

BUJAK II.7

In the autumn of 1982, the myth cherished by so many evaporated— the myth of the ICC as the commander, laying down a strategy that is carried out by the disciplined ranks of union members. The nation protested when it wanted to and not when we told it to. That, according to Bujak, is the lesson these events taught the underground.

We weren't equal to the task, and this led to the demobilization of the broader population. In addition, various groups—for example, the Inter-Regional Committee of Resistance led by Konarski—proclaimed that the ICC had lost all authority and that they were now taking over.

We drew a number of ideological and organizational conclusions from the disaster. Nevertheless, some problems can't be eliminated immediately. The ICC doesn't have a horde of activists ready to do its bidding. The machinery seizes up. It's no use at all drawing conclusions, no matter how wise, if the groups responsible for communication between regions are arrested one after the other. Some arrests resulted in the elimination of entire structures, and there were few alternative emergency channels. The whole system depends on people. You may or may not be able to count on finding them, because they go out shopping, to work, to birthday parties. If a courier doesn't work regularly, he eventually loses his contacts. Some people naively imag-

179

ine that it's enough to set up an operative, give him a password and a telephone number, and everything works like clockwork. But people aren't capable of sitting in the same place for two months at a time (and that's frequently what their work amounts to) waiting for something to do over the next six months. A structure that doesn't function continuously simply doesn't function at all. Only now, in 1984, have we succeeded in forming some kind of emergency communication network.

After all these disasters we had a difficult period. A lot of people left (although many of them came back after a time), especially those who thought you only had to give the military authorities a good kick and they'd fly apart. The myth of the general strike as a magical weapon also lost some of its force. We had to formulate a program that would help us regain our bearings in a new situation. A program of resistance over a long, a very long, time.

NOTES

1. To commemorate the second anniversary of the founding of Solidarity massive demonstrations were held on August 31, 1982, in sixty-six towns. In many places there were clashes between riot police and demonstrators. In Lublin and Krakow firearms were used and at least five demonstrators were killed.

2. *When reading the text before publication, Eugeniusz Szumiejko made the following comment: Bogdan has the facts wrong. It was not until Wednesday afternoon—in other words, when the shipyard strike was well and truly coming to an end—that Piotr Bednarz took part in a meeting of the Gdańsk Committee. Thus Bednarz could not have participated in the decision. Hardek's vote really was missing, because the first courier from Kraków did not arrive until Wednesday either.*

3. Lis was the only person from Gdańsk Solidarity.

4. On November 11, the day after the abortive general strike, the Polish authorities announced that Lech Wałęsa, who had been interned in a government villa since the imposition of martial law, was "no longer a threat to public order" and would be released.

5. Shortly before his release from internment, Wałęsa wrote to Jaruzelski, suggesting that an accord between Solidarity and the government remained possible. The letter was regarded by many Solidarity activists as too conciliatory.

May 3, 1984, in front of St. Brigida Church in Gdansk.

BORUSEWICZ BOGDAN

s. Konstantego, ur.11.I.1949 r.
zam. Sopot ul. 23 Marca 96 m. 24.

<u>wzrost</u> 172 cm, krępy, <u>włosy</u> ciemnoblond
<u>oczy</u> piwne.

<u>Kontakty:</u>
Sreniowski Józef - Łódź ul.Laurowa 2/2
Zych Stanisław-Sanok ul.Batorego 48
Bieliński Konrad-W-wa ul.Joteyki 22/2
Czyński Lech-W-wa ul.Racławicka 28/56
Napłoszek Danuta-W-wa ul.Elektoralna
               nr 14b m.15
Stankiewicz Grażyna-Białystok
             ul.Nowy Świat 14/11
Skrobotowicz Jacek - Kraków
             ul.Krowodorska 45/2
Abakanowicz Władysław - Słupsk
             ul. Z.Augusta 4/20
Pietkun Zdzisław - Dzwierzuty-Szczytno
             ul.Szczecińska 7/4

FRASYNIUK WŁADYSŁAW

s. Stanisława, ur.25.XI.1954 r.,zam.
Wrocław ul. Sienkiewicza 131 m. 8.

<u>wzrost</u> 175 cm, średnia budowa, <u>twarz</u>
pociągła, <u>włosy</u> ciemne,gęste,<u>nos</u> śred
prosty, miał sumiaste wąsy.

<u>Kontakty:</u>

rodzice - Wrocław ul. Żelazna 51 m. 2
Frasyniuk Józef-Wrocław ul.Curie Skłodowskiej 47 m.
Jędryka Tadeusz -Wrocław ul.Kościuszki 4 m.4
Ircha Józefa -Wrocław ul.Powstańców 51. m.6
[...]Józef-Chęrzyce Ulęgnic woj.Wrocław
[...]Bogdan-Cieslin[...] Chęrzykowa woj.Wrocła

JANAS ZBIGNIEW

s. Wojciecha, ur. 2.VII.1953 r., zam.
Warszawa ul. Hawajska 12 m. 69.

<u>wzrost</u> 179 cm, szczupły, wysportowany,
<u>włosy</u> ciemnoblond, faliste,ma wąsy,
może mieć brodę.

<u>Kontakty:</u>
Lenczewski Władysław-W-wa ul.Keniga 11/
Janas Wojciech -W-wa Międzylesie ul.Połaryskiego 20/2
Broniarek Emil- W-wa ul. Kulidłowskiego 11/80
Kieliszczyk Witold-W-wa ul. Keniga 4/59
Ciundziewicki Janusz-W-wa ul.Broniewskiego 22/14
Cieslikowski Ryszard - Brwinów ul. Biskupicka 51/12

Most Wanted List: Bogdan Borusewicz, Wladyslaw Frasyniuk, and
Zbigniew Janas (1983).

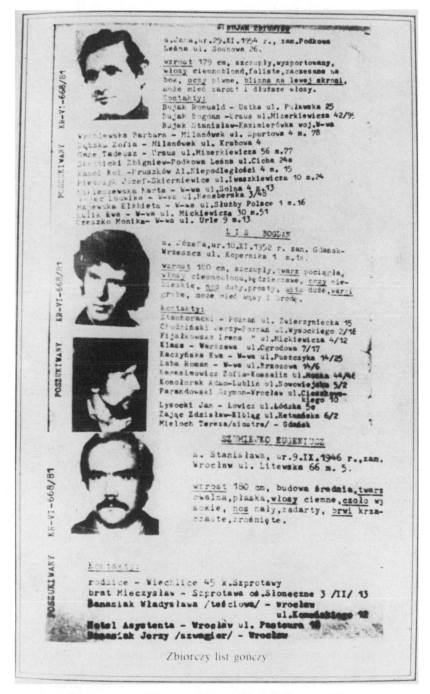

Most Wanted List: Zbigniew Bujak, Bogdan Lis, and Eugeniusz Szumiejko (1983).

The authors of *Konspira:* (from the left) Maciej Lopinski, Mariusz Wilk, and Marcin Moskit (Zbigniew Gach) (June 1984). Photograph taken in the Table Mountains where the authors were at the time preparing the manuscript of Konspira.

Why do we need a program? The implementation of the "underground society." Is there a future for "Solidarity Today"? The advice of experts. To whom are these words addressed?

SZUMIEJKO I.12

In general, the ICC's efforts to produce a program evoked nothing but criticism. The most serious complaint was that the underground had produced no real ideas, that all the talk about "long marches" or "short leaps," about the underground society, about "Solidarity Today"—or even the day after tomorrow—didn't add up to anything. The ICC was criticized for its lack of any global vision that would also address the current situation in specific, objective terms rather than in empty generalizations concerning the need to love one another and gain independence. Eugeniusz Szumiejko is aware of people's expectations and their criticisms, but he doesn't attach too much weight to them.

It's true that many people are waiting for the ICC to come up with a recipe, but there's one short answer to this: it's Jaruzelski who ought to be upset, because he's the one who doesn't have a program. This is clear to everyone, and it wasn't us who promised the nation its salvation on December 13, 1981.

Seriously though, given that Solidarity had a program that was passed at the First National Congress, we have to ask ourselves whether this program is still valid. The documents passed by the Congress were worded in the spirit of the August Agreements, in which we declared that we wouldn't overthrow the political system but would simply incorporate into it some independent regulating mechanisms. The program passed by the Congress was based, then, on the assumption that cooperation with the regime was possible. Since this is no longer the case, we have to ask ourselves whether it's possible to achieve our goals on our own, particularly within the framework of the broader question of what kind of Poland do we want. It's not enough to answer: self-governing and democratic. We assumed, for example, that the education system should function in a particular way. However, we not only demanded autonomy for teachers but also recognized the state's continuing role in relation to education. If we haven't thought up any better vision of a future Poland, then we need to force the Communists to implement the things they previously agreed to. But in this case, all we need is an improvised plan of how to respond to the authorities' successive moves, a plan that can be updated every few months or every year, depending on the situation.

Those people who demand that we draw up a new overall strategy can be divided into two groups. The first group opts for a program that is much more modest, one that it hopes the other side will find acceptable—in other words, a strictly trade-union program with some elements of a social movement (but without calling it "Solidarity" and without most of what Solidarity stood for).

The second group considers that the first group has capitulated and advocates the opposite strategy, a radicalization of the program: no tinkering with the system but its complete abolition. We want a genuinely independent Poland, they say, but since this is a long way off, for the time being let's work out a plan of current struggle. Here they see eye-to-eye with the advocates of the Congress program who also favor a short-term perspective. The only difference is that the former say we already have a long-term goal, and the latter—perhaps we don't yet have one, but there's plenty of time to draw one up. They draw a link between immediate and long-term goals, nevertheless, insofar as they see the future sovereignty of the nation as depending on the inner sovereignty of the individual, which needs to be forged here and now.

If we were to follow this line of reasoning, we could easily end up provoking serious disputes, because some people would be absolutely unwilling to associate themselves with such a program. In this situation is it really up to the ICC to come up with a program for a future Poland? Isn't it better to tell people: "By all means, produce various programs and visions of the future, let the people read them and become politically aware. We, the underground leadership, will support every initiative (well, perhaps with the exception of Communist and fascist proposals), and we'll help to promote them in the West. In the meantime, however, we're going to formulate only short-term plans."

LIS II.14

Solidarity brings together people with different views. For each group you have to formulate different goals because each has its own economic, social, and political ideas. This is a job for various political parties, not for Solidarity. We should aim simply to bring about a situation in which it's possible to advance different political programs.

Nevertheless, we're not just sitting with our arms folded doing nothing. From the very beginning we've tried (for better or worse) to meet society's need for a sense of direction.

BUJAK II.8

The first official program published by the Interim Coordinating Commission was "The Underground Society," dated July 28, 1982. As its title suggested, the document drew on statements that Bujak and Kulerski had written in their dispute with Jacek Kuroń's proposals set out in his "Theses" as well as other discussions that had taken place during the early days of martial law. The document emphasized, first and foremost, the importance of independent culture, education, and publishing, as well as assistance to the victims of repression; it called for a boycott of official social and political institutions and appealed for demonstrations, the observance of anniversaries, and various kinds of protest actions. It thus articulated what were the main ideas of the time.

The declaration—and even its name, "The Underground Society"—gave rise to numerous misunderstandings. For this reason, Bujak considers it necessary to define the term more precisely before assessing the effectiveness of the program itself.

The notion of the "underground society" did not, of course, mean that the whole population should organize its existence separately from any kind of state institution and thus—to use the metaphor—go underground. The number of people who are willing to undertake activity above and beyond their own work is always limited, even when they're not threatened by repressive measures for doing so. Generally speaking, such people account for ten percent of the population; in other words, they're a small group, an elite from various social strata and groups. We reckoned that this percentage gave us approximately three million people, including a smaller, more radical group of potential leaders and organizers. We intended to propose various forms of new activity to precisely these people, who were the most energetic (at least, that's how I saw it at the beginning).

According to my current calculations, there are now about 300,000 people directly involved in union work, while some 1.2 million read the underground press and pay their union dues. If we add these two figures (which are based on my own direct observations and calculations of probability), this gives us about half of the theoretical ten percent.

During the first period of constructing the resistance movement, the term "underground" was in widespread use. When martial law was suspended, it became somewhat anachronistic, despite the fictitious nature of this "suspension" and the following "abolition" [in July 1983]. The term "underground society" was thus replaced by the more accurate "independent society," although what was meant by the term remained the same.

It's not difficult to show how this idea has been implemented in practice. Of course, the ideal situation would be a return to the situation as it was before December 13, 1981, when about 1 million people (ten percent of the Solidarity membership) were active. This is what we are aiming for. Of course, we have to take account of the overall quality and level of activity, but 300,000 is an impressive number of activists in today's conditions.

BORUSEWICZ III.1

Bujak's approach was greatly influenced by the ethos of the independent society formulated by KOR and—if we go farther back—by the anarcho-syndicalist ideas of Edward Abramowski. This formula, which was particularly dear to the heart of the leftish groups that had been active within the pre-August opposition in Warsaw, not only indicated a course of action for today but also called attention to these ideological foundations. The theory was undoubtedly a beautiful one, but in practice (when the authorities' repressive apparatus aimed to crush with absolute ruthlessness every independent initiative) it was completely utopian. In a totalitarian regime it's hard to imagine that society could organize itself without having in its hands some means of neutralizing the violence exercised by the state. In reality, then, the idea caught on among elite groups within the intelligentsia and creative circles; it energized them and gave a long-term meaning to resistance, but on the whole it was an unrealistic approach.

If you don't agree with me, you only have to take a look around you. It's been two years since the idea was launched, and what do we have to show for it? Where is the underground society? Of course, there may be a few organisms, which I call structures of an underground state, but the idea that you can involve tens of millions or even a few million people in conspiratorial activity is absurd!

Alongside the idea of the underground society, another notion was formulated—that of the underground state. It was articulated by the group associated with the journal Niepodległość *[Independence]. In Borusewicz's opinion, neither program took account of what people were actually doing.*

We are implementing bits of one program and bits of the other. Our structures are reminiscent of the cells typical of the underground state; groups have emerged that have specific tasks, and we have foreign agencies a bit like embassies. On the other hand, groups that are active aboveground (educational groups, charitable commissions) function according to the scenario of the underground society. It is paradoxical that Bujak—a proponent of this idea—actually functions according to the second, apparently opposite, program. This has been brought about by the evolution of conspiratorial circles that, in order to achieve maximum efficiency, have been forced to abandon improvisation in favor of commands and subordination. Thus the programs of the underground society and the underground state, although seemingly opposed to each other, in fact have become intertwined.

Perhaps we were right to come out with "The Underground Society" declaration in the summer of 1982, but now I'm somewhat critical of it. Our goal was, and is, to build a normal society possessing the right to pursue its own goals. On the other hand, an underground society is a political anomaly (leaving aside the utopian nature of this program).

The next document, "Solidarity Today," was different. It made no mention of creating a national underground but talked about creating a foundation on which Solidarity could function in the then current situation. We repeated some of the earlier arguments about the need for independent education, culture, and information, but at the same time called on people to consider the possibility of activity within official institutions. In this way, we opened the door to open activity, so that people could become involved not only in the "front of refusal" but also, for example, in worker's self-management. At the same time, we left it up to the workers to decide, since they were the ones who could best assess the possibilities for the autonomy of self-governing bodies in their factories.

Bogdan Lis found his opinions confirmed by documents ironically issued by one of the ministries which stated that although the self-management movement should be viewed positively, there were cases in which workers' councils engaged in illegal activity. Among other things, self-management councils took action in defense of political prisoners, criticized various decisions taken by management, prevented the dismissal of some people and the hiring of others, and had been known to dissolve themselves ostentatiously as a sign of protest. Of course, the author of this report stressed the "marginal nature" of these phenomena, but the meaning of this term in Party jargon is well known.

The "Solidarity Today" statement was a step forward and a challenge to all those who wanted the underground to call for only destructive protests. Actually, as Lis observes, it's a great oversimplification to talk about positive and negative forms of activity, since the real division is between open and conspiratorial activity.

In the illegal sphere, nearly all the activity involving some form of independent organizing was oriented toward "positive" goals: the creation of union cells in the factories, the organization of editorial groups, the printing and distribution of the underground press, and so

on. On the other hand, what was new in the "Solidarity Today" declaration was the possibility of positive legal activity.

BUJAK II.9

*"Solidarity Today" was written during a specific time, at the end of
1982 and the beginning of 1983, right after the underground's greatest
disaster—the missed opportunity of the October strike in the Gdańsk
Shipyard and the proclamation of the protest action on November 10
(which was doomed to failure from the very start). At that time various
underground groupings formulated dozens of proposals, even though
the supply of such proposals far outstripped the demand for them. This
stormy discussion resulted, however, not in a more detailed program
but in numerous demands regarding its content.*

*Once again, people expected a vision of the ideal Poland that
would set out the means and map out the road leading to our goal
and—in addition—that would tell everyone precisely what to do. In
Bujak's opinion, it was absolutely ridiculous to hope for such a glorious
recipe, and he had little patience with attempts to define overall, long-
range tasks and goals.*

We have to realize that there's only one vision of absolute happiness (divided into precise stages and with clearly defined roles for
individuals)—the Communist vision. We in Poland have become fully
acquainted with it. In light of this, I suggested it would be better if the
Solidarity press argued against this constant search for a program, because it demobilizes people and allows them to blame everything on
the leadership. Nevertheless, thirty or forty different programs had
first to emerge so that some people could give vent to their creativity
and others could display their critical passion, and only afterward was
it possible to start looking for a different model.

"Solidarity Today" presented a clearly defined goal: the overcoming of the existing power system. At the same time, it also defined
clearly the basis of this system and how we should struggle against it.
It identified a number of areas of resistance—a universal boycott,
economic struggle, the development of an independent social consciousness, and preparations for a general strike. Of course, the destruction of the Communist dictatorship in the literal sense, sending
the army back to the barracks and demobilizing the secret police—all
this is a distant prospect. But the essence of the Communist system

187

consists in the fact that people abandon the struggle, that they participate in the farce of constructing a dual reality. And in this respect,
the document proposed going over to the attack.

The ICC declaration was criticized from many sides. The critics included those who wanted Solidarity to abandon its format as a
trade union and social movement and become a political, or even a
national-liberation, movement. The passage of time brought into
question the merit of these initially sharp criticisms. First, the harsh
critics were themselves unable to point to any significant achievements; second, the effective organization of people in the defense of
their basic rights (which was precisely what we proposed in "Solidarity Today") constituted the optimal strategy, since such action provides a basis for all other kinds of activity. Of course, the notion of
"basic rights" is a broad one. To a worker, for example, it includes
fair wages and working conditions; to a teacher—the possibility of
transmitting unfalsified knowledge to his pupils; and to a writer—
creative freedom without censorship.

The program itself remains valid, although some things have
changed. Some demands that were raised previously have now become reality. An example: we envisaged only in general terms the development of underground publishing, but within a year there were
decided improvements in both its content and technological level.
Weak publications fell by the wayside, because the publishing movement began to function according to the law of the market. We can,
then, make a kind of inventory of what we have. *Niepodległość* can
write all it likes about the need to achieve independence, but what
counts in the political arena are forces that are backed by real people
and measurable results. There were so many calls for the creation of
political parties, and what happened? There aren't any! Not because
I'm against them; if there were a genuine need, neither I nor anyone
else could prevent people from forming them.

HALL I.11

I've already stated my opinion about "Solidarity Today" in the Gdańsk
regional press and I can only repeat what I wrote then. First, the
document contained some clear shortcomings in terms of its analysis
of the political situation. (Instead of providing a sober political analy-

sis, it attempted to raise morale: we've demonstrated our unity, people have proven equal to the test, they've become hardened, the struggle continues, and so on.) Second, I considered it a mistake to present a general strike as the main goal of struggle. All in all, I thought the document inadequate, despite the fact that there were some strong passages, particularly those that dealt with the formation of an independent social consciousness, economic struggle, and the boycott of official institutions.

BORUSEWICZ III.2

The program outlined in "Solidarity Today" was a compromise between staying in the trenches and engaging in pitched battle against the authorities. Nevertheless, there was much greater emphasis on the theory of the so-called long march, whereas the general strike was dealt with as though in passing, without much conviction. Borusewicz points out that even these proposals were largely irrelevant in light of the changing situation.

Supposing there came a time when, for example, there were frequent demonstrations; the ICC would issue a statement about demonstrations. There's nothing wrong with this. Just the opposite. But I couldn't detect any general guiding principle in official underground statements, and I think this was due to the divisions within the Solidarity leadership. Some people staked everything on long-term struggle, and others argued that we ought to get it over with as soon as possible, that we had to be prepared to take the risk: either victory or defeat.

The "Solidarity Today" declaration (like the previous one) essentially described what had already been done. But is it possible to propose anything more if you postpone the decisive confrontation with the authorities to an unspecified time in the future? In the meantime, the people have nothing to do apart from collecting union dues, publishing the press, and maintaining the boycott . . .

BUJAK II.10

When talking about the ICC's program, we mustn't leave out the question of our advisers. For a long time the underground was deprived of

189

the advice of experts, since some of legal Solidarity's advisers were interned, and most of the others had abandoned cooperation or had attached themselves to other opinion-forming groups. According to various estimates, only fifteen to twenty percent of advisers, at the most, continue to be politically active.

Solidarity's leading advisers play only a minute role in the work of the underground. It is probably because they understand too well the enormous complexity of the situation that they hesitate to try to find a solution. They are simply paralyzed by their overdeveloped sense of responsibility. It's not so much the intellectuals but rather regular members of the intelligentsia who are helping us. If I were to run through the names of people who have come up with various proposals, analyses, expert opinions, it would turn out that ninety-five percent of them are people who are completely unknown.

I form my own opinions by talking to activists from various structures. Apart from that, I find myself in a specific—one might even say, luxurious—situation in that I work with Wiktor Kulerski, Konrad Bieliński, and Jan Lityński, who are experienced politicians. But they, too, arrive at their opinions on the basis of talking to people involved in practical, organizational work.

Essentially, every member of the ICC brings to meetings his own baggage, consisting of the opinions voiced in his region, and it's usually these that form the basis for our decisions.

LIS II.15

We don't have easy access to the "older" union experts. Actually, it wouldn't be worth making use of all of them today. In passing, it's worth remembering that the current minister for prices, Krasiński, was once adviser to the Bydgoszcz region, but when he started giving advice, Rulewski threw him out of Solidarity and Jaruzelski immediately gave him a place in the government.

Another problem is that the people with whom we've been working since the imposition of martial law—whatever their intelligence and even, on occasion, brilliance—don't yet have enough of the right experience. We're the ones who bear the responsibility for taking decisions and we thus have the duty to take account of the broader social implications of every issue.

BORUSEWICZ III.3

I'm not an expert, but when I read some of our advisers' proposals, I used to go weak at the knees. They're like the man in the moon; they don't understand the situation—for example, they did an overkill in attacking the Yalta agreement. I'd need a magnifying glass to find a real expert who knows what he's talking about. An academic title and a head for politics are two completely different things. The new advisers are people without any political experience. On the other hand, the former advisers—Olszewski, Geremek, and others—are following their own line now, independently of the ICC and not necessarily in accordance with us.

SZUMIEJKO I.13

The need to continue work on a program, together with the fact that the ICC was seeking advice on legal, economic, and social problems, gave rise to the idea of forming a so-called program council. The form and scope of its activity was never precisely formulated, but its goal was clear from the very beginning: to provide studies of particular issues for the use of the ICC. Some members of the council as it's currently constituted first emerged when "Solidarity Today" was being drawn up. I think the idea originally came from Warsaw, but the general outline was drawn up by experts from Kraków and Silesia, who were then joined by people from Lublin, Poznań, Warsaw, Gdańsk, and Wrocław. It was these people who laid the foundations for "Solidarity Today." For a week the ICC struggled with the various materials, until finally there emerged a compromise document, more rounded but less subtle than earlier versions.

The council's style of work hasn't really changed since then. In each region there's an honest, competent intellectual who gets together a group of academics, engineers, and lawyers, people with "access," who discuss the issues, carry out opinion polls (frequently in the factories as well), and then sit down and write it all up. Then the members of the council meet (each region has a representative on the council), choose the common features from the various studies, and put it all together for the ICC. The draft program that was circulated in two versions, A and B, at the beginning of 1984 originated in

191

this way. The so-called B version contained numerous theses transcribed wholesale from the council's own draft, to which we only added an "opener" to the effect that the goal of Solidarity is to achieve national sovereignty—and we changed the ending as well. But because some people didn't like this version (especially the new "opener"), we quickly came up with version A and circulated both versions among activists to get their opinion. Now we're collecting the results (which are extremely interesting and highly critical of both versions) and in the second half of 1984 we'll publish the final version.

BUJAK II.1

The role and tasks of the council of experts have never been completely defined. The council has never acquired the formal status of an advisory body to the ICC because Bujak is against it.

My view of how such a body should function was completely different from that of Szumiejko and Hardek (when Władek was still with us). They wanted the ICC to ask the council to produce reports on specific issues, then the council would produce a number of versions and we would choose the one we thought most suitable. I thought this was the wrong approach, because a draft statement (and I mean the substance, not just the language) would have been the product of discussion within the advisory group, not the ICC. There would have come a time when we would have ceased doing anything apart from putting our names to documents produced by the council—in other words, we'd have handed over the reins to others and yet been left with responsibility for maintaining whatever course of action they decided on.

In any case, the ICC was in no position to formulate tasks for the council. Several years ago someone in the United States asserted that no one is competent to develop a meaningful project for a particular research body unless he is involved in the work of that body itself. And I'm in favor of precisely this kind of autonomy. The council should first of all investigate the need for its expertise on particular issues, then assess its capabilities, and only then produce an independent report. It simply ought to be an independent operation.

LIS II.16

In the final analysis, the underground's program finds expression in communiques, declarations, and appeals. What kind of language do these documents contain?

Often it's really turgid. Living in Communist Poland, we've picked up the kind of sloganeering vocabulary that's pumped out by the official mass media. It's implanted in our consciousness and comes out in various situations. Actually, when we use formulations similar to those to be found in *Trybuna Ludu* or the evening television news, perhaps it's easier to reach people, since their minds are saturated with propagandistic phraseology. Specific terms and phrases have specific connotations. On the other hand, we teach people to be innovative when we change the terminology. If we don't do this often enough, it's because time is always limited at ICC meetings, and we tend to concentrate on the substance of our documents. In general, we don't let anything through that doesn't correspond fully to our intentions, but it's a different matter when it comes to style.

BUJAK II.12

At the beginning, our statements were concise, simple, and no one could have any doubt as to whom they were addressed. Currently, our peculiar—I'll admit it—language comes from the fact that our documents generally aren't addressed to the people but to the authorities. Every phrase comes wrapped in cotton wool, so that the addressee shouldn't take offense; who knows, maybe at this very moment they're considering coming to an agreement, so why burn our bridges? In other words, render unto Caesar . . . But you can't do this. You have to write either for the authorities or for society. It was late in the day when we realized this, but better late than never.

BORUSEWICZ III.4

The majority of communiques have been published on the occasion of anniversaries of one kind or another, but what can you think up that's new in a situation when you basically have to keep saying the same thing? From the linguistic point of view, many of the statements are poorly edited, but then they're not written by specialists in Polish language. Szumiejko is the only one on the ICC who has a higher education (and a degree in astronomy at that!). The others are all real workers. If you don't have a scribbler at your side (sorry! I mean someone who knows how to write well), you have to cobble something together yourself. Apart from that, working in conspiratorial conditions means that, once a text has been approved, it's difficult to withdraw it because of stylistic errors.

The enigmatic nature of many statements, the vagueness of many text formulations, suggests a lack of clear ideas on the part of the ICC. I've already said why the language is akin to newspeak. Too many statements are issued on special occasions, when there's yet another demonstration (and when, moreover, the ICC has little faith in the outcome) or when there's yet another anniversary. On the other hand, there are too few documents dealing with specific issues, with particular measures introduced by the authorities, with social and economic policy. We exist only when we make our voice heard, and we do this, unfortunately, too rarely. For example: the reintroduction of butter rationing in the fall of 1983 was an enormous loss of face for the authorities. Everyone protested except the underground; organizational problems prevented us from speaking out for a week—by which time the issue had died.

The ICC's program, the advisory body that tried to articulate it, the linguistic style of ICC statements—all these are, however, secondary issues compared with the population's determination to resist. As long as this resistance is maintained, Borusewicz emphasizes, everything is all right; the moment it disappears, even the most eloquent declarations are no use at all.

The demand for a program essentially comes down to the demand for a panacea. Most people consider that before you can do anything you have to have a theoretical basis for your actions. As far as I'm concerned, a program is superfluous. All you need is a broad outline of the goals and values that you want to realize. You don't really need a detailed program in order to struggle against a regime that oppresses its citizens, a regime that constantly lies, that throws people into jail for publishing independent newspapers. All you need is moral opposition to the things that are going on. In a country where the regime infringes all the basic human rights, it's ridiculous to call for a program, it's turning the problem upside down. Actually, the ones who shout loudest about a program are those who think that ideas can replace action. But they can't! That's why I couldn't care less about a program, that's why I'm not going to sit down and write one! Maybe my opinion isn't representative, but I've been toiling in the opposition for ten years without any theoretical basis and I seem to be managing quite well.

12

The ICC in a new role. The chairman. Factories and factions. The knitting of the Network. Upper Silesia after awakening. The maturing of underground agencies. "Let's be professional!" The papal pilgrimage. The 1983 amnesty and disappointed hopes. Who leaves the underground and with what. General strike. A Nobel Prize for Solidarity.

SZUMIEJKO I.14

Each of the numerous documents issued by the ICC can be viewed not only as shaping or informing public opinion but also as illustrating the degree to which the underground leadership reacted to rapidly changing circumstances. To what extent was the ICC able to adapt its underground structures to the changes that took place aboveground in 1983?

During the whole of the first year of martial law, we were more or less on our own, because everyone (including Wałęsa) was in prison or internment camp. Moreover, we initially claimed credit for the successful demonstrations of May 1 and 3 as well as August 31, 1982. At that time the Church didn't aspire to an independent political role. Its first powerful statement, the Theses of the Primate's Social Council, supported our line of action. Its second such statement—Cardinal Glemp's appeal in connection with the protests planned for the anniversary of the Gdańsk Agreement—didn't support us, but people followed the ICC, not the Primate, which strengthened our position even further. Then, however, we lost ground. A couple of times the Episcopate took a position that differed from ours, and a lot of people followed the Church. Its prestige rose even further as a result of the Pope's visit, although one shouldn't interpret the Holy Father's pilgrimage solely in terms of current politics. Time also worked against the ICC. Since the idea of a general strike (not to mention a national uprising) had come to nothing, the apparent need for an underground leadership declined.

In addition to all this, Lech Wałęsa was finally freed, together with many former activists and advisers who were important and respected people. I can't deny that this filled us not only with hope but also with insecurity.

BORUSEWICZ III.5

From the point of view of the authorities, the decision to release the Solidarity chairman might have been highly beneficial. In fact, it wasn't, since the junta was unable to capitalize on the move. This was yet another example confirming Borusewicz's view that, in a situation where a breakthrough seems possible, the Communist regime is unable to take the next step, to make genuine concessions, even if such a step were to guarantee its total victory.

I think this irrational blockage is their basic mistake. The release of Wałęsa was a smart move that should have been followed by efforts to persuade him to come to some kind of agreement. But they did nothing, absolutely nothing! In politics, if one side adopts an inflexible position too early it often turns out that it's lost its freedom to maneuver. Of course, the authorities are now going to talk about how their position has evolved, they'll grudgingly hand out a few freedoms, grant us democracy like the King of Prussia granted the constitution, and nobody will see this as anything more than enlightened absolutism. But the likelihood of an uncontrollable social outburst would be much less if there were no political prisoners and if Wałęsa had been coopted into some kind of arrangement. Rakowski, however, just couldn't bring himself to do this, because, even though he's a smart gambler, he simply hates Wałęsa.

BUJAK II.13

Most underground activists viewed the release of Wałęsa as a political maneuver on the part of the regime. The authorities apparently saw an opportunity to counter the authority of the Interim Coordinating Commission with the influence of the union chairman. No one in the underground leadership doubted that Wałęsa and the ICC had different possibilities for action, that their tasks were different, and that there should not, therefore, be any problem or conflicts between them. Nevertheless, Zbigniew Bujak felt himself in an awkward situation.

Even before December 1981, some people saw me as an alternative candidate and rival to Wałęsa. The situation in which Lech was free and I was underground was perfect for the regime. That's why I trembled at the thought that anyone might accuse me of being a rival to Wałęsa. After Lech was released I pressed the ICC to issue an unambiguous statement that would put an end to any speculation about any possible differences of opinion between us and Wałęsa. Here I'd like to point out that I'd previously received a number of offers from Kiszczak, the minister of internal affairs: they weren't going to talk to Wałęsa, but they'd be willing to talk to me.

LIS II.17

The ICC's first meeting with Wałęsa, in the spring of 1983, came as a great shock to the authorities and as a surprise to the rest of the population. According to Bogdan Lis, the meeting also provided proof of the underground's organizational efficiency.

It was important for us that the meeting have propaganda value, but we had to take every conceivable kind of security measure. If they'd caught us all together, it would have been possible to blame Wałęsa. We worked everything out, therefore, to the last detail. For some time Lech had been suggesting in public that he would go to Warsaw for the fortieth anniversary of the Warsaw Ghetto uprising. He played out this intention so well that all the Western journalists rushed to the capital (after, of course, they'd filmed Wałęsa leaving Gdańsk) in order to immortalize his arrival in Warsaw. But he never arrived! At the appointed place outside Gdańsk he got out of the car, thanked his driver (who never knew that Lech was going to a meeting of the ICC) and ordered him to carry on in the same direction for another half hour so that the Security Service checkpoint in Elbląg would flag the car. Wałęsa himself, together with our courier, was taken to the meeting place by other means of transportation. It wasn't until two hours and twenty minutes after Wałęsa and his driver had parted company that the Security Service set up roadblocks. After our meeting, we simply put Wałęsa in a taxi and he went home without any further problems.

Apart from taking the opportunity to socialize (pass on greetings from others, exchange notes about what everyone had been doing), we discussed the current situation in Solidarity and the country as a whole. The main difference of opinion concerned the issue of a general strike. We had come to the conclusion that the international situation favored such a confrontation. The East–West disarmament talks that were still continuing, the suspension of martial law in Poland, the official talk of normalization—all this, in our opinion, made it difficult for the authorities to launch another attack on society, since this would have completely undermined Jaruzelski's policies in the eyes of the outside world and would have hindered Moscow's attempts to negotiate with the West. Wałęsa, on the other hand, argued that we shouldn't call for a strike but simply take part in it when it erupted. I didn't like this argument, because if we waited for the optimal moment on our side, the authorities in the meantime could provoke a conflict at a time that suited them. Apart from that, the point of having an organization is precisely so that it can, somehow, direct people and give shape to their activity.

HALL I.12

Since his release from Arłamów, Wałęsa has, on the whole, proved equal to the situation. As a symbol of Solidarity he enjoys widespread trust. So far he hasn't taken a single compromising step. Nevertheless, he finds himself in an extremely difficult situation. The nation expects a lot from him, but he actually has—if we remain realistic— very few possibilities in terms of action. I think his situation will become even more difficult in the future. People are going to demand from him greater activity, ready-made solutions, and real successes because what he's been doing so far (giving interviews, issuing statements, and attending political trials and funerals) is no longer enough. He has to think up something new. The times won't allow the

199

chairman of Solidarity to retire into the shadows of political life as Piłsudski once did. This time, there's no return from Sulejówek.[1]

LIS II.18

It's difficult to say whether Wałęsa's regaining his freedom of movement restricted the ICC's own freedom of movement. On the other hand, it's worth analyzing the reciprocal influence of an individual–symbol and an organization–symbol.

Regardless of the unavoidable differences of opinion, we always stressed that Lech was—and remained—the union's chairman. At the same time, we never thought that he ought to join the underground. Just the opposite! Nevertheless, I guess there are what I'd call tactical differences between us. Apart from the one I've already mentioned, we don't see eye to eye on the issue of economic sanctions. Another example is the question of demonstrations; Wałęsa isn't opposed to them, but he'd prefer that they were organized by the people themselves rather than by us.

But these are secondary issues; what's most important is the fact that the "extremist" underground would strengthen Wałęsa's position in any possible discussions with the government. Of course, the relationship works the other way as well: Wałęsa's position strengthens that of the ICC.

SZUMIEJKO I.15

If the Interim Coordinating Commission wanted only to bask in Wałęsa's reflected glory, this would be a mistake in Szumiejko's view.

What do we have to do in order to remain a force that both Cardinal Glemp and Wałęsa still take seriously? In my opinion, we have to continue organizing in the factories, because this at least safeguards us against losing touch with the masses. Whenever I'm at a meeting of the Lower Silesia Regional Committee, surrounded by the leaders of clandestine factory commissions who go to work normally day after day and listen to what the workers are saying, I'm not worried about becoming alienated from society. A cadres organization easily becomes alienated, but not a factory-based organization.

To put it briefly, any idiot knows that whoever has the factories on his side has a weapon in his hands; whoever doesn't is nothing more than a symbol, a moralist, a myth. Therefore, the greatest danger for us is that the union's influence among workers will decline. What good will it do us that activists warn us in good time that morale is falling if we lose our access to the workers? The silent majority won't move an inch. So what are we to do—wring our hands? No. We have to sustain this silent majority (in the last analysis, it's on our side, not with the regime), we have to arouse its consciousness. We're now moving in this direction, and the authorities are helping a little. At the beginning, everyone believed that "once Jaruzelski puts his foot down, the economy will take off." It hasn't, and it's hard to imagine that it could. Of course, the authorities have grown wiser since Gierek's time. This is clear from the latest price increases. They engaged in some pseudo-consultations and strung out the whole operation over a longer period of time, which made it difficult to organize counteraction.

We might lose our authority precisely if we don't struggle against the rising cost of living, against disastrous working conditions—in other words, if we lose our function as a trade union, if we stop flooding the factories with independent publications that address the issues closest to people.

Recently the Network of Leading Factories—an organization that goes back to the time of legal Solidarity—reemerged. It came into being as a kind of service organization for the ICC, with the aim of taking up such issues as wage agreements and working conditions. But some people in the underground leadership had a somewhat ambiguous attitude toward the Network. They praised the idea and immediately gave the new body responsibility for organizing the enterprises. I think it would be better if the Mazowsze Regional Committee itself expanded the factory structures.

BUJAK II.14

Thanks to—or as some would have it, in spite of—the ICC, the functioning of the factory union cells in the Mazowsze region achieved a qualitatively new level. Zbigniew Bujak sees a clear strengthening of the clandestine factory organizations alongside the decay of the PUWP primary organizations, which are still losing members.

The Party doesn't really have anywhere to retreat to, because the army is still competing with it in one area, and the Security Service has long since taken over the other. In this unstable disposition of forces, industrial administrators are in a particularly difficult situation. That's why, in some places, enterprise managements have come to a kind of vague understanding with Solidarity activists: management will abandon some of its claims if the clandestine Solidarity commission does likewise. This kind of arrangement has existed in one medium-sized Warsaw plant for several months now. I didn't expect, for example, that it would be so easy for us to win the elections to the workers' self-management in the Warsaw Steelworks. I know of several enterprises in the Mazowsze region where the workers' councils and Solidarity commissions are becoming quite powerful. Often management is unable to get rid of a worker even though it's known that he's involved in "conspiracy" and is distributing leaflets in the factory. Even in Ursus, where the administration is so subordinate to the Party apparatus, they don't even try to deal with many of our activists, although they're really causing a lot of trouble.

The ICC needs competent observers in the factories, and I'd hand this task over to Network activists. They ought to bring to our attention specific issues we may have overlooked.

It was Tadeusz Jedynak, the Upper Silesia representative on the ICC, who proposed that the Network be reactivated. Those who took part in the revival included delegates from Ursus, the WSK plant in Świdnik, the Lenin Steelworks, and the Fadroma plant in Wrocław, as well as the Katowice Steelworks and the Wujek Mine, which gave Solidarity an opportunity to expand its base in Upper Silesia. Actually, the fact of Jedynak's joining the ICC itself testified to the progress made in organizing this region. Already, in the middle of 1982, the ICC began to try to include Upper Silesia within the scope of its activity. There was even a proposal to join it to Lower Silesia, which was then the best-organized region. With the successive arrests of the leadership, however, which greatly weakened the Wrocław underground, and the increasing activity of the miners, the proposal lost its rationale.

TADEUSZ JEDYNAK I.1

To give a complete answer to the question of why the most industrialized region of Poland for so long was not represented on the ICC you have to go back several years. The Upper Silesians were the last to join the struggle for Solidarity, since under Gierek they had achieved high wages and numerous privileges that they didn't want to lose. As soon as they realized the underlying significance of the movement, however, they joined in wholeheartedly. The imposition of martial law deprived the miners and steel workers once again of the right to think their own thoughts.

The Silesians are such stubborn creatures that once they become convinced of something, they won't let go. This is why resistance in our region was so strong, that's why we had bloodshed. When they shot at people, the authorities made an enormous mistake, because Upper Silesia, which had hitherto been lulled into passivity, had undergone its baptism of fire, so to speak, in the Polish People's Republic and for the first time had joined with those regions that had rebelled previously, in 1956, 1968, 1970, and 1976. The people who were killed in Wujek became heroes, and those who survived never forgot the bestiality of the ZOMO and the subsequent repression of those who had resisted. When I was under arrest, just after December 13, they threw into my cell some guys from the Piast and Ziemowit mines who had been on strike for several days underground. They were semiconscious, covered in filth, black and blue from the beatings they'd received. Later, when I went through three internment camps one after the other, I saw people who were still severely injured. I'll never forget a guy who'd been scalped by a projectile and another one who had a plastic bullet in his spine. Although I myself was never a victim of physical violence, I know of a case where people who'd been arrested were subjected to outright torture. I even heard of someone having his spine broken. But then the Katowice police and Security Service have long had a reputation as the most degenerate in the country.

When they took up the fight against the regime at the beginning of the "war," the Silesians were convinced that the rest of the country was on strike too. When they heard about the fleeting wave of strikes, and particularly about the pacification of Gdańsk, they were swept by bitterness and a sense of isolation. Since even the city that had become the symbol of Solidarity had failed, they too gave up the struggle. The authorities took full advantage of people's deep sense of frustration: knowing that many Upper Silesians have relatives in Germany, they began a campaign of forcible emigration. First of all, they offered passports to Solidarity leaders in internment (unfortunately, one person who allowed himself to swallow this bait was the chairman of the Silesia–Dąbrowski Region, Leszek Waliszewski) and to the heads of many factory commissions. Later, it turned out that there'd been a bribery scandal connected with this campaign: people who'd never been active in Solidarity and who wanted to go abroad bribed police officers—on average, seventy thousand złoties—to get a place in an internment camp and, at the same time, a passport.

Before December 1981, our region had 1.5 million Solidarity members, so it was very important for the regime to cool things down in this colossus. But this passivity lasted no longer than six months. The emergence of the ICC and the formation of regional committees in Gdańsk, Warsaw, Wrocław, and Kraków heartened the miners too. From the fall of 1982, the calls for a "regular" underground in Upper Silesia became increasingly insistent. People also began searching for someone who could act as leader of the region (Cierniewski was out, as a declared supporter of the regime, and Rozpłochowski was behind bars).

Some time after my release from internment, which took place just before Christmas 1982, I was suggested as leader, but I hesitated for quite some time. Silesians' strongest attachments are to people whom they know directly—for example, activists of the factory commissions. But many of these activists (at least two hundred) had been intimidated and packed off to the West. I realized that we were going to be short of people, but then others convinced me that the factory structures were rapidly rebuilding themselves and that everything was improving.

I finally reached a decision in the early spring of 1983, after several hours talking to Zbyszek Bujak. I said goodbye to my family (I have a wonderful wife) and went underground. In May 1983 I began to sign ICC documents as the chairman of the Upper Silesia Regional Executive Committee.

We began organizing the underground by strengthening the factory commissions and our printing facilities, in which we were greatly helped by Warsaw. Then we established procedures that would allow the Executive Committee to replace quickly any of its members who might be arrested. Finally, the time came to set the whole machinery in motion.

People from outside Silesia often don't understand the specifics of underground activity in this region, which involves the coordination of many densely populated and highly industrialized cities. If a demonstration takes to the streets in Gdańsk or Warsaw, it's immediately visible to everyone. In our region, you can have a considerable number of disturbances in Gliwice or Jastrzębie, but people living in Katowice, Sosnowiec, Bytom, Chorzów, Zabrze, and other places won't hear about them. In addition, in order to get people together for a demonstration you have to have them close by, but many miners and steel workers travel long distances to work and after work they're in a hurry to get home. It's difficult, too, to organize a mass meeting or a strike in the mines, because people live several kilometers away from one another and work in small, isolated groups.

In order to avoid the error of the Solidarity period's "gigantomania" (the Silesia–Dąbrowski region had more members than any other), we returned to the previous form of regional delegations, as we now call the microregions loosely associated with the center, the Regional Executive Committee. Actually, to be precise, I should add that since the beginning of martial law an autonomous Regional Coordinating Commission has also been functioning, together with about thirty other independent groupings, whose activity is confined, by and large, to individual towns and cities. With some of these groups we have only limited contact; with others—none at all. Nevertheless, we support their activity, because we're in no position to serve an entire region of nearly four million people on our own.

The specific characteristics of Upper Silesia have also given rise to specific forms of underground activity. Apart from regular publishing of papers and journals and the distribution of publications from other parts of the country, we've concentrated on two main areas: broadly conceived aid for the families of people who have suffered repression (largely with the support of the Church) and a series of educational programs. Our charitable activity demanded a great deal of preparatory work, because the Katowice voivodship is divided into four dioceses. Our educational work is partly determined by the possibility of getting premises for the classes and, of course, competent lecturers. During the legal Solidarity period, we simply would select an honest guy from the Regional Board, and after a couple of months we would be completely lost because he didn't have the faintest idea about labor law, cooperatives, finance, and so on. So we decided that this had to change, that when Solidarity or free trade unions exist once more, our people will already be trained, that they'll be prepared.

In Szumiejko's opinion, the increasingly widespread view that the move-
ment must decentralize does not undermine the position of the ICC.

We might lose our influence if the movement that we lead stops
being a trade union. On the other hand, there's absolutely no need to
bring all independent activity under our wing. In any case, we don't
even try to do so, and that's why I don't take seriously the arguments
about how, by our very existence, we restrict other people's initiative.
If competitors are emerging (in a positive sense, since everyone who
fights the bolsheviks is our ally), all the better! For example, I've
heard that Stefan Bratkowski is reviving the "Experience and the Future" discussion group; why should we try to prevent this? Any such
suggestion is just nonsense! It's obvious that we support it. This
is the kind of thing we've been counting on since the beginning of
the "war."

Or take the Helsinki Committee, which is clearly an agency of the
ICC. Its first report on human rights violations in Poland, which was
sent to the Madrid conference, was all but signed by us. But even
those underground who had close ties to the Committee (people who
gave it money and equipment) didn't think that we ought to take it
over. At a certain point the Committee began to publish its own material and collect its own funds; in other words, it emancipated itself.
The same thing happened with the National Council for Culture (and
the Council for Education); they already have their own sources of finance and channels to the West. It's easier for these groups, because
academics and other intellectuals travel abroad a lot and have many
acquaintances there whom they've known for a long time.

We need to exercise only the most general supervision—to know
what kind of statute these various bodies have, how they distribute
their funds, and so on. Of course, if they start to do something we
disapprove of, we tell them we no longer wish to be associated with
their activities, and inform our people abroad. But if, for example,
they get money from the French Academy of Sciences instead of the
International Confederation of Free Trade Unions (as was recently the
case with one group), that's their business. During the time of legal
Solidarity also we gave priority to the creation of various councils,
commissions, and associations.

BUJAK II.15

Of course we support autonomous initiatives. For example: we organized the Social Committee for Scholarship, which provides better grants than the government does (eventually it'll be able to provide scholarships abroad as well). Unfortunately, despite the fact that the availability of these grants has been widely announced, so far we've received only a dozen or so applications—and we're in a position to provide tens or even hundreds. I suppose it's possible that the idea that there are hundreds of scholars dying to do genuinely independent research is just a myth. But we hope that after we've awarded the first few grants and published the work funded by them, the number of applications will increase. In any event, the Committee is prepared for this.

In our region there are many groups of varying degrees of independence—from structures associated with the Regional Executive Committee to groups that are entirely autonomous. The standard of their activity is clearly improving, they're becoming more professional—in the positive sense of the word. People who eighteen months ago didn't have the faintest idea how, for example, to obtain supplies of paper for their publication are now ready to organize all the printing for a new factory or interfactory group. They've simply learned how to divide up the work, who has to do what, and where to find supplies. The existing editorial groups have created a regular labor market for those who know how to write or print. I know, for example, that the CDN publishing house pays writers a fee amounting to twenty percent of gross sales. With 10,000 copies of a book that sells for 400 złoties, this means a fee of 800,000. This shows that we've become professional.

The many months spent on organizational work have had positive results. As I've already mentioned, the demonstrations on May 1, 1983, showed that we'd achieved a fair degree of efficiency.

HALL I.13

In Alexander Hall's opinion, during the spring of 1983 the only time the underground truly showed its capabilities was on May 1.

As far as the call for independent May Day demonstrations was concerned, I was completely in favor. We needed to show how many supporters we had before the Pope's visit. On the other hand, at this crucial time we failed to take advantage of the possibility for open activity. The joint campaign involving Solidarity and the former autonomous and branch trade unions was only just getting under way. And the idea of setting up the so-called anti-PRON, a body that would have a genuine social mandate, before the arrival of the Pope never got off the ground at all.

SZUMIEJKO I.17

The underground awaited the Pope's visit with great tension. It was hoped that this pilgrimage of the head of the Catholic Church would strengthen the population spiritually, but there were also fears that people were putting all their hopes in heaven and expecting a miracle.

We realized how important the situation was and we didn't want to anticipate the course of events. In our open letter to John Paul II we wrote that we were praying for him and awaiting his arrival. This wasn't a diplomatic gesture but a sign of genuine happiness. In any case, we're not exactly diplomats. Next to him we're a bunch of noisy lightweights.

I knew that the Pope's visit would yield enormous benefits. The sight of his homeland would only confirm his political and religious line, and he'd have a number of strong things to tell our Episcopate. In my view, any fears that the authorities would succeed in intimidating people into not displaying their political feelings during the visit were completely unfounded. Obviously, if it had been the Papal Nuncio, Luigi Poggi, who'd been coming to Poland, I'd have been very much afraid; although Poggi has had the Polish situation explained to him many times, he still doesn't understand a thing. But Karol Wojtyła?! It was inconceivable that he could allow himself to be taken in by Jaruzelski or let the people down. You can't imagine the crowds on the Błonie Fields in Kraków. I was there and could see everything from above, from the embankment. I saw two million people raise their hands in the V sign. It was the most unbelievable sight—a sea of black heads suddenly giving way to a wave of white fists.

BUJAK II.16

Unfortunately, my people wouldn't let me go to see the Pope. They thought the crowds would be crawling with Security agents. I was pissed off because, after all, the average Security man can't remember every "suspicious" face he's supposed to be looking for. Anyway, the decisive argument was that if I got caught, everyone would say how stupid I'd been, how could I have pulled such a number on the Pope?

It was clear to us that the underground shouldn't interfere with the pilgrimage or we'd find ourselves under fire from the Church, which would claim that we were trying to score points, to capitalize on the occasion. In avoiding accusations of this kind, we fell from the frying pan into the fire. People were angry that we seemed to keep ourselves apart from everything that went on during the visit, from the flags, the banners, the parades. I guess they were right, because the people demonstrated their attitude toward Solidarity in front of the Pope.

LIS II.19

In June 1983 the population showed its true face. Not the one you see on the television screen, but its authentic face. The crowds cheering the Pope, the Solidarity slogans, the helplessness of the Security Service— all this was caught by the foreign correspondents. On the other hand, Poles were able to hear broadcasts of the Holy Father's sermons only on Polish-language Western radio stations (largely Radio Free Europe and the Voice of America). The fact that the regime's first television channel didn't broadcast complete reports of the Pope's second pilgrimage gave the authorities the worst possible testimonial. In Lis's view, the Church could have adopted a stronger position on this issue.

Apart from this, the fact that John Paul's meeting with Lech Wałęsa was organized by the Security Service speaks volumes. It's obvious that the regime decided it was going to take all the credit for the Pope's visit. The Holy Father's second conversation with Jaruzelski (in Wawel Castle) was intended to counterbalance somehow his earlier meeting with Wałęsa. It was also supposed to create the impression of idyllic relations between the Communist dictatorship and the Church. We don't know what went on at this meeting. If it had yielded some benefits to society, then of course it would have been worth it.

But more than six months have gone by since the Pope's visit and nothing has changed! I don't think the Church can ignore this and proceed as though it were business as usual.

HALL I.14

I myself hoped for two things from the pilgrimage. First, I hoped that it would incline the authorities to undertake a significant, perceptible liberalization, to proclaim an amnesty, and to create a certain space for independent activity (of course, not on the same scale as Solidarity). This hope was not fulfilled, but my second one was. This was that the nation would come together in truth, in a genuine collective experience. John Paul's calls to action, proclaimed in profound words, will continue to bear fruit for a long time to come. The Pope also dispelled all illusions about a speedy resolution of our problems and appealed for people to work with the conditions that exist.

BUJAK II.17

Although everyone claimed to realize that the pilgrimage wouldn't yield any direct results, everyone was expecting them. This lasted for months after the visit, and that's why our region hit its lowest point in terms of organization. During the summer of 1983 we just limped along, as people dropped out of underground work for a time. Nevertheless, we survived. Moreover, in the longer term it turned out that the Pope's visit had actually helped. People soon returned to clandestine activity, and emotions subsided.

BORUSEWICZ III.6

The atmosphere encouraged people's expectations of some kind of concessions. But for the regime to have been trusted by the population, it would have had at least to release the political prisoners. To deprive people of freedom for their convictions is evidence of the authorities' lawlessness, it's a violation of morality that makes any agreement impossible. The Church even announced that an amnesty would be proclaimed, and if the regime had taken advantage of people's willingness to compromise, it could have solved once and for all the whole problem of the underground and mass resistance. As it was, it soon became clear what they were up to. The amnesty turned out to be a trick, and martial law legislation was retained under another name.

At the same time, a conflict arose between the authorities and the Church. Up to this point, the authorities had been spinning the Episcopate a line about how any moment now the army would return to barracks, Jaruzelski would shed his uniform, and all political prisoners would be freed—but in stages, because you couldn't do everything all at once. And what happened? Instead of a human face, the authorities kept the same face, the same red face, as before. Following a visit by the Pope's envoy, Father Dziwisz, the Church finally reacted. The Episcopate refused to sign the agreement on the Church's legal status, and a month later the press began in all out attack.

What was crucial about the lifting of martial law on July 22, 1983, was the way it was perceived by the population. If this farce had been taken for the real thing, we'd have found ourselves in a much more difficult situation. In fact, this measure, which was intended to elicit universal applause, didn't fool anyone.

The authorities hoped to use the amnesty in their political game with the West and their own population. They were aiming for a reduction in external economic restrictions and the elimination of internal resistance. So, it was by no means a humanitarian gesture deriving from Poland's tradition of tolerance (as Urban and Jaruzelski maintained), but rather an example of cynical manipulation. It's clear that, from the authorities' point of view, the most important part of the operation was the amnesty for those who abandoned the underground and turned themselves in to the police. What's more, the minister of justice actually proposed an exchange: if all underground activists turned themselves in, the authorities would release all political prisoners. But no one from the underground leadership paid any attention to this, although we reckoned that some people would take advantage of the regime's offer, simply because they wanted to go home. The Security Service was held responsible for the results of the amnesty, so what did they do? They arrested a whole bunch of people against whom they'd already collected some incriminating information and announced that these people had turned themselves in. A typical case was that of two people from Gdańsk, Piotr Kapczyński and Krzysztof Wyszkowski (former secretary to the editorial board of *Tygodnik Solidarność*). They were picked up on July 22 in some Kashubian village, and the next day they heard on the radio that they'd turned themselves in voluntarily. The same thing probably happened all over the country.

LIS II.20

The regime claimed that eleven hundred people had taken advantage of its noble-minded gesture. But regardless of the song that Urban sang for the television cameras, Bogdan Lis considers the real number of people who turned themselves in to be no more than one-tenth the official figure.

Yes, of course, there were some activists who really did turn themselves in—usually for family reasons or because they couldn't take it any more. Others had already been identified or even seized by the Security Service (in one of the interviews I gave to the underground press, I actually thanked the authorities for having protected our people). The funniest incident was described in *Tygodnik Mazowsze*, though: this fellow was supposed to go abroad on business, but he postponed his trip for a couple of days for family reasons; while he was still in Warsaw, he opened *Trybuna Ludu* and read that he'd apparently turned himself in. Of course, the Party paper didn't publish a correction.

HALL I.15

You shouldn't attribute the same significance to all the cases of those who turned themselves in. People who appeared on television shouldn't be treated the same as those who simply wanted to return home to their families without at the same time abandoning independent activity. In my opinion, you can't apply rigid moral criteria to these situations. One thing seems clear—the whole operation was designed to divide society and to destroy, or at least to undermine, the underground leadership. However, like all the regime's thinly disguised maneuvers, it yielded few results. Actually, people were much more critical of those who turned themselves in earlier on—and this had been going on since the autumn of 1982—than they were after the amnesty. The authorities had made various advances to the underground leadership even earlier.

BUJAK I.22

The first of these advances was made by Rakowski at the beginning of 1982. It was formulated in a fairly devious way: Bujak was to make it seem like it was he who had asked for the meeting, and the deputy premier would graciously agree.

Rakowski is incredibly vain, and a coup like this would have made him look very important: here's someone who's managed to talk with an underground leader. Apart from this, he'd have acquired an important propaganda argument: of course we talked, but the "extremists" refused to compromise. I received another proposal from General Kiszczak, who even issued a guarantee of safe conduct to the effect that they wouldn't arrest me between May 1 and May 3, 1982, if I kept quiet and did nothing. This was nothing but a crudely cunning move. Later he tried to sound me out a few more times. Among other things, he summoned Jan Józef Szczepański, the president of the Polish Writers' Union, to his office. Before Szczepański arrived, Kiszczak had all the papers cleared off his desk, covered it with a tablecloth (the desk, damn it!), and had supper served. There was something farcical about the whole show: a police general talking to a distinguished writer about conditions for the revival of the Writers' Union. The conversation was dragging along, and suddenly Kiszczak started on about the underground: Bujak didn't need to stay in hiding, since he hadn't really committed any political errors, and anyway the Ministry of Internal Affairs knew where he was and had taped and filmed him living underground. So, he really ought to give himself up, and he would appreciate it if Jan Józef would pass the message along. Szczepański said of course, he'd be only too happy to, but the minister would have to give him Bujak's address, ha, ha!

Kiszczak's last offer came via Andrzej Wielowieyski. I replied in writing (Wielowieyski was to read Kiszczak the letter) that, of course, I welcomed this interesting initiative, but on a number of conditions: the safe-conduct letter would have to be read out on television, the proposal that I turn myself in should be extended to include the entire underground, all political prisoners and internees had to be released, and martial law had to be lifted! After this, I didn't get any more proposals.

SZUMIEJKO I.18

The authorities did not come back to the subject until the Sejm passed the amnesty law. Then ICC itself never really discussed the possibility of its members turning themselves in. Someone asked whether anyone thought it a good idea. No one did, so there was nothing to discuss; they were going to carry on as before.

Not everyone, however, maintained his initial resolve. The regime unexpectedly scored a spectacular coup. In the middle of summer, 1983, the media announced with great satisfaction that Władysław Hardek, who represented Małopolska on the Interim Coordinating Commission, had turned himself in to the authorities. Of all the accounts of this event, Szumiejko says, most convincing is the one that Hardek himself subsequently sent the underground leadership.

They caught him in Piła and then for five days transported him by helicopter between Security headquarters in Kraków and the Rakowiecka Prison in Warsaw. High-level officials from the Ministry of Internal Affairs talked to him, and he was treated very well. They didn't ask any detailed questions; they didn't need to since they supposedly had everything worked out. They fed Hardek one or two facts from which he concluded they did indeed know a great deal. In reality they possessed mostly only unimportant details. Anyway, they kind of whispered in Hardek's ear that they had really wanted to go all the way with the amnesty but Moscow wouldn't allow it, and that if only they could talk with the underground, maybe they could work something out together.

They too were Poles, full of good will, they claimed. And Hardek bought the whole spiel. He gave a television interview and even agreed to act as a go-between for the ICC and the Ministry of Internal Affairs!

You have to admit it, they played him along very cleverly. Hardek always said he wouldn't be able to stand it in prison. I think we underestimated this. He was incredibly edgy. When he slept, he'd toss and turn the whole time. Once we were spending the night at the same place, and I suddenly heard Władek call out, "Let me go, you son of a bitch!" I gave him a shake and said, "It's OK, Władek, they've gone." He practically jumped out of bed and asked, "What's going on? They were really here?" His dream and reality were all mixed up.

LIS II.21

The Hardek affair was a moral disaster for Solidarity. His "puppet-show" appearance on television has to be unambiguously condemned. Later, in fact, he tried to explain his motives to us. He'd simply wanted to believe what they told him. And in the end, he came to believe that underground activity was pointless and that he had a duty to save all those who were still active.

It was a real waste; we'd worked well together. He's gone back to work at the Lenin Steelworks, but no one will talk to him. Apparently, he's started drinking.

BUJAK II.18

The psychological losses that the union suffered through Hardek are simply incalculable. If a national leader breaks down, what is a rank-and-file leaflet distributor, for example, supposed to do? Squeal on everyone, I suppose! Of course, a few people really did turn themselves in, and in some cases this hindered underground activity, but the only case that achieved national prominence was Hardek's performance. The others were soon forgotten.

BORUSEWICZ III.7

It seems to be the rule that verbal radicalism generally doesn't go together with consistency in action, strong character, or willingness to sacrifice oneself. In any case, radicalism isn't a virtue in itself; it's just a means to a goal.

On the surface, Hardek was the most hardline member of the ICC. It was as a radical that he got to the top, just like that guy from Silesia who got onto the Solidarity National Commission because of

215

the fuss he made about the price of cigarettes. You remember how he criticized the price increases and government policies in general at the Congress? He's long since left the country. Nowadays, the only thing you hear about many of these radicals is that they're sitting in the West—particularly those who used to shout the loudest that the Party was on its last legs, that the authorities didn't stand a chance and couldn't do anything to us!

Any activist at the level that Hardek had achieved who gets caught ought to go to jail like a man. He mustn't think that after turning himself in he can dive into the underground and take up his activity as though nothing had happened. Clandestine work depends on people's credibility. A man lives in a particular place, he has contacts, and he has to safeguard his reputation. If he turns himself in in this way, he loses face. Who's going to trust him again after this? In general, the first iron rule is that you never engage in political negotiations after you've been caught; the second iron rule is that you never negotiate with the police about anything.

SZUMIEJKO I.19

Even before July 22, 1983, the ICC received information to the effect that the lifting of martial law would not lead to any significant changes.

That's why we issued a statement saying the amnesty wasn't an act of generosity but an obligation on the part of the regime, because it was a scandal that so many people were behind bars. The Ministry of Internal Affairs was not only pressing for a bargain—the freeing of political prisoners in exchange for the ICC turning itself in—but even suggested talks about an independent trade union (a second union in the factories). Hardek later learned firsthand what it means to conduct political negotiations with policemen.

Thus, although the situation remained difficult (we weren't making any progress), not everyone lost energy. Bogdan Lis, for example, aided by Borusewicz, argued strongly that this was the best possible time for a general strike. He argued a possible scenario that had the demonstrations on August 31 sending the commies running for refuge in the cellars—which we would be coming out of. During our discussion, we were evenly divided on the subject: two in favor of a strike, two against, and two abstentions (it's not hard to guess that Bujak was one of the two who were undecided). Then we began to speculate that perhaps it was our destiny to bring about a general strike and to lose it. After all, what did it mean to lose a strike? If they caught only the factory leaders and the ICC, it wouldn't be a disaster, because the underground structures and the technical base would still be there. The ICC would have lost but not the underground. Apart from that, in crushing the strike by force, the regime would once again find itself opposed by the entire population and would have to abandon its strategy of quietly buying off the silent majority. In other words, we'd have entered a new stage. To hell with it—we're going to be relegated to the sidelines anyway. But at least we would put an end to this wretched stalemate.

But what about Wałęsa? We felt that the ICC couldn't manage on its own, but Lech might get sick and not come to work. . . . We decided, then, to go ahead with the strike if Lech would climb aboard and shout "Strike" along with the rest of us. Borusewicz felt we'll haul Wałęsa in, we just had to make sure he won't jump ship. The problem was, how could we tell Lech about our plans? I think he must have known, because he avoided a meeting at all costs. He wrote to me saying that we wouldn't meet until October 31 (that is, after the first deadline for underground activists to turn themselves in), because "the situation will have changed completely by then." After getting this response, I had the feeling that nothing would come of the strike. Just in case, however, I suggested that each of us on the ICC cut our little finger and write a promise in blood: if the strike went ahead, all of us would join in—one would go to the shipyard, another to Ursus, the others wherever they were needed; and then no one would be able to claim he couldn't make it because the streetcar was late, or the ZOMO had mounted a blockade, or there was an eclipse of the sun in Warsaw.

Gradually, however, the idea of the general strike died away. I comforted Bogdan with the thought that the idea would catch fire again in the spring of 1984. After all, I said, every "spring will be ours." Somehow we'd get through the next few months. In the end, we could always call a general strike. Ha, ha, ha!

LIS II.22

The swing in public morale, dangerously low after the frustrations brought about by July 22, 1983, moved in the opposite direction in the

fall of that year. Wałęsa received the Nobel Peace Prize! The impor-
tance of this fact cannot be overestimated, says Lis.

It was, and is, significant not only for Solidarity, or Poland as a whole, but also for all the independent movements in countries governed by a Communist dictatorship. Of course, Wałęsa's prize isn't going to eliminate international conflict, and the Afghans, for example, aren't going to abandon armed struggle in favor of passive resistance, because they'd simply be signing their own death sentence. On the other hand, everywhere there's a possibility of introducing peaceful methods, Solidarity will become a model now that its political line has received the seal of approval in the form of the Nobel Prize.

On the national level, the prize confirmed that Wałęsa still exerted a substantial influence on the situation in Poland, on the population. That's why the attempt to compromise him can only be attributed to extreme political stupidity. Actually, the Communists have stopped attacking Wałęsa himself. It looks as though they've finally realized that it doesn't make sense.

BORUSEWICZ III.8

The decision of the Norwegian parliament strengthened the tendency in our movement which, in my opinion, had gone from one mistake to another. The Nobel Prize helped turn this tendency into dogma, particularly for the activists in Warsaw. Currently, even the majority of underground activists accept the line that we won't use force or even the threat of force.

Wałęsa has lived up to my expectations only in part. I hoped that he'd manage to place the issue of Solidarity squarely in the international arena—and in this respect he's done quite a good job. Most of all, however, I hoped that he'd pull together all the threads of anti-regime activity, particularly in relation to information (at one time, the Kurońs played this role). In my opinion, there's too little concrete information about who's in prison and what for and what prison conditions are like. After all, Wałęsa is able to transmit this kind of information to the West. Journalists aren't particularly interested in this, so you have to combine it with other things—a little bit of gossip, a few statistics about the level of repression. We can't do this because we don't have easy access to the West, but it's very important that somebody should. In the first place, the people who are behind bars play an important symbolic role; second, they and their families need more help than they're currently receiving; third, it's a way of compromising a regime that claims everything is in order, that normalization is proceeding.

Unfortunately, Wałęsa isn't fulfilling this function.

SZUMIEJKO I.20

Underground activists were divided in their assessment of the significance of the prize and the role of the Nobel laureate himself. Only a few days after the prize had been awarded, Szumiejko stated that the underground would reap little benefit in the international political arena.

The West has no serious interest in the Polish question. It's inconvenient to declare publicly that the Nobel Prize was awarded to the whole Polish nation. Such statements commit people to supporting the Poles, so, instead, they say, "Here we have a hero, Wałęsa; let's name a street or square after him."

When I say "the West," I don't mean the trade unions or the ordinary people. For their solidarity and support we're enormously grateful. I'm talking about all those politicians. They know perfectly well that "the cold wind comes from the East" and that we constitute the first barrier. But they won't do anything more than send us some aspirin, shoes, and warm underwear. We Poles aren't interested in acquiring still warmer clothing; we simply want it to stop freezing.

As far as the ICC was concerned, at our second meeting with Lech we greeted him with respect and courtesy. Of course, we had some cognac in honor of the prize-winner and a cake with one candle (if he gets a second prize, we'll get him a cake with two). After the formalities and the congratulations, however, we began to work on Lech. We said he'd evaluated the situation correctly, that now that he had the prize he could begin to go all out, and that everything was working against the regime. He just had to be careful that the regime didn't start praising him!

You could see that Lech was determined to take a stronger stand on political prisoners and so on. Unfortunately, I could also see the other side of the coin—the growing influence over him of certain people around him. Eight months before, these people had already suggested that the ICC suspend its activity; because its prestige was bound to decline they wanted to preserve underground Solidarity's myth intact. This was the same line of thinking that had been represented during the legal Solidarity period by advisers to the National Commission. As usual, they analyze the Polish question in a global context—the configuration of forces within the Kremlin, the new military divisions on the banks of the Dnieper, the situation in Lebanon, and the latest natural disaster in Arkansas. And somehow it then turns out from that context that Poland will be saved if the underground abandons all activity, that it has to abandon its activity because it's clear that Poland . . . These people have become infected with backstage politics and they're incapable of changing. They really are concerned about Poland. Whether they're sitting down drinking tea (or something stronger), or fishing—they're always thinking about Poland!

So, anyway, Lech spoke about the hopes he had of the ICC—this "symbol of resistance"—without the same degree of enthusiasm as during our first meeting. Then he proposed that we allow him to appear at the Gdańsk Monument on December 16, 1983, to read out the ICC program and a statement saying that, from now on, it was he who was going to continue activity. So then I told him that we, too, had a proposal: we should appear with his program and declare that it was us who would continue further activity. He replied, "Brother, don't pull the trigger on me."

After a time, he came back to the subject in a different way. He suggested that if (God forbid!) two of us were arrested, the next two should write something like the last will and testament of the ICC. And then he started going on about how the work had to continue, how people can't stand a vacuum. This was the first time I'd come across such a shrewd fox. He didn't say we couldn't work together because we were heading up a blind alley and he, Wałęsa, wanted to become immortal. No. He praised us excessively, and only from time to time mentioned that he'd give money for our souls. A real diplomat . . .

What we feared most of all were disputes over the program, because, on the one hand, our council of experts was putting the finishing touches to its proposals and, on the other, Wałęsa announced that he'd appear at the Monument with proposals of his own. We couldn't allow a situation to arise in which the two versions differed markedly from each other, but it soon turned out that we had nothing to fear, because neither Lech nor we were going to come out with a program. Lech, as you'll remember, got the flu, and we just gave up on our program. So, we were able to carry on quietly working.

NOTE

1. Sulejówek was Piłsudski's country estate from which he launched his coup of May 1926.

Self-examination. The balance of profit and loss. There are no victories without victims. Views of the future. When to leave and how to return. "This is our last chance."

LIS II.23

The balance of underground Solidarity's disasters and successes cannot be reduced imply to an assessment of particular actions: successful or unsuccessful demonstrations, strikes, and protests. For this reason, Bogdan Lis tries rather to answer the question of whether the union has retained the people's trust that it had before December 13, 1981.

As a whole, we didn't allow ourselves to be corrupted, and that's the most important thing. Regardless of what you think about the activity of Wałęsa or the ICC, Solidarity has remained true to itself; it has remained a trade union, and at the same time a pluralistic social movement. That's how the movement was shaped by its members during the years 1980–1981. Of course, the regime makes it difficult for us to fulfill our trade union functions, but we haven't given up; we still get involved in such issues as collective bargaining and work safety. We can't possibly allow the workers to be represented in such important areas by tiny groups of new trade unionists.

The authorities haven't managed to buy off any of those whose names mean something to society. The fact that the seven from the

National Commission—Gwiazda, Jaworski, Jurczyk, Modzelewski, Pałka, Rozpłochowski, and Rulewski—as well as the four from KOR—Kuroń, Michnik, Romaszewski, and Wujec—stayed behind bars for so long without trial and wouldn't agree to be exiled has increased Solidarity's moral authority. The fact that during his nearly year-long internment and total isolation Wałęsa didn't succumb to any pressure also testifies to our strength. The fact that, since the beginning of martial law, society has stubbornly struggled on behalf of those people who have led the movement has allowed us all to keep face. Despite the raids, arrests, and repression, there's no shortage of volunteers ready to bear witness to the truth under their own name. As far as real disasters are concerned, I think one of the greatest has been the emigration of some activists, largely from Upper Silesia. Another blow was Władysław Hardek's appearance on television. We've also lost a few rounds when the Security Service managed to destroy individual underground structures. Finally, our own erroneous political decisions have also had a negative impact on the overall balance.

It's hard to say to what extent we're closer to our goal with respect to December 1981. Our goals are no longer the same as they were during the first strikes against the imposition of martial law. Solidarity will never be the same as before the "war," and not because the authorities will forbid it. It's simply that it would be a mistake to create a movement with an identical political, and perhaps, organizational framework. A trade union isn't enough, because the regime can always dissolve it whenever it likes. What we need are structural changes in the system, and this is what we have to struggle for. Only with the passage of time will we be able to say whether we're farther from or closer to our goal. Since we've caught up in the center of events, we're not able to analyze objectively what's going on, to distinguish clearly between profits and losses.

BUJAK II.19

On the negative side I'd include, first and foremost, the delegalization of Solidarity. Our gains, on the other hand, can be seen on two levels: national and regional. We've managed to preserve our organizational continuity as a trade union despite proposals to transform ourselves into a political party or a movement for national liberation. Of course, a lot of people have given up, but the union and its leadership still exist. This is an undoubted achievement of the ICC.

As you can tell, I'm fairly satisfied with my region, although I can take very little of the credit for its organizational efficiency. Zbigniew Janas, for example, had real problems coping at the beginning, but now he is way ahead of me on many issues. I really envy his achievements in aiding the victims of repression and in putting together the Network of Leading Enterprises.

On a more personal level, I regret that I haven't written very much. Although I think I have something to say, I haven't managed to get it onto paper. The greatest gain of my two years in the underground, though, is the enormous number of experiences I've been through, the knowledge I've acquired, and the people I've met. No one will ever be able to take this away from me.

JEDYNAK. I.2

I gave an interview to the underground press. In it I said that it would be two years before the impact of a representative of Upper Silesia joining the ICC could truly be seen. We're two years behind in relation to Warsaw, Gdańsk, Wrocław, and Kraków, but we're clearly catching up fast. At the beginning, we didn't have any safe apartments—now we have more than enough; in terms of printing, we were limping along—now we're publishing nearly thirty titles; we were stagnating—now we have an estimated ten thousand activists in the region.

We've revived such traditional activities as plastering the towns with posters at night, painting slogans on walls, and conducting masses on the sixteenth of every month (to commemorate the massacre of the Wujek miners). In the near future, Radio Solidarity will be starting up in Katowice. We're also planning to start our own publishing house, since people are so keen to read the underground press—unlike the time of legal Solidarity, when they generally hoarded it away. We're continuing with the boycott of the official unions and we're broadening the scope of our educational program. We still have a long way to go in terms of reviving the factory commissions and organizing the payment of union dues, but the fact that people have stopped being frightened gives us reason to be optimistic.

In my opinion, our basic achievements are the continuing social resistance, oriented on the long term, and the absolutely unprecedented press and publishing activity. Even the underground press of 1939–1947 can't be compared with what we have today.

As far as losses are concerned, I'd point only to a single fundamental one: we didn't manage to win out, that is didn't manage to prevent the authorities' unceremonious assault on society.

The most probable scenario for the future is that the current situation will continue, with a slight tendency for morale to decline. In other words, resistance will decline, but the authorities will become increasingly isolated. Eventually, people will become completely indifferent to all public issues.

What more should the underground be doing? Above all, it ought to use the underground press to arouse the will to fight. That's all. It's best not to delude oneself or the population in general that it's possible to beat this regime without victims. People keep repeating the same refrain: we all want to win but nobody wants to die. This is absolutely understandable, but this approach isn't going to change anything. The only thing to do is wait—perhaps in ten years, perhaps in fifteen . . .

We're on a downward slope. We have to make society aware of this. I've talked with many people who don't understand the situation at all. Some guy says what he likes about the underground or where the underground has made mistakes, but he doesn't understand that in this struggle sacrifices are needed—including the highest sacrifice of all. Otherwise there's no way to force the authorities to make positive changes, because they have staked everything on the use of brute force. After two years of this, I don't have any illusions.

SZUMIEJKO I.21

Solidarity has shown the world great things. It's impossible to overestimate the innovative nature of Solidarity as both a movement and a trade union. Of course, its innovativeness derives from the fact that it emerged within a totalitarian system; in a democratic system many of the functions that Solidarity took upon itself are fulfilled by numerous organizations, clubs, and other institutions. But our idea deserves deeper consideration also because it may in the future have enormous significance for the Western (and not only the Western) labor movement. To date, however, we haven't worked out a "theory" of our movement; all we have to sell is the raw material.

On the other hand, there are enormous practical achievements. We haven't corrupted the ideals of August and of Solidarity. Quite the opposite: we've strengthened them. It's a fact that the regime has helped us a bit in this, because without martial law it's possible that solidarity between people would have been nothing more than a myth. Never before have we helped one another on such a scale; never have we defended our dignity to such an extent (for example, by opposing the loyalty declarations). An enormous number of activists have emerged. In this sense we're organizationally stronger than we were before December 1981. Other People's Democracies—the Czechs or Hungarians—will take years, God willing, to achieve this level of independent organization, and the Bulgarians probably never will. It doesn't matter that we don't yet have any clear-cut results, that the stalemate continues; given our potential, we don't need to worry about what's going to happen a few years from now.

What, if anything, has the ICC contributed to all this? Some people are going to be enraged, but I think that, despite the mistakes it has made—its contribution has been enormous. Of course, we haven't regained what we had before December 1981, but who said we had to do it in such a short time? The most important thing is that it's still within our grasp.

BUJAK II.20

Bujak has two possible versions of future developments: optimistic and pessimistic. According to the first version, in the fall of 1984 activists will be instructed to establish groups to rebuild Solidarity at the factory level.

If the thing takes off, founding committees, welfare and labor-protection commissions, and so on will be formed in the enterprises in 1985. Again we'll be in a situation where any day may see the beginnings of a mass movement; given the atomization of the authorities, this movement may acquire the same strike force as Solidarity did in 1980. Do I expect this to happen?

In my pessimistic version, I spend the next five years in the cooler. But I'll serve time and come out as a member of Solidarity, since I'm not going to change my opinions.

Nevertheless, I don't spend too much time worrying about the future. My life goes in stages, and only when I near the end of one stage do I start planning the next. This allows me to keep in shape and makes my work easier. That's why, for the time being, I see 1985 as a certain end-point. I'd like to work with others to put a few more ideas into practice. One of these involves the creation in the West of a Solidarity fund (with a little effort it should be possible to collect ten million dollars). Another is a Solidarity award that would go to an organization or individual who has aided victims of totalitarian regimes. This would enable us to repay our moral debt for the assistance we've received from all over the world. Finally, I'd like to see the publication of a Solidarity encyclopedia. Work on this is already at a fairly advanced stage, and we're planning seventy volumes.

JEDYNAK I.3

I'm a trade unionist, not a politician, so it's hard for me to talk about the future. In any event, if I didn't believe change were possible, I simply wouldn't be active. I admit that I used to be more optimistic because I thought martial law and its after-effects were going to be temporary. Now, I know that they're going to be with us for some time. How long? Earlier I said that in two years my region will be as well organized as the others, so I'm assuming a period of at least two years.

Our methods of struggle against the regime were different two years ago from what they are now. Even Lech's ideas have changed (he's thinking of Christian trade unions or something). We have to adapt our efforts to our real possibilities because we won't get anywhere by force. Nevertheless, I don't agree with the KOR approach, which aims to reform the system. Unless the system is changed, we'll achieve nothing worthwhile. I pointed out that I'm not a politician, but I realize that my work is essentially political, even if I don't call it such. During the period of legal Solidarity we acted as a trade union, but we had a profound impact on politics (it could hardly be otherwise in the case of a movement that brought together fifty percent of the adult population).

As long as we have social support, we can't allow the authorities to smash us to pieces. History teaches us that we have to leave traces behind; you can't get off the train halfway to your destination. It may be years before our dreams are realized. If we don't manage it, others will.

LIS II.24

Where we find ourselves at the moment is one thing; what we're planning for the future—another. Of course, we take account of various possible future developments. We are even considering the possibility of branch unions, joined together in a federation, which would fulfill much the same role as the National Commission in legal Solidarity (and this would be in accordance with existing law). We're also analyzing the possibility of a complete change in the law on trade unions, and probably this is what we should aim for above all else. We have a certain minimum program, but for tactical reasons, we don't want to announce it right now.

How might the situation develop in the near future? Well, Poland's situation is closely bound up with the international situation. No radical changes in East–West relations are possible until 1985, after the presidential elections in the United States. If Reagan is reelected, the Soviets won't be able to stand another four years of technological competition, sanctions, boycotts, and the clever manipulation of the Chinese threat. They will have to come to some agreement.

We have to be prepared for this possibility; in other words, Polish society must be organized and strong. We can't abandon the formation of factory structures, we can't abandon demonstrations or even, in favorable conditions, strikes. If the regime again increases the cost of living, we mustn't keep people on a leash, telling them to sit quiet. Negotiations toward détente work in our favor (no cold war is going to prevent a massacre on the Vistula). If it came to a dialogue between the superpowers, we'd have a greater chance of solving our own internal problems. We have a right to demand from the world that which is our due.

Obviously, I'm taking into account the fact that any possible success on our part is a matter for the distant future, even future generations, but, subconsciously, I don't want to believe it. Every one would like to outlive this regime.

HALL 1.16

The more or less hazy future is one thing, and the here and now, which demands an instant reaction, is another. In this light, Alexander Hall's resignation from the Gdańsk Regional Committee (in January 1984) should be viewed as an individual choice.

I don't regret it. The period after December 1981 taught me a great deal, but I'd have liked my departure from the Regional Committee to have taken place in different circumstances. Of course, I could have stayed to the end, without agreeing with the decisions made, but it's a difficult and ambiguous situation when you find yourself in the role of an internal opposition and have to put your name to majority decisions. For example, I had to put my name to the appeal for the last (1983) demonstrations, even though I thought it was a serious mistake.

I realized that there would have to be a parting of the ways (with all respect to my colleagues' position) much earlier, in July 1983. That's when we were discussing the issue of a general strike that, in my opinion, was completely unrealistic. I wouldn't like to limit our differences of opinion to the strike issue, however, because the problems went deeper than that. It's simply that it seems to me that conspiratorial structures have fulfilled their role and have outlived their usefulness. It's true that there are still some factors that speak in favor of maintaining them, but I foresee the rapid end of the underground in its present form. The role of symbol is fulfilled more or less exclusively by Wałęsa, whereas the ICC's possibilities to direct the struggle are really very limited. Although its voice will certainly count for some time to come, perhaps it would be better to depart the stage in a moment of glory rather than when everyone has forgotten about it. I wouldn't dream of comparing the future fate of the ICC with that of the London government (apart from anything else, the ICC functions within the country), but the borderline between greatness and foolishness is hard to determine. Opposed to Yalta, the London government didn't look ridiculous in 1945, but today?

What, in my opinion, has a future? Maximum decentralization of resistance and the various forms of independent activity, together with the formation of political groups. Not that I'm anticipating in advance the end of conspiratorial activity. It would certainly be impossible to eradicate all the information bulletins, factory groups, committees of social resistance, and so on.

As far as future developments are concerned, it's most probable that there will be several years of relative calm, during which there'll be time to create a genuinely strong society. And then—as one of my colleagues said—the steam engine of history will come round again.

For myself, I see three possibilities: first (and this is the most likely), I'll end up in the can; second, it will be possible to leave the underground honorably; third, there'll be several more years of living in hiding.

SZUMIEJKO I.22

The prospects for resistance. Is there an easy answer to the question of how underground activity might come to an end—the lack of social support, a radical change in the political situation, the destruction of the underground by the Security Service? After all, none of these can be precisely measured. It's also impossible to determine the precise scope of the freedoms we'd need to win in order to come out aboveground.

I've already said that independent structures are our most valuable asset. If we start thinking in terms of what we might gain by abolishing the underground (the release of political prisoners, pluralism, and so on), then we're lost. The only conceivable question is: how much would we lose by this? If you pose the issue in this way, it's clear that any emergence aboveground on the part of the ICC would be a loss (unless it were to take place when the authorities were very weak or when the ICC no longer had any value). We have to state clearly that we mustn't weaken or, God forbid, destroy underground structures. They have to continue existing for another three to five years—let's say five.

But we members of the ICC won't last that long, so we have to do all we can to make sure that we leave everything well sewn up. In January 1984 we amused ourselves during one of our meetings by presenting our "private" forecasts. It turned out that we can last out until the end of 1985—but not because they're going to catch us, because they can't catch everyone. The truth is that they are weak and so are we. The decisive factor in this "contest" is, then, social support. The question is: how long will we continue to be needed?

Apart from the issue of the need for the ICC, each of us has our own sense of normal human endurance. That's why we said another year or two. But another three or five years? I personally won't stand it that long, because I actually don't want to. I don't want to cross the

line that I referred to earlier. I'm not cut out to be a professional oppositionist. I'm afraid that, if I spent many years in the underground,
I'd become a maniac, that I'd succumb to a sense of mission, that I'd
get stuck and that, even if the Soviets lost the war with us, I'd just
keep right on blowing up trains.

FRASYNIUK I.26

I think we have to bear in mind that leaving the underground involves
our return to two different things: public life and family life. I also
think that the second will be the more difficult of the two, since we'll
have changed a great deal and we'll be going back to harassed wives
and children who don't understand what's been going on. The first few
moments together may be joyful, but afterward? Parents, in-laws, and
friends will all try to restrain you: "Don't go out, don't take any risks,
it doesn't make sense. You've seen for yourself: you hid for so long,
and Kowalski or Malinowski did fuck all, didn't lift a finger because
they were afraid, and now they're doing quite well." Others, on the
other hand, will try to make a hero out of you, to put you on a
pedestal.

   As far as the return to public life is concerned, at the moment we
have no idea whether we'll come out of the underground to a free Poland, a half-free Poland, or simply to prison. Maybe we'll have to
build everything all over again from scratch? There's no doubt that
most of us have had enough, at least for the time being. Although, on
the other hand, I can't imagine that we'd put up with inactivity for
very long; after all, it's precisely through struggle that we realize ourselves. Otherwise, we'd never have got involved in conspiracy in the
first place.

BORUSEWICZ I.36

Apparently, Security officials refer to me as a professional revolutionary. Maybe, but it's more the result of specific circumstances, which
forced me into action, than of any desire on my part. I haven't yet
reached the stage at which conspiracy would be the thing I valued
most, an end in itself. It's hard work, an obligation that I've taken
on consciously. If I find that the time has come when I can leave the
underground, I'll do so with great happiness. I'd like, I really would

like, to get involved in some other activity. I've spent so many years going flat out in opposition, I've gotten to know various people (some of whom have changed in the most startling way), and I know how the authorities and the Security Service function. Nothing surprises me any more. My experience could still be useful, but there'll come a point when I have to say: enough! Otherwise—it's just the same as drinking vodka—I could fall into a dangerous habit.

I imagine returning aboveground as something totally normal, like coming back from a long hike. It'll be harder if I land in prison first. But if it were possible (if they released political prisoners and if an independent trade union acquired the right to legal activity), I'd go home and marry the girl who's been waiting a long time for me. I'd like to teach history in a secondary school, to have an influence over young people. That kind of work would give me a lot of satisfaction.

LIS II.25

There's never enough time for me to sit and think clearly about what I'd like to do with my life (certainly not stand in line all day). More than anything else, I'd like to live to see the day the country is free. How do I imagine freedom? I can't say it in just a few words. The world is divided, and middle-sized countries like Poland can't become completely independent of one bloc or the other. The place in which we find ourselves forces us to look for a partner to the East also, but according to different principles than those currently in effect. Our sovereignty and, for example, a multiparty parliamentary system wouldn't exclude good relations with the Russians. Finland is one example.

I envisage personal freedom also within a framework of legal and moral norms, and not as something without limits. When I decide that I've had enough, and I've now done enough in politics, I'd like to find some worthwhile field of work. Maybe I'll write my memoirs. Ha, ha, ha! In any case, I'd take a trip around Poland. There's so much to see. What a beautiful country!

BUJAK II.21

The trade-union underground in Poland is the achievement of society as a whole. Illegal structures are based, in large part, on emotional ties, and that's why the struggle for every individual is so important. I admit I've thought more than once of giving up conspiratorial activity; everyone would like to go home. But I've set a condition: as long as I know there's even one person sitting in a Polish prison for his politics, there's no point in anyone even trying to talk to me about leaving the underground. If this condition is met, then I'll think about it. I'm not going to prejudge the issue, because there's still the question of free trade unions.

Today's underground is the best, the largest, and the most extraordinary in the history of our country. We belong to the last generation that has the opportunity to experience something like this. Nobody after us is going to create underground structures, because why should they? That's why those who haven't committed themselves to underground activity are missing a great deal.

Friends, this really is our last chance![1]

NOTE

1. The Polish police arrested Bogdan Borusewicz in January 1986 and accused him of preparing a coup d'état; he was, however, amnestied later that year. Zbigniew Bujak was arrested in May 1986 but likewise released in late summer 1986. Arrested twice, Władysław Frasyniuk spent three and a half years in prison: following his October 1982 arrest, he was sentenced to six years, but he was amnestied in 1984, only to be rearrested in February 1985, sentenced to four and a half years and released, like the others, as part of the amnesty of summer 1986. Aleksander Hall and Eugeniusz Szumiejko were on the Most Wanted List from 1982 to 1984 but were never apprehended. Bogdan Lis was arrested in June 1984, accused of treason and threatened with the death penalty, but then released in December, only to be rearrested, along with Frasyniuk, in February 1985 and rereleased in late summer 1986. Arrested in June 1985, Tadeusz Jednyak was tried for treason and sedition, but released as part of the amnesty of summer 1986; his case is still pending.

All the men remain active in opposition politics. In 1989, Bujak, Frasyniuk, Hall, and Lis participated in the Round Table negotiations with the government; the talks led to elections which in turn resulted in the establishment, in August 1989, of the first noncommunist government in postwar Eastern Europe. Aleksander Hall became Minister without Portfolio in this government. Lis was elected to the Senate and, together with Borusewicz, is leading the Gdańsk Solidarity organization. Bujak, head of the Mazowsze (Warsaw) Region Solidarity organization, is a likely eventual candidate for mayor of Warsaw. Frasyniuk heads Wrocław Solidarity, while Szumiejko is rumored to belong to a second (still secret, fairly marginal) Wrocław Solidarity network. Tadeusz Jedynak, former chairman of the union in the Upper Silesia (Katowice) Region, was not reelected to this post and now heads the local Solidarity group in the factory at which he works in Zory.

POSTSCRIPT [1]

Perhaps you should begin, Zbyszek, since you probably have the most comments.

BUJAK: I guess I do. What concerns me most of all about the book is the exaggerated emphasis on emotions. A number of important substantive issues are presented in *Konspira* largely in terms of personal games or conflicts rather than in terms of differences of opinion.

Are you trying to say that games and conflicts don't exist in the underground?

BUJAK: Of course they exist, but not on such a large scale. In trying to make the book more interesting, you've dragged in a disproportionate amount of emotion and you've ignored a number of objective truths, including fundamental differences of opinion concerning the reconstruction of Solidarity and its program.

We suspect that you're trying to secure an escape route just in case Konspira *were ever to come under the negative scrutiny of public opinion. Then you'll be able to say, "From the very beginning, I said there was no truth in this sensational scribbling."*

BUJAK: Don't exaggerate. I only want to stress my feeling that there's not enough attention to matters of substance. This is all the more regrettable since, after the initial disputes in the underground leadership, we soon arrived at a consensus, which continues to hold good.

235

Let's agree on the following: that what has materialized here in the form of nearly three hundred pages of manuscript is a reflection of opinions at a particular historical moment.

SZUMIEJKO: I share some of Zbyszek's criticism, but I also want to defend the authors. After all, they didn't always get from us the kind of material needed to present all the nuances.

And were there really so many differences?

SZUMIEJKO: Of course there were some. We realize that you're journalists and that you engage in various tricks of the trade (after all, that's your job), so you should admit it—you didn't want to bore the readers with too many ideas. You took a magnifying glass to only the most striking, sensational elements.

BORUSEWICZ: In my opinion, *Konspira* is a very good journalistic book in the Western style. It reads very well, and because the authors have placed the main emphasis on personal issues, we members of the underground leadership come across like normal, living human beings. On the other hand, the book doesn't present a complete picture of the union in action, with the whole army of people who actually do the work.

SZUMIEJKO: Yes, friends, you've cleverly pieced together our statements while hiding your own opinions.

That's not true. Because of the way the subject is approached, Konspira reflects, to a large extent, our perception of the underground. That's why we don't deny our responsibility for the book as a whole (as we pointed out in the introduction). We're quite prepared for any eventual criticism from readers to be directed exclusively at us.

BORUSEWICZ: As I said, *Konspira* reads very well, but this doesn't alter the fact that the book has a number of shortcomings, because it doesn't portray the people who constitute the real "fabric" of the underground. We leaders are no more than the skeleton. The fact is that in this book you have seven men talking about a number of issues in a way that makes them come off as well as possible.

BUJAK: Or rather, in the way in which the authors set them up. When we were talking, I drank fifty grams of vodka for every side of a tape we recorded. My tongue got looser and looser, and I spouted off quite openly about everything, not thinking about how it would sound. The authors were supposed to go over it all afterward, but . . .

We couldn't do that, Zbyszek, we really couldn't. No journalist could waste such material.

BORUSEWICZ: But you won't deny that you've isolated us too much, that you make virtually no mention of the couriers, distributors, and printers.

In a word, you're reproaching us for not writing a different book. Of course, we could have cooked up fifteen different things, we could have portrayed the underground from the point of view of a printer or courier. Nevertheless, we've produced Konspira *and this is what we'd like you to discuss.*

BUJAK: OK. It's not that these people don't appear in the book at all. It's just that they appear too rarely.

There's a whole chapter devoted to the people of the underground.

BUJAK: That's not enough.

BORUSEWICZ: There's another thing that I like about the book: it destroys the heroic myth.

BUJAK: Perhaps it doesn't so much destroy it as unmask it. Over the last two hundred years there has emerged in this country a myth of superficial heroism ("He joined the uprising, got a few guys together, shot at the other side"). Kozietulski, Piłsudski, Wałęsa, Bujak—it's precisely these people who are examples of easy upward social mobility. All you have to do is jump onto a barrel at the right moment and shout at the top of your lungs.

SZUMIEJKO: It's not so good if the barrel collapses.

BUJAK: The thing is, we don't have any models of heroism based on solid, long-term work. But let's move on. *Konspira* is the first book about the trade-union underground in Poland. For this reason it may well become the main source of information, the sole point of reference for this movement.

BORUSEWICZ: A journalistic work doesn't have to depict and explain everything in a profound and scientific fashion.

BUJAK: Nevertheless, some things must be clearly spelled out.

So, spell them out.

SZUMIEJKO: I'll begin with a declaration of faith. Solidarity was the best trade union in the world. It was and it is. Nevertheless, Bogdan Borusewicz's statements in the first chapter might lead one to think that the Communists did us a favor by declaring "war," because the union would otherwise have fallen apart. It's possible that the very form of the book leads to this interpretation, because some of us didn't talk about some subjects at all. Apart from this, none of us knew what the others had said, so we couldn't voice objections. As a result, it looks as though we all agree with Bogdan.

BUJAK: Some statements portray Solidarity in its pre–December 13 state as an organization evolving from democracy to totalitarianism. In my opinion this view is unjust. Because you've put Borusewicz's lengthy critical statement at the beginning, people might conclude that the totalitarian tendency dominated the union.

And it didn't?

BUJAK: Solidarity wasn't in any danger from this direction. The union was sufficiently strong to cleanse itself, sooner or later, of any dictatorial tendencies. I could cite numerous examples of an opposite tendency. One day, a guy who's clearly crazy gets hold of me and starts talking about "perpetuum mobile." I get rid of him pretty fast (after all, I'm not going to waste my time listening to obvious nonsense), but others who witnessed the incident pointed out to me, "Zbyszek, we know you have to be careful with your time, but you can't treat people like that."

Nevertheless, the resolution that Bogdan referred to, which bound a delegate to vote for everything that Wałęsa said and against everything that Gwiazda said, was an absolute affront to human dignity and degraded both the delegate in question and the regional congress and Wałęsa, Gwiazda, and the union as a whole.

BORUSEWICZ: That's how you see it, but this delegate was quite happy. And so was everyone else who was there at the time.

BUJAK: This was because of a lack of awareness rather than conscious intent. I'd like to repeat: I don't deny the existence of various extremist trends within the union; I'm just saying that Solidarity would have managed to free itself of these extremisms. You only have to recall how open it was to all groups. The workers didn't imagine that artists, actors, or singers wouldn't join the union; hence, they exchanged information with these groups about their own problems and respected them. This was a totally new development anywhere in the world, something that will always be associated with our movement.

BORUSEWICZ: I realize that, for various reasons, my view of Solidarity is unacceptable to many people. Partly this is for political reasons: because the union is struggling, because it's under attack. But the absence of criticism may well lead to serious mistakes.

BUJAK: That's why I'm not contradicting your view, just supplementing it.

BORUSEWICZ: I understand. Really, I didn't say everything I had to say, I didn't emphasize the positive tendencies in the union, I didn't emphasize that Solidarity is a value in itself—but I think that's obvious. I'm part of this group and I'm fighting precisely for the union.

Gentlemen, each of you has every right to speak in his own name.

BUJAK: Another important problem that comes up from time to time in the book without being stressed sufficiently is the difference in opinion between Mazowsze and other regions concerning the way in which the union underground should be organized. In Warsaw we declared that any kind of central bodies should be created only after the appropriate level of organization had been achieved at the lower levels. Any other approach would have, in our view, hindered initiative from below . . .

I think you're repeating yourself.

BUJAK: Wait a minute. Today, I see things a bit differently, by which I mean that I think we didn't take account of the positive side of the other approach (the proposal to create regional and national bodies at once); we didn't take account of the political importance of these bodies; we didn't take account of their inspirational role.

SZUMIEJKO: And that's the whole difference between my idea (OKO) and yours.

BUJAK: Yes, yes, I know. We underestimated the issue also because we didn't see any chance for effective action on the part of higher levels. Our lack of suitable contacts, both here and abroad, left us in a situation in which the creation of a national body would have been a purely symbolic act.

BORUSEWICZ: For my part, I think that Warsaw's antipathy to institutions was a legacy of opposition thinking from before August 1980. But the real difference of opinion between Warsaw and the rest of the country concerned the general strike, which we'll talk about in a moment. The differences between Gienek (sorry, OKO) and the others were mainly related to the issue of pseudonyms . . .

SZUMIEJKO: You guys just won't give up. I never said that we had to use pseudonyms!

BUJAK: But you have to understand, Gienek, that if you sign the first statement with a pseudonym, it looks to us as though you have a policy of using pseudonyms.

SZUMIEJKO: Anonymity was necessary so that everyone could get on the train of history. Apart from this, you really don't remember the letter in which I proposed that Borusewicz should sign on behalf of Gdańsk, Bujak on behalf of Warsaw, and so on?

BUJAK: We remember.

BORUSEWICZ: We remember.

SZUMIEJKO: Then why do you keep coming back to these pseudonyms?!

BORUSEWICZ: OK, we're all together now, and the problem no longer exists. I knew Zbyszek and I knew that as soon as we got together, everything would be all right, you understand. But you guys from OKO I didn't know. I was afraid of infiltration.

BUJAK: The second fundamental difference regarding the problem was, you're right, the issue of the general strike. For a long time Warsaw considered that to call such a strike would get us nowhere. In general, there's no way you can provoke such a strike artificially; it erupts spontaneously, as it did in August 1980, as a result of a specific sociopolitical situation. And the last chance to call successfully for a general strike was lost during the time of legal Solidarity, after the Bydgoszcz events of March 1981.

But my attitude wasn't determined only by organizational considerations. We were unable to answer the question of whether, and to what extent, a strike would resolve the country's political problems. Apart from this, such an undertaking contained an enormous danger if the regime were to use force. During the first days of the "war," it's true, I myself opted for a strike and encouraged the shipyard to call for one in the spring of 1982, but I treated it more as a threat, as a means of exerting pressure on the authorities.

With hindsight, I think that the hopes I had then were completely unjustified. The authorities were pretending to confer with various of our advisers—Rakowski talked with Lech—but at the same time, left, right, and center, they were talking about Solidarity as a thing of the past.

Unfortunately, the myth of the general strike weighed heavily in our thinking and activities.

BORUSEWICZ: I disagree (and not only on this issue either), although, like you, I think that the general strike has become a myth. This myth fitted us like a wooden leg: we needed it, but it was a hindrance. Because of it, our stride became uneven; at the ICC, we couldn't come up with a coherent approach. Some of us voted for a strike, but in the same way as you did, Zbyszek. In other words, as soon as it was time to make a decision, they laid down their arms.

BUJAK: You can't say "like you did," because in October '82 I was ready to go all out, and if Gdańsk hadn't missed . . .

BORUSEWICZ: October '82 is another matter.

BUJAK: When I now read the statement I wrote when Solidarity was delegalized, I burst out laughing.

Historians can't hear you laughing.

BORUSEWICZ: I also thought it was funny. Surprising but funny. For the whole time you'd been talking about the "long march," the "underground society," about hanging on, and suddenly, in October '82, you issued a statement that was diametrically opposed to all that and at a time when the shipyard strike was dying.

BUJAK: I'm sorry, but at the time that I issued the statement (on the Tuesday morning) anything was still possible.

Once again, please: don't repeat things you've already said in the pages of Konspira.

BORUSEWICZ: OK. The point is that the ICC didn't adopt a single, clear-cut approach (either a marathon struggle or a general strike with all its consequences). We got together equipment that would be useful in the event of a strike, but we didn't undertake any of the necessary organizational work. For the whole time there was a kind of dualism in force which lasted until about six months ago.

BUJAK: Listen, you simply can't decide in advance that you're going to follow this road and not the other. You have to consider various possibilities. In the Mazowsze region we consistently implemented the line of the long march because we saw it as preparing us for all eventualities. Today I can honestly say that it did prepare us, but not enough.

BORUSEWICZ: The idea of a general strike did make sense. At the beginning of the "war" people's willingness to fight was enormous, and they would have answered our call. Would we, though, have been able to win a confrontation with the authorities? I think so. We just had to assume that the decision to call a strike would be final and that we'd subordinate all our activity to it and create a situation of all or nothing.

BUJAK: Unless you're certain of sucess, you should vote against a strike because of the consequences of failure.

No one can ever be a hundred percent certain of anything in politics. There is, though, a notion of acceptable risk.

BUJAK: On the pages of *Konspira* both of us, Bogdan, talk about the negative consequences of passive resistance; I in relation to the business at the Fire Fighters' School, and you in relation to the behavior of those factories that went on strike in December '81. But the example of the Wujek Mine shows that active resistance wasn't successful either (it came to a tragedy, people were killed). Probably a better tactic was that adopted by other mines, where the miners simply refused to go down.

BORUSEWICZ: Do you think that the level of society's resistance on December 13, 1981, was high enough?

BUJAK: No. Solidarity turned out to be weak, and people reacted with enormous restraint. Compared with the union's ten million members, the number of people prepared to strike was disproportionately small. This is all true, but I'd like to ask whether, when you criticized the shipyard for its passive resistance, you took account of what happened in Wujek? And if you did, do you still stand by your comments?

BORUSEWICZ: Yes. In my opinion, it was possible to try to change the situation after the imposition of martial law, but resistance would have had to be greater. And, of course, you couldn't have excluded the possibility of victims in advance, which by no means signifies that I would have advocated attacking tanks with sticks. It was simply that the authorities were aware of the weakness of our defense (passive resistance just led to people holding hands and singing songs), and for this reason they so easily decided to pacify the factories. You cited the example of Wujek, and I'll cite the counterexample of the Gdańsk docks: nine hundred determined men organized some serious means of defending themselves, and this was enough to dissuade the authorities from attacking. Isolated, the docks lasted out for a whole week. So, it was absolutely necessary to take the risk; we had so much to lose. In such a situation you have to be prepared to make the highest sacrifice because, otherwise, you lose out to a bunch of gangsters.

Time's passing and Zbyszek still has a number of points he wants to raise. Let's speed things up a bit.

BORUSEWICZ: And add some color to the discussion?

BUJAK: I really would like to raise a few more points. Firstly, I have doubts about Bogdan Lis's assessment of the Young Poland Movement.

Bogdan is in jail and can't answer back.

BUJAK: And that's why I don't have any intention of attacking him; I only want to comment on his views. Obviously, I understand that Bogdan's view of the YPM was influenced by the organizational situation in Gdańsk and by the fact that the YPM issued a statement declaring it would help the underground while, in fact, it did nothing at all. Of course, I was rather surprised when I read about these promises, since I'd heard earlier that the YPM's approach to activity was completely different from ours. From the beginning of the war, they made it known (especially Wiesław Chrzanowski, their spiritual father) that they were staking everything not on underground activity but on coming out into the open and working, as far as possible, legally. It's difficult to judge how far this approach was realistic, but you can't dismiss it out of hand. It was simply another style of political thinking. And I don't say this as a sympathizer of the YPM (which I'm not) but as an advocate of a variety of independent activity. Criticism of the YPM of the kind advanced by Lis reflects too much concern with personal issues and almost completely ignores the genuine substantive differences in points of view.

244

SZUMIEJKO: Yes, Bogdan Lis's position might be taken as suggesting that all the members of the ICC thought that the ICC had a monopoly on political activity and ideas.

Why do you think that every statement made by each of you is made in the name of the whole ICC?

BUJAK: Because that's how it looks. Remember the serious complaints made about me—that everything I say is immediately identified as the position of the ICC.

We, for example, don't have this perception and absolutely refuse to treat Konspira *as a collection of official statements.*

BORUSEWICZ: If I represented the YPM line of thought, would that bother you?

BUJAK: And how would you behave?

BORUSEWICZ: In keeping with the views I would have.

BUJAK: In that case, given your position in the ICC or even within the region, it would bother me.

BORUSEWICZ: You see. Every individual and every group ought to have, of course, the possibility of choosing their own direction of activity, but I don't agree with the view that we were indifferent to the line of the YPM.

BUJAK: The problem simply didn't arise in Warsaw.

BORUSEWICZ: Because you didn't have any personal contacts.

BUJAK: OK. I have some more reservations, this time relating to one of the statements made by Władek Frasyniuk.

Who's also in jail.

BUJAK: It's just that, when he's talking about the last session of the National Commission on December 12, 1981, Władek jokes about

245

Jacek Kuroń and Karol Modzelewski, who didn't go home at the end of the meeting but stayed in Gdańsk to "decide who should be included in the provisional government." This is a really sarcastic joke . . .

BORUSEWICZ: It adds variety to the story.

BUJAK: . . . although to some extent it corresponds to the truth, by which I mean Jacek's proposal to create a government of national unity (not a provisional government!). The distinction is fundamental, particularly if *Konspira* is translated into English . . .

God willing.

BUJAK: Then it'll be extremely important what kind of government it was supposed to be. Władek's joke makes it sound as though Jacek and Karol were in favor of overthrowing the Communist system, seizing power, and so on, and that isn't at all true! I was familiar with Jacek's proposal, which was an attempt to find a solution to a situation without a solution, and I know that he regarded it as virtually impossible but, still, the only solution.

My last comment concerns Bogdan Borusewicz's statement about his conflict with the Solidarity commission in the Gdańsk Shipyard. You suggested, Bogdan, that the members of the commission gave vent to anti-Semitic prejudices. The thing is, if you're going to refer to tendencies of this kind, you also have to mention that there were very strong countertendencies (for example, the campaign on behalf of the Jewish cemetery in Warsaw or the consistent condemnation of the Grunwald group).

BORUSEWICZ: You have to say the following: in Solidarity, as in society as a whole, there are various tendencies. I referred to the matter only in passing, but I now want to repeat directly that anti-Semitism was fairly strong within legal Solidarity, although this wasn't revealed in public. In addition to this tendency . . .

BUJAK: . . . which met with massive opposition . . .

BORUSEWICZ: This was evidence of the union's moral health, but, on the other hand, there was constant whispering about the fact that someone or other was something or other . . . and so on.

This argument could go on forever because you two differ in your perception of not only the past but also the present.

BUJAK: Insofar as our chances weren't very great in the past, we're now experiencing a turning point. It may last a year, or even several years; in any event, the regime, which reached the height of its power in the first months of martial law, is clearly weakening. The destruction of the entire power apparatus is clearly visible; and not just the repressive apparatus but also the state and economic administration and the Party. Through the right kind of activity, we can strengthen society's organization and raise morale. In other words, we can stimulate a process similar to that of the late seventies, when society's readiness to act increased. In addition, today we're both organizationally stronger and wiser for our recent experiences. The international situation also favors us. Today it seems highly improbable that the entire power apparatus could consolidate itself sufficiently to carry out a repeat of martial law.

BORUSEWICZ: A repeat is actually unlikely. It'll be even worse, that's what! The regime hasn't weakened at all. After all, it doesn't depend on social support but on means of repression—and these exist, as they did before. On the other hand, the level of active resistance in society has undoubtedly declined. And our increasing organizational efficiency is no substitute. An authentic mass movement cannot remain in a state of full alert for a period of years, and if it is forced to wait long enough, it will lose to the state—until the next explosion. This is normal. Currently, though, the level of social mobilization has stabilized to an extent that allows further activity.

BUJAK: So what? So far, we've discussed our previous activities, we've defined clearly our current differences of opinion . . .

So, it's time to talk about the future. You've taken the decision to remain in the underground.

SZUMIEJKO: After analyzing recent events, after asking the opinion of various groups, and after numerous conversations with our advisers and the eleven who were recently released,[2] we came to the conclusion that the existence of the underground is a condition of Solidarity's continued existence. The underground means also the ICC, which ought to cooperate well with Lech and other groups, and be strengthened in terms of personnel. Personnel changes mean not only the co-optation of new members but also the departure—for family reasons, let's say—of one person or another. I say "for family reasons," because within the ICC there aren't any differences of opinion so great as to make it impossible for us to work together.

BUJAK: The union's attempts so far to fight its way to openness haven't yielded satisfactory results. Solidarity members think that day-to-day work can be directed only by the ICC, regional bodies, and clandestine factory commissions (in other words, by the underground). We're not at all happy about this. We would like other possibilities to emerge—for example, the creation of an open union leadership. But such a possibility is slight.

BORUSEWICZ: In general, there haven't been any real attempts at anything else, despite our attempts to persuade many people. The existence of the ICC is simply useful to many people—as an alibi.

SZUMIEJKO: Those who, a year ago, were trying to persuade us to end our activity on the grounds that our authority was declining and it might be a good idea to salvage the myth for posterity while we still could, now say that only the ICC will do!

BUJAK: I see some purpose to our continuing activity, since—as I said earlier—the regime's power has weakened. The point is that we, society as a whole, should know how to take advantage of it. People's faint reaction to the rearrest of Frasyniuk and Pinior (for laying flowers to commemorate the fourth anniversary of August 1980) show that we still have a lot to do. But many courageous and determined people will undoubtedly emerge. Before us we have elections to the Sejm. The authorities certainly aren't going to introduce a democratic electoral law, so—a boycott, which will present the underground with specific organizational tasks. The tactics of open activity aren't appropriate in this case. We came to this conclusion on the basis of elections to the People's Councils.

The authorities are taking care to ensure that underground bodies have something to do: they're preparing a further rise in the cost of living, limitations on workers' rights and the powers of self-management. But these are only some of the areas in which we're active . . .

BUJAK: Let me add one more thing. What is the basis for our political perspective? In large part it is the firm stand of the West, which, for the first time in many years, has been so consistent in relation to the socialist bloc. This has an affect on Poland . . .

BORUSEWICZ: . . . where repression has come to a kind of halt midway, where they declared an amnesty two years running, and where the authorities, who clearly want the United States to lift its economic sanctions, have little room for maneuver.

BUJAK: If, however, the West were to abandon this policy, the regime would immediately appropriate the abandoned territory and would start to tighten the screws. So, how, in this context, can we interpret the current visits to Poland on the part of Western diplomats? As long as—as in the case of the head of the Austrian Ministry of Foreign Affairs—they keep asking about Solidarity, we can only applaud. We'll voice objections when they start to ignore the issue of human rights violations in our country.

BORUSEWICZ: The very existence of the underground forces the authorities to moderate their policies. The ICC, like all previous temporary structures in Poland, has proved to be a permanent element of our landscape; it's already been functioning twice as long as the National Commission of legal Solidarity.

SZUMIEJKO: In light of which, you, dear authors, have a chance of further future earnings.

You mean further years of underground activity and additional volumes of Konspira?

SZUMIEJKO: Of course. Our successors will undoubtedly provide you with new material. But seriously, it's not the case, I repeat, that the ICC (like the Sejm of the PPR) has extended its term of office all on its own. The fact is that those in whose name we function have given us a further vote of confidence.

October 22, 1984

NOTES

1. After reading the manuscript of Konspira, *some of the heroes who appear in its pages felt the need—out of concern for historical truth and the desire for a balanced assessment—to comment on statements made by others. Had we carried on with polemics of this kind, we would have found ourselves having to edit comments made in response to other comments. To avoid this while also allowing our heroes to voice their criticisms of the form and content of this book, we decided—on our part, without much enthusiasm, because we'd already said all we had to say in the thirteen chapters of this book—that all further comments and additions would be expressed in an open but principled discussion.*

The following discussion, in which, apart from the authors, only three people finally took part, does not constitute an integral part of the book. Rather it should be regarded as a supplement or appendix, or, best of all, as a postscript.

2. Szumiejko is referring to eleven Solidarity activists who were interned under martial law and, while interned, were charged with conspiring to overthrow the state and transferred to prison to await trial. Four of the eleven were members of the Workers' Defense Committee (KOR)—Jacek Kuroń, Adam Michnik, Jan Lityński, and Henryk Wujec—arrested on September 3, 1982. The remaining seven—Andrzej Gwiazda, Seweryn Jaworski, Marian Jurczyk, Karol Modzelewski, Grzegorz Pałka, Andrzej Rozpłochowski, and Jan Rulewski—were all members of Solidarity's National Commission and were arrested on December 2, 1982, shortly before the "suspension" of martial law and the release of all internees. No indictment was ever completed in the case of these seven. The trial of the KOR activists finally opened on July 13, 1984, but was adjourned following opening proceedings. A week later, on July 21, the Polish authorities granted an amnesty to nearly all political prisoners which resulted in the release of the eleven, who had spent a total of two-and-a-half years of detention.

AFTERWORD

I write these lines, having just reread this remarkable manuscript, in the waning days of the astonishing autumn of 1989. Throughout East Central Europe—from Budapest to Leipzig, from Prague to Sofia—crowds have been surging and governments toppling. Or, not so much toppling as melting, seemingly, into thin air: totalitarian regimes suddenly emptied, totally pithed, of their dread onetime authority. The phenomenon is so relentless that it has begun to seem inevitable—and yet it was far from inevitable: history, as Marx taught, is made by people, and as for this particular history, the protagonists in the current book would have a larger claim than most if they chose (as, emphatically, they never would) to claim much of the credit for recent developments.

I say this in two senses. To begin with, though it has become fashionable to suggest that the single most important factor in the ongoing democratic upwelling along the fringes of the Soviet Empire has been the benign disposition toward those developments displayed at the very center of that Empire, particularly in the person of Mikhail Gorbachev (and, of course, this is undeniably true)—what tends to get obscured in such a formulation is the extent to which Gorbachev himself rose up in the first place largely as a response to Poland's Solidarity movement. There is already considerable evidence (a final accounting will naturally have to await the eventual opening of the Kremlin's archives) that the example of Solidarity horrified several key sectors among the ruling elite in the Soviet Union of the late Brezhnev period, particularly among the intelligence circles that had

251

the most consistent access to reliable assessments of the depth of the phenomenon. The prospect of a revolution from below—of workers seizing control of the foremost bastions of worker's power and then going on frontally to challenge the very state and party that had heretofore supposedly ruled in their name—shocked those Kremlin officials to the core. They decided that the only way to head off any similar developing challenge to their own domestic hegemony was through a concerted program of reform *from above*. This was indeed the program envisioned by Yuri Andropov, the former head of the KGB, when he took over following Brezhnev's death, and though he died long before he came anywhere near fulfilling it, he did manage to position his protégé Gorbachev for an eventual rise to power (following the brief recidivist interregnum of Konstantin Chernenko). The protagonists of this book were all seminal players in the initial upsurge of Solidarity and hence they deserve a fair measure of credit in that regard.

But more to the point, Brezhnev didn't die until almost a year after the December 13, 1981, coup, engineered at his insistent behest by General Wojciech Jaruzelski and his colleagues in the Polish Communist party. (In fact, Gorbachev, for his part, didn't rise to power until a full half year after this manuscript was originally completed.) In December 1981, East Central Europe was still in the thrall of Brezhnev's neo-Stalinism—perhaps more desolately so than at any time in the previous decade. Berlin 1953, Hungary 1956, Czechoslovakia 1968, and now Poland 1980–81—yet again, a tentative, hope-swelling opening had suddenly been closed down with a vengeance; once again the passed torch seemed on the verge of guttering out completely. In Berlin and Hungary and Czechoslovakia the neo-Stalinist forces did succeed, at least for a time, in "normalizing" the situation—-expunging, at least for the most part, the living spirit of resistance. This, however, did not happen in Poland—in part because of the remarkable efforts of the individuals portrayed in this book. The fact that they and their colleagues were able to keep that spirit of resistance alive through the dark months following December 1981 would prove to have a direct bearing on the shape of the world in December 1989. The unraveling of the neo-Stalinist hegemony would probably have occurred eventually in any case, but perhaps not as soon, nor as quickly, nor as peaceably.

The fact that these people were able to sustain that resistance at all was (as gets revealed over and over again in this manuscript) purely a matter of contingency. A certain number of individuals happened not to get caught, as they were supposed to have been, on that particular December night: one had turned left instead of right, another had gone out drinking instead of returning to his hotel, another had skipped the meeting altogether. . . . Contingency, and yet, given the nature of the Solidarity movement, inevitability as well. For just as it was probably inevitable that the regime was never going to be able to capture every single one of its opponents straight off that night, so it was also highly likely that several among those whom the regime failed to capture would prove themselves activists of exceptional sophistication, intelligence, and daring. Such was the *depth* of the movement Solidarity had become by December 1981. A few months later, President Reagan would make his preposterous assertion that the Nicaraguan Contras were "the moral equivalent of our Founding Fathers"; but halfway around the globe, Poland had indeed spawned a generation that could lay proper claim to that awesome analogy. In the same eerie way that a farflung colonial outpost on the furthest edge of the Empire, back in the 1770s and 1780s, managed to produce a generation featuring the likes of Washington, Jefferson, Franklin, Adams, Hamilton, Paine, and Madison—so Poland in the 1970s and 1980s produced Wałęsa, Michnik, Kurón, Borusewicz, Karol Wojtyła, Miłosz, Lipski, Frasyniuk, and the others. Had Frasyniuk and Bujak been captured on December 13, but Wujec and Michnik not, the regime would probably have had every bit as great a problem on its hands.

This book was itself the product of sheer contingency—specifically the fact that Mariusz Wilk, one of the leading journalists in the Solidarity movement, happened to be in Warsaw and not Gdańsk that terrible night. Though only twenty-six years old, Wilk was a veteran of the democratic opposition, having edited several underground publications in the Wrocław area during the late seventies. In August 1980 he happened to be vacationing along the Baltic coast when the country's proliferating labor troubles first spread to the Lenin Shipyards in Gdańsk. He managed to squirrel himself into the yard, and together with two colleagues (Konrad Bielinski and Krzystof Wyszkowski) launched the strikers' daily information bulletin, which they dubbed "Solidarność." A few weeks later, following the triumph of the strike, the suddenly legalized independent national trade union adopted that bulletin's name as its own. After that, Wilk continued

253

on, editing the union's bulletin and serving as spokesman for the union's Gdańsk regional office. By the end of 1981, however, having grown disgusted with the union's increasingly tense and fractious environment and the way he was continually being accused of favoring or betraying one faction or another, Wilk had resigned from both of these involvements. "If not for martial law," he recently told me, "I'd probably have continued to drift away from Solidarity. I'd begun working for a more independent journal, and I was playing with the idea of moving back down south and raising sheep." He laughed. "But martial law made me mad. They went and arrested all those people I'd been having so much trouble with, and it really got me furious."

That December night, he was in Warsaw covering the Cultural Congress taking place, the same weekend as the union's National Commission was meeting up in Gdańsk, but he was staying with friends instead of at the hotel where the authorities were expecting to grab him. He immediately went underground, initially smuggling himself back to his hometown of Wrocław, where he stayed with his parents for several days while he tracked down Frasyniuk and some of the other activists who'd already started operating there. On Christmas Eve he decided to head back up to Gdańsk (an hour after he left, the police raided his parents' home for him). Within a few weeks of his arrival in Gdańsk, Borusewicz got in touch with him. (Like Wilk, Borusewicz had been pulling away from Solidarity during the months just before December, though, again as with Wilk, the imposition of martial law immediately reignited his earlier passions.) By that time, Borusewicz had managed to locate Lis, but the two of them had yet to figure out a way of making contact with Frasyniuk—this was in fact why Borusewicz had initially sought out Wilk, and through him they were indeed presently able to connect with the Wrocław underground. Wilk meanwhile threw himself wholeheartedly into the work of the underground in Gdańsk.

Gradually Wilk's old journalistic instincts rose to the fore: he realized he was living an incredible story, and that intimately involved as he was with many of the most important players, he'd been vouched a unique vantage point from which to tell it. Inspired in part by the example of Maria Esther Gilio's book on the Tupamaro guerrillas of Uruguay, he evolved the idea of trying to record the observations of the principal conspirators themselves, right there in the midst of their conspiracy. When they in turn agreed to go along with his project, he decided he would need to collaborate with at least one other writer, someone who was not himself as directly involved in underground activities and hence would be able more safely to store tapes and generate transcripts and so forth, as the project went along—so he made contact with Zbigniew Gach, a contributor to the aboveground periodical *Pomerania*. Two years later, when *Konspira* was eventually being published, Gach adopted the clever pseudonym Moskit—Mosquito. The Gdańsk police went into a frenzy trying to track down the exasperating Mr. Mosquito, interrogating dozens of individuals in an effort to crack the code, hoping in turn through him to get to the Prize Quarry—Borusewicz, who was still successfully at large. But even though they interrogated Gach as part of that search, they never plumbed his true identity. (This was in part perhaps because physically, Gach was the least mosquitolike person one could imagine: had he adopted the moniker "Falstaff," they would have had him nailed in a minute.)

Wilk and Gach in turn realized they'd need at least one other collaborator, someone who had more familiarity with book-length prose, and they turned to Maciej Łopiński, another writer who was editing his own underground bulletin. "When the two guys originally came to me with the proposition," Łopiński recalled for me, "I couldn't at first make up my mind. I was already living with enormous day-to-day pressures, what with my bulletin, and I really didn't need anymore. But I guess I have a feel for the theatrical. We were sitting there in this big old house which we'd chosen for our secret rendezvous—old armchairs, an old brown round wood table covered with lace—huddled together, drinking our tea. There was no samovar, but we were all bearded and suddenly it felt exactly like the *narodna wola* [?], one of the legendary old Russian socialist conspiracies—it made a big impression on me, and I decided to go along."

Their first sessions were with Frasyniuk, in June 1982, which was a good thing because by October he'd been arrested and was hence unavailable for any further collaboration thereafter. In October and November they interviewed Bujak and Borusewicz—a particularly dramatic time to be doing so, since the parliament had just delegalized Solidarity and the TKK was in the midst of calling for its November protest strike. In the wake of the disastrous failure of that action, the police redoubled their efforts to crush the underground, and on December 11, during a lightning sweep of clandestine networks in Gdańsk, both Wilk and Łopiński were themselves apprehended. The police had apparently still not gotten any wind of their developing

255

project, for though both men were extensively interrogated, the subject never came up. Łopiński served three months in prison, after which he was released on health grounds. Wilk served seven months, that is until his release as part of the limited amnesty of July 1983. Gach meanwhile spent the hiatus transcribing tapes.

The project lapsed during the latter half of 1983, but in early 1984, the collaborators resumed work, interviewing Bujak and Borusewicz again and now taping conversations with Lis, Hall, Szumiejko, and Jedynak as well, between January and April. The meetings were carefully plotted so as to avoid detection. Contacts were made through couriers, and the final approach invariably occurred across a series of checkpoints where others could ascertain if anyone was being tailed. Łopiński, for example, told me how, when he wanted to make contact with Borusewicz, he'd frequently head out into the forest surrounding Gdańsk, having arranged for three or four separate cars and drivers to be stationed at different exit points surrounding the forest. Entering the woods, even he wouldn't know which car he'd eventually end up deciding to take. One evening, the forest was suspiciously crawling with drunks and other odd characters and he ended up deciding not to take any of the cars—a good thing, as he later discovered, since the police had mounted a particularly intensive effort that evening to capture the ever-elusive Borusewicz. Wilk for his part was interviewing Bujak one day in Warsaw when suddenly a guard rushed in to warn them that the apartment complex was being surrounded by security police; Wilk and Bujak both scampered for cover. Later it turned out that the police were closing in on someone else in an altogether different apartment. But generally, as Gach told me, "There weren't that many particular situations. We were all so cautious it was boring." Interview sessions would last between eight hours and two days and were generally conducted by Wilk and Łopiński. Afterward the tapes would be brought back to Gdańsk and hidden by Gach.

By May 1984, the three journalists had collected all their material—over fifteen hundred pages of raw transcript—and they now went into deep hiding for the three months it would take them to distill the final manuscript. To begin with, they repaired to a friend's private hotel in the small spa resort of Polanica in the mountains south of Wrocław. The season had yet to begin, so they pretty much had free run of the place. They impishly informed inquiring townspeople that they were part of a team "building the new road." No restaurants were open; every day they went out and bought milk, cheese, and eggs, and for forty days they lived on that and nothing else. Working ten hours a day from three carbon copies of the complete transcripts, they systematically honed and shaped the material. "We were trying not to fall into hagiography," Gach told me. "We preferred to prick our characters rather than throw ourselves prostrate before them. And this worked: had we done it the other way around, the results would have been unreadable already today."

In June they received word that back in Gdańsk, Bogdan Lis had been captured by the police. Meanwhile their own security was becoming increasingly tenuous with the fast approach of the resort season's opening. Another friend packed them up, crammed them into the back of a truck, and transported them to a delapidated seventeenth-century castle in the nearby Klodzko [?] district, a ruined mansion which was in the process of being refitted for eventual reopening as a museum. The castle was located on the boundary of a busy state farm, so for several weeks they left the building only late at night for brief walks in the garden. Otherwise they had virtually no contact with the outside world: they never used the lights, they had no radio or television, they played dice with cubes they whittled from a piece of wood, they never used the stove in the kitchen. Each morning an old lady who knew they were up to something but never asked precisely what brought them the day's ration of food. Mainly they worked.

By August they'd completed and retyped their manuscript, which they now circulated among the protagonists, or anyway those who were still out on the loose. "The whole project had taken two years," Łopiński recalls. "In the early period we'd had to break through the blockage, the shy reserve of our young, fresh protagonists. 'Why me?' they'd ask. 'Maybe somebody else would be more appropriate. Really we're not that important.' By 1984, however, they had become different people—more careful, more canny, more circumspect: they'd become politicians. We had to convince them to let us keep certain passages." Somewhere between five and ten percent of the original transcripts was retained in the final manuscript. The authors had themselves censored a good deal to protect their subjects and the wider common project: the ongoing clandestine movement as a whole. They made a few more additional cuts in response to the specific concerns of their protagonists. And in October they gathered several of them together for a last conversation, which they included as a postscript.

Then, finally, in December, they published the book in two simultaneous editions, one underground (with the Spotkania press) in Poland and the other with an émigré house (Przeşwit) in Paris. The book proved a sensation from the start—it was both enormously talked about and quite controversial. (It was eventually republished by over a dozen separate clandestine publishing outfits in Poland, only three of whom paid royalties to the authors. It was also quickly translated into Hungarian, Slovak[?], and Russian for samidzat distribution abroad.)

The latter half of 1984 saw the beginning of a very confusing period in Poland. On the one hand, most of the remaining interned figures (including Kuroń, Michnik, and Frasyniuk) were released during the summer as part of a general amnesty. Lis, however, remained incarcerated and was indeed facing charges of treason which carried a possible death penalty. In October, perhaps the foremost clerical ally of the oppositionist movement, Father Jerzy Popiełuszko, was kidnapped and savagely murdered by renegade security agents. But then, in December, Lis was released after all. No sooner had this relative thaw set in than Frasyniuk, Lis, and Michnik were all rearrested while attempting to meet with Wałęsa. Several others, including Wilk, were also arrested at that meeting, though they were all released following the standard forty-eight hours detention, whereas Frasyniuk, Lis, and Michnik were held over for trial and presently were sentenced to between two and three years each. Both Wilk and Łopiński were frequently detained and interrogated as police tried to locate Borusewicz and the others through them; they never broke, and nor were the police ever able to decipher Moskit's true identity (when he himself was being interrogated, Gach helpfully volunteered that he'd heard Moskit was *a woman*). Still, the security forces gradually succeeded in netting their prey. In June, Jedynak was arrested. In January of 1986, the Gdańsk police finally bagged Borusewicz (there followed a crackdown on Gdańsk area clandestine journalists at which time Łopinski was once again briefly detained). On April 30, Wilk was arrested and accused of consorting with foreign agents (in connection with his attempts to arrange further foreign publication of *Konspira*). And on May 31, Bujak was finally captured, after having managed to sustain himself underground for over four-and-a-half years. A few months later, however, a new amnesty was announced, and this time, by September, virtually everybody was released.

During the next year-and-a-half, the underground continued to function—the leadership met and issued statements (the TKK reconfigured itself under a new name with a somewhat revamped membership), and the publishing movement continued as dynamically as ever. Repression became somewhat more sporadic, although as late as October of 1988 the editorial board of *Tygodnik Mazowsze*, the foremost underground weekly, suffered a terrible raid, with virtually the entire staff (most of them women) being hauled to police headquarters and subjected to full body searches. But for the most part detentions were limited to the forty-eight hour variety, particularly on the eve of important anniversaries. In part, the repression subsided because the regime became convinced that, for all intents and purposes, it had won—that after over six years of sometimes withering repression, it had outlasted Solidarity and achieved a sullen acceptance on the part of the body politic, or at least it had succeeded in enforcing an apathetic resignation.

And then, in May 1988, everything started up all over again. With the national economy downspiraling into an ever more desperate crisis, a new generation of workers burst forth upon the scene, youngsters much too young to remember the glory days of 1980 who nevertheless made the reinstatement of the union—*their* union—their principal demand. Across two waves of strikes—in May and then in August, in Gdańsk and Nowa Huta and Stawola Wola and the Silesian coalfields—they chanted their insistence that "There can be no freedom without Solidarity." Although the reconstituted successor to the TKK had in no way anticipated the force and strength of this new upsurge, its members now quickly maneuvered to lend their support and offer their guidance to this radical new generation. Borusewicz in particular was back in the thick of things, in his element, actively organizing the Gdańsk strikers—and Wałęsa, of course, joined in as well. (Many of the rank-and-file veterans of the 1980 period, for their part, sat out this series of strikes.) On August 31, 1988, precisely eight years after the initial Gadńsk agreements through which Solidarity had been legalized in the first place, the regime offered Wałęsa the prospect of a series of roundtable talks with the opposition in which everything, including the status of the union, could be brought up for discussion. With difficulty Wałęsa convinced the young strikers to go along with the proposal. With a maximum of resistance and a minimum of grace, the regime lived up to its side of the agreement, finally convening the long-delayed talks in February 1989. Virtually all the protagonists in this book played key roles in the ensuing negotiations that culminated, in April, with the relegalization of Solidarity as an independent trade union, and the calling of a sudden snap election, to be held on June 4, 1989.

Against formidable odds, Solidarity swamped the much better organized Communist party in those elections. Meanwhile, on the very same day, on the other side of the globe, the Chinese Communist party violently lashed out against its opponents, slaughtering hundreds and perhaps thousands of young people in the bloodbath of Tiananmen Square (and incidentally affording the Poles a chilling vision of an alternative future). In Poland, however, a new process had been decisively set in motion. The party had guaranteed itself control of the government no matter what the outcome of the vote (so that even though Solidarity captured all but one of the 261 parliamentary seats for which it was eligible, the party and its allies still retained control of 65 percent of the seats in the crucial lower house, as agreed to in advance in the roundtable agreements); nevertheless, the actual outcome, when it finally registered, was so staggering to the party's morale that it began to cave in from the inside. By the end of the summer, Solidarity was taking command of the levers of power in Poland, and by the end of the year, similar sorts of astonishments were occurring throughout the rest of East Central Europe.

About a week after the massacre in Tiananmen Square, I happened to attend a meeting at the New York offices of Human Rights Watch—a group of shell-shocked Chinese students conferring with some veteran Eastern European clandestine activists who just happened at that moment to be in town: a Hungarian, a Russian, a Pole. It was like watching Deng Xiaoping's worst nightmare come to life: the Chinese students asking how, how specifically, you operate a mimeograph machine, where you get the paper, how you fashion the distribution networks, what sorts of information are the most important to circulate— how, in short, you learn to conspire. From out of those talks came a project to translate several seminal documents from the Eastern European dissident movements into Chinese and then to smuggle them into China. *Konspira* has now been slated to become one of those documents. This splendid historical record thus seems destined to play a considerable role in the making of future history—here, in the Chinese instance, but also, one hazards to guess, in countless others. (I can already envision the smudgy, tattered typescripts getting passed from hand to hand, in Asia, in Africa, in Latin America. . . .) From these pages, those Chinese and other future readers will derive all sorts of clever technical secrets (my own favorite perhaps involves the packets of leaflets suspended in midair, swaddled in string smeared with baconfat so that after a while the birds end up pecking it free). But in the process they'll also pick up something considerably more valuable: a tenor of being that radiates throughout this text, just as it radiated throughout the entire Polish underground experience, both before Solidarity was born and after it was (momentarily) extinguished.

At the time *Konspira* was published, some movement sympathizers were bothered by its continual tendency to debunk the almost mythical stature of the underground's most cherished heroes—to portray them debunking themselves, critiquing their own performance, expressing their myriad doubts and hesitations. Several critics worried about the manuscript's corrosive effects on the Myth of Solidarity (and in fact, the regime happily reprinted some excerpts from the book in official journals). But the book's authors—and its protagonists—saw precisely that process of subversive demystification as central to their whole project. That's why they did it: that's what they were all about. The underground required heroes, but the future required that they be heroes of a certain sort. Heroes who were human, and fallible, and *civil*. Heroes who were already behaving like the kind of open democrats they hoped one day to be able openly to be. At one point in the manuscript, Bujak tells the story of how an old veteran of the clandestine Home Army gave him a handbook, seemingly devoted to the pruning of apple trees, "only when you read it carefully (skipping part of the text), it became clear that its real subject was sabotage." *Konspira* is a book which purports to be about the arts of conspiracy and sabotage, but if you read it carefully, it turns out to be about the planting and maintenance of a certain kind of orchard—the orchard of civil society.

Lawrence Weschler

December 1989

Studies in Society and Culture in East-Central Europe

General Editors: Jan T. Gross and Irena Grudzinska-Gross

Designer: Sandy Drooker
Compositor: G & S Typesetters, Inc.
Text: 11/13 Bodoni
Display: Futura Extra Black
Printer: BookCrafters
Binder: BookCrafters